God, the Devil, and Divorce

Advance Praise

I was drawn in by this positive and life-affirming story about a woman who finds herself and her strength as her marriage deteriorates. She fights for her marriage, her husband, and herself, battling unseen enemies. This is an engaging book about the struggle of knowing when to fight, and when to give up and make a new life for oneself.

—**Susy Flory**, *New York Times* bestselling author or co-author of over a dozen memoirs, and director of West Coast Christian Writers Conference.

In this compelling, readable, and highly relatable memoir, Linda M. Kurth takes us deep inside what could be so many American homes and reveals the pain, joy, and discovery of motherhood, womanhood, and sexuality. Looking at Christianity from both the inside and outside, Kurth writes honestly about how her faith supported her, as well as the challenges she faced when the choices she made conflicted with some of her fellow Christians' mores.

—**William Kenower**, author of *Fearless Writing: How to Create Boldly and Write with Confidence*

Linda Moore Kurth is a soulful, big-hearted survivor whose suffering has somehow not made her bitter but passionate—passionate to help others escape abusive situations and to cultivate advocates for those who are suffering. I'm honored to know her and pray you will be blessed by this fierce, vulnerable book.

—**Chad R. Allen**, writing coach, blogger, speaker

One of the greatest gifts we can give another person is to do the hard work that turns our pain into their gain. Linda Moore Kurth has taken the time, the energy and put in the work to do just that. Her gift in sharing the process of her pain and her insights into what you might gain from her experience makes her book worth reading and sharing. Divorce is rampant in our culture and help in dealing with it is invaluable. Make this resource a gift for yourself and others.

—**Cliff Tadema**, President, Christ The King Network,
Ministry Made Simple

If your heart aches over your broken marriage—even one filled with crazy mixed messages, a tug of war between love and hate, and abusive neglect—*God, the Devil, and Divorce* is for you. If you've felt judged by those who don't know the full story, this book is also for you. Linda invites us on her honest, vulnerable journey from love to heartache as she battles first to save her marriage and then to let it go. Writing as a trusted friend, Linda shares journal entries, encouraging bible verses, and inspiring quotes from her step-by-step healing journey. Even if your story isn't exactly like hers, you will experience understanding, renewed faith, and assurances you are not alone.

—**Rebecca L. Mitchell** Author of *From Broken Vows to Healed Hearts: Seeking God After Divorce Through Community, Scripture, and Journaling*

A divorce is a death—a death of a marriage you expected to last a lifetime. Linda shares her journey working through the difficulties encountered in marriage and two divorces before finding that lasting marriage. She shares her struggles with lack of church and Christian support for what she is going through. She writes her story to enlighten other Christians who may be struggling for support and understanding surrounding divorce and marriage issues.

—**Marlene Anderson**, mental health counselor,
motivational speaker, author

In her memoir, Kurth bravely shares her journey of faith, heartbreak, and crushing judgments from segments of her Christian community after leaving a marriage fraught with crazymaking and loneliness as she works to rebuild herself.

—**Lizbeth Meredith**, author of *Pieces of Me:*
Rescuing My Kidnapped Daughters

Emotional and spiritual abuse can often be worse than physical in that there are no obvious scars. Linda M. Kurth's writing is raw and honest, making her story feel authentic. She exposes her own vulnerability while presenting her husband in a realistic, multidimensional way. Her characters come alive on the page. Her story will give hope to countless women who feel trapped in an abusive relationship.

I highly recommend this well-written memoir to women who have been abused, to health care providers who care for them, and to anyone who would like a glimpse of emotional and spiritual abuse.

—**Kathleen Pooler**, author of *Ever Faithful to His Lead:*
My Journey Away from Emotional Abuse and *Just the Way He*
Walked: A Mother's Story of Healing and Hope.

Marriage isn't for the faint-of-heart. Linda M. Kurth knows that all too well, yet over time she has triumphed over failures, lack of faith, and disappointment. *God, the Devil, and Divorce* explores wide-ranging issues—practical, emotional, and spiritual—as well as providing a wealth of resources concerning these issues. If you're a Christian in a troubled marriage, if you're divorced, or a church leader, you'll want to read Linda M. Kurth's inspirational read.

—**Linda K. Thomas**, author of two memoirs, *Please, God, Don't Make*
Me Go!: A Foot-Dragger's Memoir and *Grandma's Letters from Africa*

In her memorable memoir, Linda M. Kurth describes the intimate and gradual breakdown of her twenty-five-year Christian marriage. She looks for help and guidance, but when one faith counselor threatens, "If you divorce, Satan wins!" she prays for enlightenment. You can sense the author's joy when she finally allows God to light her way and leads her to the man of her dreams. In an engaging and authentic style, Linda shows how things went wrong, and what it took for things to go right!

—**Larry J. Dunlap**, author: *Night People* and *Enchanted*, Books 1 & 2 of *Things We Lost In The Night*, a memoir of love and music

In reading *God, the Devil, and Divorce*, I was privileged to join author Linda M. Kurth on a fascinating and sometimes agonizing emotional roller-coaster ride of love, joy, happiness, adventure, sadness, helplessness, futility, and hope. I found myself experiencing a deep sadness coupled with huge frustration that, at times, people of faith offered her little help and in some cases, more disillusionment. Linda's beautifully vulnerable sharing of her life is so real and relatable that you can't help but find yourself walking alongside her in her journey towards hope and freedom.

—**Vic Woodward**, co-founder and leader, Marriage Mosaic

God, *the* Devil, *and* Divorce

A Transformational Journey out of Emotional and Spiritual Abuse

Linda M. Kurth

NASHVILLE

NEW YORK • LONDON • MELBOURNE • VANCOUVER

God, the Devil, and Divorce

A Transformative Journey out of Emotional and Spiritual Abuse

Published in New York, New York, by Morgan James Publishing. Morgan James is a trademark of Morgan James, LLC. www.MorganJamesPublishing.com

Unless otherwise noted, Scripture is taken from the Holy Bible, New International Version®, NIV® copyright ©1973, 1978, 1984, 1985 by Zondervan Corporation®.

Scripture marked NLT is taken from the Holy Bible, New Living Translation, copyright © 1996, 2004, 2015 by Tyndale House Foundation, Tyndale House Publishers Inc., Carol Stream, Illinois 60188. All rights reserved.

Scripture marked KJV is taken from the King James Version of the Bible, public domain.

Scripture marked NKJV is taken from the New King James Version®. Copyright © 1982 by Thomas Nelson.

ISBN 9781631951503 paperback
ISBN 9781631951510 eBook
Library of Congress Control Number: 2020938864

Cover and Interior Design by:
Chris Treccani
www.3dogcreative.net

Morgan James is a proud partner of Habitat for Humanity Peninsula and Greater Williamsburg. Partners in building since 2006.

Get involved today! Visit
MorganJamesPublishing.com/giving-back

CONTENTS

A Note from the Author   xi
Acknowledgments   xiii

Part One   The Beginning of the End   **1**
Prologue   3

One   Jesus Freak   7
Two   Hot in the Kitchen   13
Three   Merged   18
Four   Moving into Faith   27
Five   Life in La La Land   34
Six   Sunshine and Shadow   42
Seven   On My Knees   48
Eight   Home to Oregon   53
Nine   My Cheating Heart   60
Ten   What-A-View   65
Eleven   Our Dream Jobs   69
Twelve   Promise Keepers   76
Thirteen   Guacamole   80
Fourteen   Decision Time   86
Fifteen   For Sale   91
Sixteen   Farewell Bend   97
Seventeen   All Over the Map   102

Eighteen	Dish Detail	109
Nineteen	Will Satan Win?	113
Twenty	Breaking Up Is Hard to Do	120
Twenty-one	Pushed Off the Fence	125
Twenty-two	Job Hunting	132
Twenty-three	Beyond Belief	137
Twenty-four	Drama Queen	143
Twenty-five	Pants on Fire	150
Twenty-six	Truth Will Out	155
Part Two	**Trusting God and Doing the Next Thing**	**163**
Twenty-seven	God in the Dark	165
Twenty-eight	A Moving Experience	174
Twenty-nine	Forgiveness	181
Thirty	Substitute	189
Thirty-one	Dance Lessons	196
Thirty-two	A Home of My Own	201
Thirty-three	Revelations	209
Thirty-four	Dating	215
Thirty-five	Tough Calls	221
Thirty-six	Dance Code	227
Thirty-seven	Falling	235
Thirty-eight	God Bless My Broken Road	242
Epilogue		247
Reflections		251
Suggested Reading & Resources		258
Endnotes		260
About the Author		263
Other Books by the Author		264

A Note from the Author

Memoirs invariably involve persons who would rather not be identified for various reasons. I've changed the names of many people here, but I've also used the real names of those I consider to be the heroes of my story. (You know who you are!) For the last ten years of my marriage, and the first three years of my single life, I kept a journal. This is what I relied upon to construct scenes and dialogue. They are by no means a perfect replica of those times, though I did my best to keep to the truth of the incidents I've portrayed.

Acknowledgments

To Bill, who shows me love every day, and whose support for the writing and publishing of this book has meant everything. The Lord meant us to be together.

To Ros, my "sister-cousin" who held me up during the most difficult time of my life. I miss you so much.

To Lorraine, my spiritual anchor during the end of my marriage and the beginning of my new life.

To all my friends and relations who came alongside me as I struggled to let go of the past and forge a better future for myself.

To David, whose prodding helped me regain a healthy lifestyle, and to whom I could depend on to keep me on schedule.

To Pastor Cliff, who read my entire awful first draft and yet encouraged me in meaningful ways to keep writing.

To my critique group, who suffered through two revisions of the memoir, and especially to Meghan, who gave me the title for this book.

To my editor, who kept me encouraged and challenged as I wrote, and rewrote, and again rewrote this memoir.

Part One

The Beginning of the End

Prologue

The most confused you will ever get is when you try to convince your heart and spirit of something your mind knows is a lie.
–Shannon L. Alder

Bend, Oregon, 1998

Approaching the church located in a small business park, I wonder how this latest counseling could possibly be of help. When my husband suggested I see Pastor Susan, I suspected he hoped she'd straighten me out. In the last fifteen or so years of our twenty-four-year marriage I've been to Gestalt therapy, couples counseling, family counseling, individual counseling, a women's support group, yoga therapy, tried valium and other antidepressants, and even talked with my gynecologist. *What more is there to learn? And from a conservative pastor? Still, a woman pastor in a conservative church is a bit unusual ...*

Susan ushers me into her office and beckons me to a comfortable chair. I settle in, studying her attractive yet simple style, weighing the timbre of her voice, and noticing the smile wrinkles around her eyes. Feeling an immediate connection, I sigh in relief and pour out the frustrations that have been building in me over the last several years.

"I don't know how to be with Jim anymore," I begin. "I don't know if he dislikes me or is just too distracted to think of me. Whatever it is, I feel disregarded and disrespected, and I'm hurt and angry."

Susan listens to my story, nodding her head encouragingly. When I finish, she hands me a tissue. I hear compassion in her voice as she asks a few questions, jotting down my answers in her notebook.

"Has Jim ever hit you?"

Her question startles me. "Oh, no, he wouldn't do that."

"How about other physical intimidation?"

I pull up scenes in my mind. "He has bumped into me. Our last counselor suggested he help me with the cooking on occasion. I was pleased when he volunteered a few days later, but he bumped me a couple of times while we were working. Nothing hard, but it seemed odd. After I complained, he stopped, but he also stopped helping me. He's bumped me on our infrequent walks together too. I've wondered if he's just clumsy or trying to make me uncomfortable. I don't know—his behavior is confusing. He never forgets my birthday or Mother's Day, and he's good at cracking my back when it gets out of alignment."

"Is that enough?"

I shake my head no.

She continues with her questions. Has Jim ever incited me to anger? *Definitely.* Played on my sympathies? *Oh, yes.* Challenged my memory of something he'd said? *How did you know?*

She sighs and delivers her startling assessment. "I believe Jim's personality type will try every trick in the book to avoid taking responsibility for sabotaging your marriage. His type is good at keeping the opposing party off guard and off-balance. That's what's called 'crazymaking.' Crazymakers want their victims to feel confusion and shame, making them believe they're the bad or crazy ones. All these things you've told me about Jim: saying one thing, and then later, the opposite, without acknowledging the difference, his lack of empathy for your physical and emotional state, making you the bad one in the relationship, encouraging you to doubt your feelings—they convince me he's a crazymaker. I'm not optimistic he'll own up to his behavior."

"But ..." It's one thing for me to complain about my husband, but hearing him judged in this harsh, unambiguous manner makes me want to defend him, if only a little. He's not all bad!

Susan puts down her notebook with a decisive thump, her gentleness gone. Her eyes lock onto mine. "Don't buy another house with Jim until you've seen a good counselor in your new area and get clarity on the state of your marriage. Promise me!"

I leave Susan's office in a daze. Her words, "I'm not optimistic he'll own up to his behavior," play over and over in my mind as I drive to the hilltop home I will soon have to leave. I'd promised Jim I would go to counseling with him one last time. What I want from him is an awakening, a realization that will turn him back around to me. Am I foolish to hope he will do that?

One

Jesus Freak

1972

Jesus Freak: a member of any of several fundamentalist groups of chiefly young people (Jesus people) originating in the early 1970s and emphasizing intense personal devotion to and study of Jesus Christ and His teachings.

—Dictionary.com

My blind date arrives at my rented Albuquerque bungalow to pick me up for a movie. It's been two years since my divorce from Rex. I'm twenty-seven, and I've changed. Back then, I was a straitlaced, church-going college student, but the Almighty hadn't protected me from the pain of my husband's rejection and the loss of my green stucco ranch house with the big cottonwood in our front yard. Whether God had ignored my cries, or had purposely let me suffer, it didn't matter. He was not the loving God I'd been taught as a child, and I burned with anger against Him. Since my husband had divorced me, I would divorce God.

Set adrift just as the Age of Aquarius was dawning, I became curious how its tenets of free love, drugs, and rock and roll might apply to me. The prevailing philosophies of the day were, "Do your own thing" and "Love is the answer." A person could do almost anything as long as it resulted in peace for the individual and the world, letting it "all hang out" without fear of being judged. Christianity was seen as a man-made construct, a part of the deadening machine manifested in big corporations. "The man," who represented the machine, was to be mistrusted and resisted. Materialism was rejected, and psychedelic drugs were an aid to true enlightenment.

I dabbled in this new way of thinking, growing my hair long, wearing prairie skirts and bell-bottoms, and throwing away my bra. I felt groovy in my tie-dyed clothing and granny glasses. The Moody Blues became my favorite music group. I camped in the mountains of Colorado at a Rainbow People Gathering, and joined an encounter group, a quasi-psychotherapy gathering where we expressed our emotions without inhibition. It became my tribe, something to hang onto while I navigated this new world of singleness.

My post-divorce boyfriends had been disasters. I whined to Naomi, my college weaving instructor who had become a friend, "Where are the good eligible guys?"

She shook her head. "I still can't believe you were thinking of marrying that guy who was living with you."

I laughed. "You mean the one who began following me around the duplex and calling me 'Mama'? Thank goodness I finally came to my senses when I found myself hiding in the clothes closet to get some space from him."

"Yes, that one. Looks like I'm going to have to save you from yourself. There's a guy who works for my husband as a stereo repairman."

Good. He's not into computers like Rex. Those darn machines meant more to him than I ever could.

"His name is Jim. He's a little heavy and has a long blond ponytail, but he's smart and funny. I'll see if he'd be interested in meeting you."

I answer the door and am immediately pleased by Jim's appearance—tall, broad shouldered, round wire-framed glasses, a puffy-sleeved shirt tucked into bell bottom cords. I smile and invite him in.

His weight and small mouth—not handsome by conventional standards—don't keep me from appreciating his pleasant voice, gentle demeanor, and kind smile. In fact, his extra weight seems teddy-bear-huggable. He sits down on my pink-and-avocado-green striped couch, and Yum Yum, the little dog-of-my-heart, suspicious of most men, jumps onto his lap.

"Cool," he says, scratching behind her ears. "I love animals. I rescued a pregnant cat, and she gave birth to her kittens on my bed." His face softens in wonder. "Such an amazing experience."

Animal lover. A good sign.

After the show, we chat in his car. "I went to the University of Virginia," he tells me, "but I didn't enjoy being there. My father is an attorney, and Mom went to Smith. They expected me to follow in their footsteps, but I wanted something different. I dropped out, joined the Air Force to escape the draft, and got sent to Turkey. I didn't much like it, but it kept me out of 'Nam. Since my parents moved from the Washington, DC, area to Santa Fe, I moved to Albuquerque when I got out of the service. Life is a lot less confining and regimented here than back East."

"You should know I'm a Jesus Freak," he continues. "I'm a born-again Christian and belong to a small house church. I feel the Holy Spirit when I'm with those people. You should come with me sometime."

"Maybe," I reply. "But tell me what you mean by being 'born-again.' I remember reading that term in the Bible when I was younger, but I never quite got what it meant."

Jim smiles. "That's okay. When I was growing up, we didn't talk much about that in the Episcopal Church either. Going to church was my parents' thing, and I left it when I went into the service. But then a few months ago, I picked up a couple of girls hitchhiking, and they were all afire for the Lord and so full of joy! I wanted that joy too. When they invited me to their house church, I accepted. The words of the pastor rang true, so I invited Jesus into my heart and was born again, repenting of my sins and accepting Christ's forgiveness. Now, I have a personal relationship with Jesus and can look forward to being with Him in heaven when my time comes."

Different strokes for different folks. I steer the conversation in another direction, telling Jim of my heartbreak over my divorce and that I'll soon be entering my second year as a junior high art teacher. He seems sympathetic and encouraging, and I feel comfortable with him. We laugh as we agree his hippy factor exceeds mine because of my full-time job and washer and dryer.

I surprise and delight Jim when I initiate sex on our second date. He's a gentle, yet passionate lover. The next morning, we laugh and joke as he helps kill the tomato hornworms in my substantial garden with his size-twelve Frye boots. In the ensuing weeks, I'm impressed with his eagerness to spend time with me, helping with projects for the summer art class I'm taking to complete my master's degree through the University of New Mexico.

Having a steady salary, I obtain my first loan and buy a turquoise 1969 Dodge van with a spare tire on the front and an air conditioner on the top. I hippie it up, making curtains and fuzzy seat covers, and strap a wicker pet bed to the engine between the front seats for Yum Yum. Jim builds a seat-bed platform for the cargo section while I tie-dye sheets to cover the foam pad that goes on top. As a young girl, I loved working with my dad in his shop and garden, and Jim's help reminds me of those times.

Jim's friends call him "Easy." He seems easy to me too, as we go dancing at hippie bars, hiking on the trails around Albuquerque, and camping in the mountains. We drive to Santa Fe so I can meet his parents. I'm surprised to hear him address his dad as "Father." Instead of the embrace I always share with my dad, they shake hands in a formal manner. His mother seems the opposite of this stiff man, giving us both a warm welcome.

I feel comfortable in their adobe-style home as Jim and I become regular overnight visitors, enjoying and exploring the unique shops, art galleries, museums, and restaurants of Santa Fe. His mother and I discover a common interest in the arts, and I enjoy his father's sense of humor, which reminds me of Jim's.

My eyes are opened to a darker family dynamic one evening, however. Jim's mother serves us a lovely dinner in their antique-filled dining room with Jim's sister and husband also in attendance. Jim's father becomes drunk during the meal and begins an argument that leaves us all uncomfortable.

Later that night, Jim explains that his dad's behavior is not uncommon, and he lays bare his difficulties growing up with an alcoholic father. "He'd call me a 'worthless piece of garbage' when he was drinking," Jim relates matter-of-factly. "I made a point to be in bed when he got home from the bar at night so I wouldn't have to see him. He may have been an outstanding attorney and an important member of my parents' upper-crust society, but he was a lousy father. Back then, I made up my mind I'd never be like him."

My heart aches for Jim as a young boy, and I'm glad he's become a different kind of man. I've had the opportunity to observe Jim with his friends' children, playing games with them and making up silly songs. I conclude Jim will make a great dad, his behaviors lining up with everything I want in a husband—kind, gentle, loving kids and pets, a great sense of humor. I relish his involvement with me and our activities, both at home and in the outdoors.

I'm amused by Jim's little-boy charm, and a few months later, when he says in his Donald Duck voice, "I wuv you, Linda," I realize he's captured my heart. I invite him to move in with me, and we quickly develop a routine. In the mornings he makes me breakfast, sends me off to teach, and does the dishes before going to work himself. In the evenings I cook, and we wash dishes together.

I write my parents and tell them about Jim. They beg me to reconsider my decision to live with him, sending me Bible verses against premarital sex. I write back and tell them I don't appreciate their trying to interfere with my life.

A short time later, Mom and Dad announce they're planning a trailer trip from their home in Oregon, and that Albuquerque will be one of their stops. Jim doesn't say so, but he must be extremely nervous because he cuts off his beautiful ponytail. I'm sorry he feels a need for that, but I take it as a good sign he cares what they think. I imagine many men in this situation would run far, far away.

We don't know what to expect when Mom and Dad arrive. Jim is his sweet and funny self during the visit, and they make no mention of their disapproval of us living together. *Phew!*

Life with Jim seems perfect.

Two

Hot in the Kitchen

I have made a lot of mistakes falling in love, and regretted most of them, but never the potatoes that went with them.
—Nora Ephron

I've carefully selected the menu and set up a table on my front porch with a nice tablecloth and proper place settings, setting a small vase of vibrantly hued nasturtiums in the center for Jim and his mother's birthday luncheon. Bamboo shades provide privacy from passersby. Jim's parents are from East Coast society. This is the first time they've been to our home, and I want them to know I have good social and domestic skills.

"So sweet of you do this for us," his mom remarks after getting settled in one of the folding chairs I've painted bright pink. "It seems I'm always the one to arrange our birthday celebrations."

So far so good. I pass the watermelon, cantaloupe, and honeydew salad with pieces of sweet dates and fresh green mint sprigs in a citrus honey dressing.

13

"This salad is really good," Jim's father offers. I glance at Jim, hoping to see some sign of pride—proving to his father that he is capable of attracting an accomplished girlfriend. Instead, my boyfriend focuses his attention on his plate, picking out the dates in the salad. *Okay, so not everyone likes dates, but couldn't he have been less obvious?* Taking a sip of water, he looks up at me. "This ice is old," he declares, a slight frown on his face.

Hot embarrassment floods over me. Taking a deep breath, I fight to diminish my feelings of betrayal. *He's just thinking out loud. He didn't mean to hurt me.*

"How's your garden coming?" I ask his father, changing the subject. Soon he and I are comparing gardening triumphs and failures, Jim's behavior all but forgotten.

Upon leaving, his mom gives me a warm hug. "Such a lovely time, and such good food. I'd love a copy of your salad recipe."

Jim's father stands back, his smile genuine. I breathe a sigh of relief, believing I may have passed a significant test.

Jim's behavior that day leaves me with a vague unease, and I vow to open his eyes to my culinary skills. A week later, I clip a recipe for Deviled Crab from the newspaper. Since I'm from the Pacific Northwest, home to the famous Dungeness crab, it sounds scrumptious. Singing *"You make me feel like a natural woman,"* I sauté chopped onions in butter, and stir in flour the way Rex's grandmother taught me. I'd been a top home economics student in my high school class, and, after marrying Rex, I'd been further tutored by his mother and grandmother, both excellent cooks.

The temperature in the room increases from the preheated gas oven, and I push my glasses up my perspiring nose with the back of my hand as I continue working. While the dish bakes in the oven, I rinse and tear fresh lettuce and slice a perfectly ripe tomato from my garden for a salad. Jim walks in the door as I pull the fragrant dish out of the oven. I run to greet him, standing on my tiptoes to receive his warm embrace and sweet kisses.

"What's cooking?" he asks.

"It's a surprise. Doesn't it smell wonderful? Are you ready to eat?"

Jim washes his hands at the kitchen sink and pulls one of the heavy upholstered chairs up to the old round oak table that crowds a corner of the kitchen. I set the table and sit down, tucking my long skirt under me. Digging into my dish with relish, I savor the rich taste on my tongue. Jim hasn't touched his dish. In fact, instead of taking a bite, he stares at it as if it might bite him.

"What's the matter?" I ask

"It looks funny."

"You're kidding, right?" *He must be joking. Who, but a child, would complain about a dish looking funny?*

He glares at me. "No, I'm not kidding."

"Come on, give it a try. You might be surprised at how good it tastes." *Why am I begging this guy to eat my food?* Somehow, though, I can't help myself.

"I don't like surprises. What's in it?" he demands.

"It's a crab dish."

He sighs. "All right." He picks up his fork again and gingerly places a bite in his mouth.

I hold my breath, watching his face.

He grimaces as he put his fork down. "Well, I didn't think I'd like it and I don't." He pushes his plate away.

My chest hurts and I feet confused as I take in the stubborn set of his jaw and the defiant look in his eyes. His attitude toward my efforts doesn't seem consistent with his otherwise caring behavior. Just now I wouldn't call him "easy." The comfort I've felt from his large presence in my small kitchen crumbles.

"Wow, this isn't the first time you haven't seemed to like my cooking. Maybe we should discuss it."

"You don't have to make a big deal out of this!"

"I'm sorry, but it is a big deal to me." Heat rises in me, hotter than the oven heat.

He shrugs his shoulders. "Oh, well."

"Oh, well? What do you mean, 'Oh, well?' It doesn't bother you I'm upset?" I raise my voice a notch or two.

"I don't have to listen to this," he mutters. His chair scrapes on the worn vinyl floor as he rises from the table.

I follow in disbelief, watching as he gathers his things.

He stomps out the front door, slamming it behind him. *Did this just happen?*

The door opens again, and for a split second, hope springs in my breast. Will he apologize? Instead, in sails my house key, skittering across the hardwood floor and coming to rest at my feet. He slams the door again.

I can't believe what has just transpired. I pace the floor in shock, trying to process our fight. Attempting to sooth my battered emotions, I take a hot bath with Dr. Bronner's Peppermint Soap, finally allowing my dammed up tears to flow. How could this "nice" guy be such a jerk?

Alone again, I cry myself to sleep for several nights, remembering the sense of abandonment and pain I'd experienced when Rex left. It should have been obvious Jim's distaste for my cooking and his refusal to discuss it meant he'd just failed my suitable-husband test. Yes, I wanted a man who was smart, had a good sense of humor, was a good hugger, and enjoyed spending time with me, but he'd have to appreciate my cooking too! Still, I grieved for the good times we'd had.

One night, a few weeks after our breakup, I climb into bed and turn out the light. On the window shade in front of me appears the shadow of a man. I stifle a scream. Yum Yum, who has been curled at the foot of the bed, rises and utters a deep, deep growl. Shaking with fright, I roll out of bed and crawl to the hallway and the phone. I know one number by heart—Jim's. I hold my breath, waiting for him to answer. He picks up on the third ring. "There's a man ..." I gasp, struggling to get out the words. "He's at my window, and ..."

"I'll be right there!" Jim yells before I can finish my sentence. He lives across town, and although he must have run a dozen stoplights to get to me as soon as he does, the man has disappeared. There's nothing to do but make crazy love. Jim stays through the night and every night after that. I'd missed his warm hugs, and delight in having him back, avoiding a discussion of our fight.

We continue to have disagreements over food and other minor issues, so I suggest we go for counseling. Jim immediately agrees. We're taught to fight fair, how to not "hit below the belt," and how to talk things out. I love him, believe we have the keys to a good relationship, and want to get married. He confesses he's afraid I'll eventually leave him. I promise I won't. We take the next logical step and get engaged, believing we've left our troubles behind.

Three

Merged

Albuquerque, New Mexico 1973

Love gives naught but itself and takes naught but from itself. Love possesses not nor would it be possessed: For love is sufficient unto love.
—**Kahlil Gibran,** *The Prophet*

Following our counseling experience, our future together looks bright. We say our marriage vows on the veranda of Jim's parents' adobe home in Santa Fe with a glowing pink and orange sunset for a backdrop. I've made a long, red velveteen gown and wear the silver and turquoise squash blossom necklace Jim has given me as a wedding present. He looks handsome in slacks, a shirt, and wool tie (the only one he owns), a tan corduroy jacket, a cowboy hat, and his Frye boots. Yum Yum attends, as well as Rex's sister (with whom I'm still friends), and Jim's sister and her husband. Jim's father arranges with a judge friend to preside. We've written our own vows, and I quote something from Kahlil Gibran's book, *The Prophet*.

At the close of the ceremony, we call my parents who've been waiting by the phone in Oregon to congratulate us, pleased we are now married.

As we take the first bites of our catered reception dinner, the judge looks thoughtful. "Your marriage license was issued in Bernalillo, but this is Sandoval County. I hate to say it, but I'm not sure you're legally married. I'll see if anyone at the courthouse can tell me what's what." He turns to Jim's mother. "May I use your phone?"

Jim grabs my hand as we wait in suspense for the answer.

The judge returns to the dining room shaking his head. "Couldn't raise anybody. I'll just have to drive you to Albuquerque."

Jim's somber face turns into a grin. "Want to marry me again?" he asks me.

Jim and I and our two witnesses pile into the judge's car and drive to the Bernalillo County line at Albuquerque's city limits. We pull over at a "Merge" sign where we again exchange vows.

Back in Santa Fe we eat our warmed-over meal. At the end of that momentous day, we return to Albuquerque where we collapse in happy exhaustion. We learn later our original ceremony was, in fact, legal. We sometimes joke that our marriage will surely last, as we were married twice in one day.

Our wedding behind us, we want to buy a house. Jim quits his part-time job as an electronics repairman and goes to work for MITS, a company that has recently developed the first handheld calculator. We find a two-bedroom, stucco bungalow with a crumbling concrete patio. Dogs have torn up the yard and soiled the avocado-colored shag carpet inside, but we see the house's potential and begin renovating it as soon as the sale becomes final.

Jim hacks out the crumbling patio and pours a new one. He helps me create a lush garden with irrigation ditches and indoor-outdoor carpeting to keep the weeds out and moisture in. I grow giant Russian sunflowers, crisp snow peas, and enough tomatoes to can ketchup and tomato sauce.

I heal an ailing plum tree, and Jim covers it with an electric blanket to save the fruit from a late frost. I strip four layers of paint off the kitchen cabinets and Jim pulls up the old vinyl and lays new flooring. We continue to hike and camp, and sing faux-operatic songs we compose while working in the kitchen. I bake our bread and we make yogurt together. We are a great team.

Being part of Jim's family has its benefits. I've been able to get college credit for private weaving lessons, and, although I loved learning many of the fiber arts, weaving has become my passion. Jim's mother works at the museum of Santa Fe, and when it acquires an impressive collection of Navajo rugs, she arranges for me to spend several hours in the vault with this fabulous collection. I observe the differences in the weave, the spinning, dyeing, and patterns up close and at my leisure. The lanolin scent of sheep wool surrounds me as I run my fingers over the rugs' textures—a rich feast for my senses.

Jim's mother's cousin Sallie, a former trader on the Navajo reservation, has an impressive Santa Fe home filled with a glorious collection of Southwest Native American art. Sometimes we stay at Sallie's guesthouse, filled with treasures from her many travels. She takes us to visit her friends in nearby pueblos, watching their dances and feasting in their homes. I love visiting in winter, bundled in my heavy thrift shop karakul wool coat, snow at my feet and the intense blue New Mexico sky overhead, listening to the *boom, boom, boom* of the drums. Delighting in the scent of piñon fires, I feel incredibly alive.

Just before our first wedding anniversary, Jim and I learn we're pregnant. In our excitement, we begin preparing for our child. Jim builds a laundry room in the garage for the washer and dryer that had been in the kitchen. This allows us to move the big loom on loan from school out of what will be the nursery and into the kitchen. I make yellow-checked drapes out of sheets, weave a blue and white rya rug, crochet a blue and yellow pillow for my grandfather's rocking chair, and paint a hand-me-down crib yellow for the nursery.

Friends ask me what I'll do if we have a girl. "She'll have to like yellow and blue," I reply. Somehow I know in my deepest self our baby will be a boy.

We agree I will be a stay-at-home mom, and I begin weaving in earnest, hoping to join the ranks of other Albuquerque craftspeople who make a living from their work.

As happy as we are, food issues pop up again. Jim has begun taking some UNM engineering classes at night, working toward a bachelor's degree. Home from teaching one late afternoon, I fix dinner, making one of my grandmother's favorite salads—iceberg lettuce, grated apple, and canned Mandarin orange segments with a mayonnaise dressing. We sit at the oak table and I put the salad bowl in front of Jim.

"What's in this?" he asks, the inflection in his voice the same as when I'd served the crab dish.

"Mandarin oranges," I answer lightly, although my shoulders automatically tighten.

"What were you thinking?" he asks.

"What do you mean, 'What was I thinking'? I thought about making a salad," I respond, my voice too loud.

His face contorts in disgust. "Don't you know fruit and lettuce don't mix?"

"You have some nerve!" I exclaim. "I'm a good cook and I don't appreciate you lecturing me on what constitutes acceptable food." I scoop up a handful of salad and throw it at him. It lands on his cheek.

He glares at me, wipes off the gooey mess and, not saying a word, leaves for his class.

Shaken, I call my mother, the first time I ask for her marital advice. "I know I shouldn't have done that, and I don't want to get a divorce over fooood," I wail.

"It'll be all right. You'll figure it out," Mom says. I feel somewhat comforted she has confidence in me, but her advice doesn't seem at all helpful. I won't be asking for her advice again.

I don't look forward to Jim's return that night. *How can we talk about the salad incident without starting another fight?*

Jim comes home with a frown on his face.

"Is everything all right?" I ask, worried I'm opening up the potential of continuing our argument.

Jim has something else on his mind. "The instructor took me aside after class, and you'll never guess what he asked me."

"Not a clue," I answer.

"You know I've been complaining that I already know the material we're studying and I'm not learning anything new."

I nod.

"Well, the instructor showed me the next unit he'll be teaching and asked me if I understood it. I looked it over, and said, 'Yes.' Then he asked me if I would meet with him outside of class and explain it to him. He doesn't understand it!"

I cover my mouth. "Oh, my gosh! No wonder you've been so frustrated with this class. What are you going to do?"

"What can I do? I need to instruct the instructor! But this is the last time I'm taking a class at UNM!"

"Wow, that's awful. But are you sure you want to quit? Are all the instructors so bad? I remember when I had an art instructor who trashed my drawing in front of the entire class, and I mean *trashed*, not critiqued. I guess he was having a bad day or something."

Jim purses his lips impatiently. "What does that have to do with me?"

I hold up my hand for him to wait. "I ran to my advisor, wanting to drop the class. He talked me out of it because I was already halfway through. It was hard going back; I had to swallow my pride. Maybe I didn't learn much, but I finished with a B-minus and was able to move on in the program. I know how smart you are, and that you don't need a degree, at least not now, but it might be useful later on."

Jim shakes his head. "No, it's not worth my time."

My husband stands beside me as our beautiful boy Travis comes into the world. He never hesitates to diaper Travis or give him a bath. He plays silly games with our son and sings and reads to him. Jim no longer spends time with me in the kitchen, but I'm okay with that. As he entertains Travis, I have some quiet time cleaning up. I often find big Jim and four-month-old Travis sitting together on the couch, Jim's protective right arm circling his son, his other hand holding the paper and reading Travis the funnies.

Shortly after our son's birth, Jim and I watch a TV news segment that features a porcupine race. The poor animals are dumped out of trashcans, prodded along the racecourse with brooms, and then shooed into more trashcans at the end. The spectators howl with laughter, but I begin crying, upset at the cruelty, my maternal instincts in high gear.

I can't get the images out of my mind. A couple of days later I decide to write to Friends of Animals (FOA), of which I'm a member, asking if they are aware of the race and if they can do something to prevent it in the future. I remember Fargo, North Dakota as being the location of the race and mention it in my letter.

A week later I receive an irate call from FOA. Without my knowledge or consent they've printed my letter in their newsletter, and the mayor of Fargo is furious. He claims his fair city has never had such a race. He wants a retraction and an apology. Unfortunately, when I contact the TV news department, they have no record of running the story. There's no such thing as the Internet so I can't Google it.

Jim can't corroborate it either. All he'll say is, "What did you do?!" At first I think he's kidding, but, when he continues to repeat his question, I realize he's dead serious. For several days I wish I could disappear like an extinct species. "What did you do?!" becomes one of Jim's teasing questions to me on a regular basis. I try to act as if I think it's funny, and I don't ask him to stop. In truth, it takes me several years to overcome my shame and to appreciate the humor.

Being Travis' mom fills me with joy and satisfaction. I'm determined to give my son a healthy start in life, breastfeeding him and making his baby food. I often load little Travis in a front carrier and walk our neighborhood of small, older houses with big shade trees in their yards. When he gets a bit older, I dress him in one of the five pairs of corduroy pants I've made, and we go to a nearby pocket park. Or, I strap him to the child seat on the back of my bike, and we ride to the nearby gem and mineral shop to admire its many treasures.

By the time Travis is two, I begin to question the assumption we'll have two children. I can't say why, but somehow, I know my son is all I need. I sit down with Jim to tell him what I'm thinking.

"Are you sure this is what you want?" he asks.

"Yes, I just know it in my bones. Although I always thought I'd want a daughter, Travis is enough."

"Well," Jim says, running his fingers through his hair, "You're the one who has the most responsibility for the day-to-day care of Travis. That would be true of another child as well. So, I'll leave that decision up to you."

I hug my husband with relief. Soon, I'm in the hospital recovering from a painful tubal ligation. Jim drops in to see me but doesn't linger.

My friend Barb pops in, a puzzled look on her face. "I met Jim coming down the hall," she says. "He seemed awfully cheerful—not at all concerned about you."

"Huh. Well, he must have something else on his mind. You know these engineer types."

Barb laughs knowingly. After she leaves, I wonder, was my husband not concerned about my pain? But his cheerfulness must have meant he feels okay with our decision not to have any more children.

Jim becomes part of the team at MITS that develops the Altair, the first personal computer. The company brings in two college dropouts, Paul Allen and Bill Gates, to create the operating system. I drive Jim, Paul, and

Bill to the airport, but I can't make sense of their conversation. I haven't changed my mind about disliking computers, and this one is taking much of my husband's time. Still, I try to be supportive of Jim's excitement over this new development, knowing his work allows me to stay home taking care of our son and working on my craft.

After getting acquainted with the families in the neighborhood, I arrange for the teenage twins across the street to babysit Travis once a week while I work. This turns out better than I'd hoped. The girls come from a large family with grandparents just down the block. Travis becomes the baby of their family and thrives on all the attention. On those days, Jim comes home from work and lifts the lid on a pot cooking on the stove. Often it contains my experimentation with natural dyes—not something edible. "Don't worry, I'm not going to make you eat it," I joke. My knowledge of weaving and dyeing grows by leaps and bounds, and I later share it with the community college classes I teach.

Since I haven't lost all the weight I've gained during my pregnancy, and Jim's weight has increased too, I suggest we give Weight Watchers a try. His positive response encourages me. I research the Saturday morning meeting times, glad they offer babysitting, and make plans for attending. On the following Saturday, I begin getting ready while Jim remains in bed.

"When do you think we should leave?" I ask him.

"What are you talking about?"

"I'm talking about going to Weight Watchers. When do you think we should leave?"

"I never said I'd go!"

"Excuse me. Of course you did!"

"You're mixed up. I never said I'd go. You go ahead. I'll take care of Travis."

Surprised, disappointed, and confused, I keep turning his response around in my mind. I thought Jim had said he'd go, but he must have implied an interest without committing. Whatever his reason, I feel puzzled and let down.

At the beginning of our relationship, Jim had mentioned he wanted to lose some weight, but now it seems he's not interested in addressing it. Like food, I'll probably do best to avoid this issue.

Four

Moving into Faith

How can you seek God if he's already here? It's like standing in the
ocean and crying out, "I want to get wet." You want to get over the
line to God. It turns out he was always there.

—Deepak Chopra

Even though I've slowly abandoned my anger with God in the early days of our marriage, I've not grown closer to Him. I simply don't feel a need for a personal relationship with the Lord. I'm content with my life, and that's all that matters. When we were dating, Jim had taken me to a service at his house church, but the leader left and the group broke up soon afterwards. Since then, my husband hasn't brought up the subject of finding a faith community. In due time, however, I learn why it's said the Lord works in mysterious ways.

Life in our little Albuquerque bungalow has been pretty sweet, but Jim changes jobs and we can afford a bigger house. Shortly before our move, I'm asked to return the borrowed loom I've been using. After careful investigation of ads in my weaving magazines, I choose a new four-harness floor model available from a shop in Oregon not far from my parents. They agree to help get it shipped, enlisting the services of an uncle who owns a trucking business.

Another uncle and aunt get wind of the project and decide to contribute, giving me a hundred dollars to help pay for my project. In addition, the aunt sends me a very special package, an indigo wool and natural cotton double-weave coverlet woven around 1835 by my great-great-great-grandmother, Nancy Ann Hall. She'd brought it with her all the way from North Carolina when she made her way over the Oregon Trail. It has been handed down in our family, and when my grandmother died, its heritage was nearly lost. Fortunately, my aunt, who is into family genealogy, rescued it, waiting to find someone in my generation who would cherish it. Learning I'm a weaver makes her decision easy. I'm over the moon with excitement and gratitude as I open the package containing the coverlet.

Our new home's living room, with its bay window full of plants, becomes my studio. Jim helps set up the loom, and I begin unpacking from the move. After a few days, I look for the coverlet, and discover it's missing. In the short time I've had it in my possession, I've become attached to it, feeling as if part of Nancy Ann's spirit still resides within it. *I have to find that coverlet!*

Perhaps it had somehow fallen off one of the pickup runs as we shuttled our household across town. I put an ad in the paper, hoping someone has found it, but receive no response.

Finally, desperate, I boldly make a bargain with the Lord Almighty. "Lord," I pray, "if you help me find the coverlet, I promise I'll go back to church, and I'll take Travis to Sunday School." I don't expect an immediate answer, and I don't receive one.

One Friday afternoon, as we prepare for a weekend trip to Santa Fe, I get down one of our suitcases. It seems suspiciously heavy, and, in that moment, I know what I will find—the coverlet. Thank you, Lord! The following weekend, Jim and Travis join me in going to a church not far from our home. It feels good returning to my traditional faith with my family, and soon I'm singing in the church choir. This all seems to be fine with my husband.

The large Sunday School facility impresses me, and knowing Travis needs some structure, I help organize a community preschool co-op to be housed there. Planning meetings fills the summer. I enjoy discovering I have organizational abilities, and I feel needed and respected.

"What does your husband think of all this time and energy you're spending on the school?" the church's administrator asks me at one of our meetings.

"It's not a problem," I answer. "Jim is busy with his work, so he doesn't miss me while I'm getting the school ready to launch."

Travis is five when I become president of the co-op. We hire a teacher and are up and running. My son loves his school time. I drive him there Monday through Friday and serve as a teacher's aide twice a week. That means he and I are "going to church" six days a week. I wonder if the Lord smiles at how my promise has turned out—I'd delivered big time. And to think, it all began with the coverlet.

Jim and I hadn't shared the same Christian faith when we first met, but I believe we now hold a mutual view of Christianity that helps bind us together.

Although Jim works long hours at his new job with TelCo, he seems happy. He lingers in the morning to play with Travis, and always comes home for dinner before returning to work. I appreciate what time I have with him, but I miss the closeness from the early days of our marriage. I busy myself with our child and my weaving, as well as taking care of the house, the yard, cooking, and shopping.

Despite Jim's work, we still manage to have fun together as a family. We never miss the Albuquerque Balloon Festival or the New Mexico State Fair. We anticipate visiting Chaco Canyon in the fall, poking around its ancient cliff dwellings, the scent of decomposing cottonwood leaves wafting around us as they crunch under our feet.

Because of Jim's schedule, I try to limit my requests for help, but a creeping suspicion he takes my "homework" for granted begins to bother me. I try to think of a way he can pitch in just a little—something that will be fair to both of us. His bathroom, which I never use, comes to mind.

"Honey," I say one day, "I've been feeling a bit overwhelmed lately, what with you at work so much. Travis, the yard, the house—they take most of my time. It would be a big help if you'd be willing to be in charge of cleaning your own bathroom."

"What? Are you kidding? You think I don't do enough for our family? Is that how it is?"

Taken by surprise, I hasten to calm him down. "No, no. That's not what I'm saying. It just seems that cleaning your own bathroom wouldn't be a lot of work, but it would make it a little easier for me, and kind of a symbol that we are still connected to one another."

Jim's face grows red with emotion. "I've cleaned enough bathrooms to last me a lifetime. First my grandmother's room, which I had to clean when she lived with us, and then my Air Force sergeant—both of them gave me a bad time."

"Really? What was that about?"

"My sergeant gave me grief about the way I cleaned the latrines in the barracks, assigned me double duty, and had me shipped off to Turkey. I'm not cleaning the bathroom!"

A ball of anger rises up from my gut to my chest. Jim refuses to do something he expects me to do! If he had at least shown some understanding of my thinking, I would have let it go. But this is war! I'm not about to clean his bathroom! I try to shut my mind to the accumulating filth.

A few months later, I scurry around the house, cleaning for a meeting of my large weaving group. I know the women will want to use both bathrooms, and I cave. True to his word, Jim never cleans another toilet, but he pays a price. A small piece of trust I've held for my husband breaks away—trust that we are in this marriage together and have each other's best interests at heart.

Jim has been working furiously on an engineering project. He finally insists on a two-week vacation, planning on spending it with my family in Oregon. My mother, who always tries to please, asks what kinds of activities we'd like her to arrange. We decide on a camping trip in the mountains followed by time at the beach. Jim, who has been fascinated with the eruption of Mt. St. Helens a few months earlier asks, "Can you arrange for the mountain to erupt again?"

Mom laughs. "I'll see what I can do."

We have a fun time camping with extended family along the McKenzie River. We spend a few days at the beach. And then Jim gets a call from his boss demanding he come back immediately. Jim is livid.

"I'm betting that when you finish that job, the business will shut down," I tell him.

Jim blinks. "Why do you think that? Do you know something I don't?"

"It's just a hunch," I assure him.

On the eve of Jim's departure, we pile into the car to go out to dinner. But Jim is missing. I go back into the house to see what the delay is. I find him sitting in front of the TV. "What are you doing?" I ask. "We're all in the car, waiting for you."

Jim points to the screen. "Your Mom must have some pull! Mt. St. Helen's is erupting again!"

We proceed to the restaurant and watch the mountain from our table. Afterwards, we drive to the hills of Portland where folks have spread out blankets on their lawns and are sipping their wine, watching the eruption. We often tease Mom about her special "connection."

Back in Albuquerque, Jim practically lives at TelCo in an attempt to meet the deadline on the project. He surprises me by coming home one early afternoon, his face flushed, his body rigid. "You called it!" he exclaims. "They sold the company and are moving our division to Florida!"

"Florida! Florida? You've got to be kidding! I don't want to move to Florida!"

"I know! I know! I don't either!" He utters a few choice swear words. "I feel so betrayed. You know I've given them my all, just to come to this." He plops down in a chair, heaving a huge, deflated sigh.

"I'm angry for you, and for me too," I say, taking a second breath. "My weaving career is finally taking off. It all goes away if we have to move!" I'd just been appointed New Mexico's state representative of the Handweavers Guild of America, I'm president of Albuquerque Designer Craftsmen, and I finally have a booth at the prestigious Southwest Arts and Crafts Festival. I'd have to give up all that and start over. Besides, I've been a resident of Albuquerque for fourteen years—most of my adult life. I might have grown up as a "webbed-footed" Oregonian, but New Mexico has seeped into my bones. And Florida? Clear across the continent from our families? No way!

Jim straightens "You know what? I'm tired of being their slave. I'm going to tell them I won't go."

"You'll do that?" I ask. Hope fills my heart.

"You bet! I'm going to tell them tomorrow! This can't be the only job I can get."

I pray this is true.

Jim comes home the next day in a totally different mood. "We're going to Southern California! I told my boss you wouldn't let me move to Florida. They offered me a job at their division in Camarillo, and I accepted. I hope you don't mind that I put the blame on you."

"California? I still don't like the idea of leaving Albuquerque and all I've got going career-wise." I take a few moments to process. "At least we'll be closer to our families than we would be in Florida and you'll have a guaranteed job," I reason.

We put the house up for sale, and Jim leaves for Camarillo, a small town between Los Angeles and Santa Barbara. Travis and I stay behind, waiting for the house to sell. The market is sluggish, and the weeks crawl by before we finally get a decent offer. Plants hanging in the front window, a cat by the fire, and the scent of spiced cider simmering on the stove has charmed the buyer. I've perfected the art of home staging.

Ready or not, California here we come!

Five

Life in La La Land

1981-1989

Real happiness is cheap enough, yet how dearly we pay for its counterfeit.
—Hosea Ballou

Jim is now a junior executive. His position allows us to upgrade to a nice new two-story home in a Camarillo subdivision. It's here that the Elfery is born, providing us with much family fun and entertainment.

The Elfery begins with a generous space under the stairs, which I secretly turn into a little playhouse with the dolls and furnishings I'd had as a child. When six-year-old Travis excitedly discovers the space's transformation, I acknowledge the playthings had been mine, but I pretend I don't know how they got there.

Shortly thereafter, I fix pancakes for breakfast, putting the little cakes that result from the dibs and dabs of batter, on a small plate.

"Let's close our eyes and count to ten," Jim suggests, giving me a secret wink. When we open our eyes, the little pancakes are gone! Jim speculates there must be small, "rascally" visitors to our home—perhaps elves. "I suspect," Jim tells us with a twinkle in his eye, "that the little house under the stairs must be a portal for their visits."

Travis and I look at each other with wide eyes. "It's an Elfery!" I exclaim.

Travis jumps up from the oak table and crawls into the little room. "Elves," he calls out, "I hope you come visit us lots."

Over time, I wallpaper the space with an old-fashioned print. Jim puts in an electrical outlet so I can install Christmas lights. When my parents come to visit, Dad and I make a little stove out of different-sized tin cans, contributing to the domestic ambiance. We attribute all of these improvements to the elves. It isn't long before "they" begin decorating the space for special occasions—Christmas, St. Patrick's Day, etc., and leave us little notes and poems.

Travis loves the Elfery and often invites his friends to play there. Our involvement with the elves amuses the three of us for some time. Eventually, Travis outgrows it, but I don't.

Even though I wasn't thrilled to move to Camarillo, I'm determined to "bloom where I'm planted." I have a love affair with mountains, and the Santa Monicas on the horizon remind me of Albuquerque's Sandias. Although I'd grown to enjoy New Mexico, a part of me longed to be closer to the sea. I relish working in our yard on cool mornings when the sharp scent of the sea flows in on the mist, and I enjoy walking among fragrant eucalyptus trees in an arroyo a couple of blocks from our house.

The three of us explore the nearby beaches in all kinds of weather. At Christmas time, we gather the fruit of prickly pear cactus growing in the arroyo, and Travis and I make prickly pear jelly as gifts for family members.

Jim seems happy with his new job and is inspired to try developing a product on the side. A colleague from work agrees to help him, and they spend loads of time and money on the project. But the colleague loses interest, and Jim has to drop it. I'm sorry for my husband that it didn't work out.

I begin substitute teaching, which still gives me time to spend with family and new friends. I soon bond with Trudy, the wife of Jim's boss. A couture seamstress, she and I decide to go into the woven clothing business together. We take a business class. We design dresses, coats, wraps, capes, and vests, dyeing wool yarns for some of the garments. I weave the fabrics, complete with embellishments on the dresses and coats, and Trudy turns everything into beautifully made clothing.

Nerves jangling on our first trip to LA, Trudy and I drive through high-speed traffic, dealing with aggressive drivers who weave in and out. Our nervousness intensifies as we approach shop owners with our wares. We whoop with joy when our vests are accepted at a crafts gallery, and we're over the moon on the exciting day when two of our dresses are accepted on consignment in a prestigious Rodeo Drive shop. One exquisite black and gold dress with silk lining is also featured in a book on the fiber arts.

We've had fun with our little business and made some fabulous garments, but our sales lag. We don't make enough money to make it worth continuing.

I miss collaborating with Trudy. I wonder if instead I can build a reputation as a teacher of woven garments and make a career out of that. What I need is name recognition. To that end, I begin writing and submitting articles to crafts magazine. My hands shake with excitement as the magazine with my first article arrives in the mail. Travis' comment, "I'm proud of you, Mom," gives me warm fuzzies.

I have a few more articles published, receiving a small check for each, but my efforts don't result in my goal of a sustainable career. Clearly, it's time for a change. I've thought of myself, at least in part, as "The Weaver." I've poured myself into this work for nearly two decades, and my decision to move on means losing a part of my identity. It takes me a few months to recover from the depression that follows.

My world comes crashing down the day the unthinkable happens. On September 9, 1984, Mom calls. "Are you sitting down?" she asks. Her voice breaking, she says, "Matthew was on a Boy Scout outing in the mountains. The kids were swimming in the lake, and … and Linda, he drowned!"

A black cloud engulfs me. Matthew is my brother's son, my red-headed twelve-year-old nephew. "Oh, Lord! Where are Les and Sandy? Are you going to drive down to Eugene to be with them? Please drive carefully. I don't want to lose you too!" I stammer.

I immediately find Jim who holds me while I cry. Finding comfort in his arms, I can't imagine what my brother and sister-in-law are feeling.

Hours later, I pull myself together enough to go to the grocery store, but I can't understand how everything seems unchanged with Matthew no longer in the world. I leave my grocery cart in the aisle, go home, and crawl into bed, wanting to make the world go away.

The next week, nine-year-old Travis and I fly to Oregon for Matthew's memorial service. We've recently lost one of our cats, and my son seems to understand death better than I do.

I desperately need some answers to the age-old question, "How could God let something like this happen?" Jim and I haven't been going to church since our move, but having been raised a Methodist, I call the local Methodist church and ask to speak with a pastor. I'm referred to Reverend Ray, the Associate Pastor. When we sit down to talk, he doesn't gloss over my questions or spout platitudes. Instead, we discuss the nature of this world and of God's part in it.

I come to understand that evil and good are allowed their play in our world because we have free will. God is a source of comfort, strength, and refuge—not a chess player moving us around like hapless pawns. We don't often have a clear understanding of God's plans, but we are promised that "And we know that in all things God works for the good of those who love him, who have been called according to his purpose." (Romans 8:28). I find this concept hard to accept, but I pray that Matthew's death can somehow have meaning. I come to view this world as a testing ground for trusting in that promise, no matter the circumstances. Although I'll never think of Matthew's death as something good, it causes me look at life in a deeper way and nudges my family back to church.

Since our family is attending church regularly, I join the choir. Not only is the director very good at directing, his drop-dead looks inspire the women who flock around him in other ways—one recently divorced alto in particular. She's entered the romance writing market, and, upon learning I'm a weaver, she asks if I will give her some information as the heroine in her next book is a weaver. I give her a quick course and read her previous book. It doesn't take me long to realize her description of the hero fits that of our director. I feel a mixture of amusement and embarrassment for her and throw the book away.

Curious as to how she handles my information, I read her next book when it is published. Her description of the hero again fits that of our choir director. I laugh to myself and throw that book away, too, deeming both books pretty trashy.

Jim's work is demanding, and his darkening mood reflects the stress he's under. His boss resigns, and Jim is promoted to Manager of Engineering. He feels appreciated doing work he enjoys. His happiness spills over into our home life, as he jokes more and becomes more present with Travis and me. This is the kind of life and relationship I've been missing.

The boost in Jim's salary means I can quit substitute teaching. After dinner one night, as we sit around the oak table, I share with Jim something I've been considering. "Honey, you know I've given up on a weaving career. I so appreciate all you've done to support me as I tried to make something of it. But I've come to see it's never going to pan out. Besides, weaving has become harder and harder on my back. It's time I look in another direction."

"Okay …"

"So, UCLA Extension has an interior design certificate program out of their campus in Santa Monica. I've wanted to be an interior designer since

I was a teenager. Maybe this is my chance to fulfill that dream. I'd like to take a couple of classes to find out if this is the path I should pursue."

"Hmm. What would that look like? Would you have to find an after-school sitter for Travis?"

"No, that's the beauty of it. The classes I'd be taking are at night. I could fix dinner for you and Travis before I go. You usually spend time in your office after dinner, so you'd barely know I was gone, and you could be here for Travis while you both do your *homework*."

I show Jim the school catalog and we talk about the details—how much it will cost, the specific hours, the number of classes, etc. "If this is what you really want, go ahead," he concludes.

I hug him fiercely. "Thank you! Thank you!"

As I maneuver my yellow VW Rabbit on the winding Pacific Coast Highway to UCLA's Santa Monica campus, my stomach jumps with anticipation. At first, the architectural drawing class proves to be a challenge, but, with Jim's help, I get the hang of it, learning to enjoy drawing floor plans and space planning. The Kitchen and Bath Design course turns out to be a favorite. I especially like our field trips to designer showrooms in the area.

One of my instructors introduces the class to the West Hollywood Pacific Design Center, commonly known as the "Blue Whale." There, we explore showrooms of furniture, fabrics, art and more, normally only accessible to interior designers. One evening, the class joins our instructor at a fancy reception there, complete with real orange trees and wonderful hors d'oeuvres. I bring along eleven-year-old Travis.

"Mom, this is really fancy. I should have worn better clothes."

I smile and give his hand a reassuring squeeze. I don't remind him I'd asked him to dress nicely.

Already having a background in art from my UNM days, I do fine with the second semester classes. However, Jim begins asking me about his "investment" in my education.

"By the end of this semester, you'll have had four classes. Don't you think that's enough? They aren't cheap you know. When are they going to pay off?"

My mouth flies open in surprise. "Gosh, are we that bad off? I didn't know there was a deadline to making this a paying career."

"Well, look," he says, his tone becoming more insistent, "you already have an Art Ed degree. That and those four classes ought to be enough to get you a job."

"I was hoping to get a certificate in interior design," I answer, my head reeling with Jim's unexpected pressure. My husband has never before been eager for me to find work.

"When we first talked about these classes, you didn't mention anything about a certificate, did you?" he asks, sounding like a prosecuting attorney at trial.

"I guess not," I weakly reply.

Jim's pressure proves to be too much, and I drop out, a keen disappointment. I don't verbalize my feelings, though, trying to rationalize that, since Jim is the breadwinner of the family, I should trust his assessment of our finances. Still, Jim's lack of empathy for the loss of my dream leaves me suspicious and unhappy. *If Jim could spend money on his failed project, he shouldn't discourage me from pursuing my interior design certification.*

Not wanting to give up on my dream, I find a job in town as an assistant at Polly's Interiors, a husband-and-wife establishment. Excited to start just as Travis' school year begins, I immerse myself in the fabrics, wallpaper, and window covering samples. I organize the wallpaper books and discover I'm good at helping in-store customers pull the decorating elements of their homes together. I learn to place orders, and I create a color board for Polly who is pitching a job and doesn't know how to put one together, glad to be a valuable asset. Every day I go to work with joy in my heart.

As I grow to understand the business, though, I become bothered with some of Polly's practices. For instance, she orders more wallpaper than is actually needed, returns the leftover wallpaper, and keeps the refund. Also, she expects me to mislead customers about when work on their job will start, how soon she can meet with them, etc.

I hate having to lie for Polly. Both Polly's husband and their secretary see my potential and encourage Polly to mentor me toward becoming a full-fledged designer. Polly, however, is not about to let the happen, apparently having come to see me as a rival rather than someone who could help her expand the business. Her attitude toward me does not engender feelings of loyalty.

I have concerns for Travis too. Now, twelve and a latchkey kid, he arrives home a couple of hours before me. My friend across the street is always home at that time for her son, and Travis is welcome to drop in. Still, his calls after school tear at my heart. "Mom, I wish you were here! Can't you come home now? Please!"

What is this idea that women can have it all? I quit when his school year ends. Jim is also glad to have me back home full time.

That summer, I enjoy taking Travis and his buddies to the beach. Our son has a wide range of interests, and we go to comic shops in LA, a gem and mineral exhibit, the Neon Museum, and Little Tokyo, where we sample our first sushi. Time spent with Travis feels much more valuable and satisfying than working at Polly's.

Six

Sunshine and Shadow

*But once in a while, you pick the right thing, the exact best thing.
Every day, the moment you open your eyes and pull off your blankets,
that's what you hope for. The sunshine on your face, warm enough to
make your heart sing.*

–Sarah Ockler, *Bittersweet*

"How does your husband respond to your chronic pain?" the interviewer at the Pain Management Center of UCLA's Medical School asks. His question makes me pause. Searching my memory, I finally reply. "I don't think he notices." *What does he notice?*

My headaches had begun in Albuquerque but have grown worse in Camarillo. Were they caused by an auto accident several years earlier in which my hippie van was totaled on my way to teaching? Was it a yoga position that left my neck hurting for days? A session at judo when I put too much pressure on my head? There's no way of telling.

After seeking all kinds of remedies and doctors, I've finally found my way to the center. There, I'm given the Minnesota Multiphasic Personality Inventory (MMPI) test, and a physical therapist examines me. When he probes a spot in my back, I immediately experience a headache. He calls it "referred pain" in which seemingly unrelated parts of the body feel the pain. At last I know the source and can prove it isn't just "in my head," as some of my doctors have suggested.

The interviewer assures me my personality profile is healthy, and tells me I have Myofascial Pain Syndrome, a chronic pain condition. "Fascia is the layer, or sheath of tissue that lies between the skin and muscles," he explains. "Most people's fascia is flexible, but yours has become somewhat inflexible. The pain can be triggered by certain physical movements or by stress-related tension transferred to your muscles."

"You may not be aware of the physical movements that harm you, since the pain is often delayed," he tells me. "I'm prescribing physical therapy, but you should know you'll probably have to deal with this condition the rest of your life. The best way is to avoid stress."

The rest of my life? This is a hard pill to swallow.

Despite this warning, I decide to start my own design business, thinking it will give me the flexibility I need to balance a career and family. I choose to begin small, concentrating on what I call "Kids' Places." Jim doesn't want me spending much money on advertising, but I convince him to let me put faux stained glass signs in the rear side windows of our new van. Camarillo is a small town, and it isn't long before Polly catches sight of the van. The look on her face is priceless. Surprise gives way to fury in a matter of seconds. At that moment, my fancy signs are worth every penny.

Mrs. Patel, my first client, finds me through business cards I have on display in a store that sells high-end children's furniture. She and her husband are building a mansion on a hill in the most prestigious part of town. My bid is for designing the bedrooms of their three children. We negotiate, and I agree to a very reasonable price, plus offer to share a portion of my designer discount on the furnishings. The Patels understand it will be advantageous to have me design their entire home. The Tudor-style exterior contrasts with the Euro-modern interior, not my personal style, but I'm up for it. Designing a large master bedroom and separate bathrooms for the couple, a bedroom and bath for each of their three children, a maid's room, a sauna, etc., consumes me.

I soon discover Mr. Patel has a shrewd business sense, and discerning how green I am, tries to nickel and dime me at every turn. My nerves extend down to my toenails. I have scant experience working with challenging clients, and I suffer from math phobia. One day, Mrs. Patel asks me the dimensions of a queen-size bed, and I freeze. Pleading illness, I leave hurriedly. *What an idiot I am, not knowing the dimensions of a bed!*

Finally, Mr. Patel pushes me too far, expecting me to pay up front for materials I order. I inform him I'm quitting. But Mrs. Patel loves my vision for her kids' rooms and asks me to reconsider. I return, but this time, on my terms. Oh, the lessons I'm learning.

I struggle to estimate materials and costs, and keeping my business books is a challenge. I see no alternative but to ask Jim for help. He reluctantly agrees, hunching his shoulders and breathing in an exasperated way, clearly expressing his displeasure. I'm not sure what his issue is, but I'm afraid to ask.

An inner dialogue runs through my mind as we work. *Is he too busy? Does he wish I wasn't pursuing this business? Does he not want to spend this much time with me?*

This is torture. I wish I wasn't so stupid, so helpless. I wish my high school counselor hadn't told me I'd never need anything beyond computation because I was a girl! It's all I can do to stand here, taking in Jim's displeasure. I just want to run away. If I ask Jim what's wrong, he's likely to get even more disgusted and quit. Then where will I be? I've got to hold my tongue.

Interior design has been my dream, and I want mightily to succeed, but I never imagined it would be like this. I feel squeezed, with no room to breathe. *God, why have you given me design talent without mathematical ability? How can I get past this?*

Even though I have problems and fears, the project turns out well. The pièce de résistance is a puppet theater headboard that I design, arranging to have it fabricated and painted to match the tall wallpaper border.

Having completed this project, it seems I'm on my way to my dream career. Since that means I need office space, and so does Jim, we decide to remodel. The living room ceiling of our home soars to twenty feet, with a tall attic space over the adjoining kitchen. Thanks to my new training, I draw up plans to turn the attic space into an inner office for Jim, and a studio for me in a new loft over the dining area. A French door separates our two spaces. One end of my office serves as a lounge area for clients, with wicker furniture and plants beneath the new skylight. I do all the painting and staining, and the project turns out to be beautiful and functional for both of us. I invite the local newspaper to take photos of the remodel, but the reporter/photographer focuses on the Elfery instead. Still, I glean a little publicity from the article.

Jim and I continue to have our problems, but things get better in the autumn of 1987, when his company takes several of its top employees to the Telecom trade show in Geneva, Switzerland. "I'm glad you're not working at Polly's anymore," Jim tells me. "That means you can go with me." Ever since I'd read *Heidi* by Johanna Spyri and discovered some of my ancestors were Swiss, I've wanted to visit Switzerland. My parents agree to take care of Travis.

We arrive in Geneva a few days before the expo begins. I'd read about the tiny village of Gimmelwald in Rick Steve's book *Europe Through the Back Door*. It sits high above the Lauterbrunnen Valley, is accessible only by cable car, and sounds like the kind of Heidi experience I'm hoping for. Jim isn't so sure, but I tell him I'll never forgive him if we don't take this side trip. He finally agrees, and we spend a night discovering that down comforters, combined with the coin-operated heater, are too much of a good thing. We laugh at ourselves as we open our window, allowing the rush of cold air to cool us down.

Back in Geneva, Jim shows me off with obvious pleasure during the several social events. "I'm glad I brought you along," he tells me, his arm around my waist as we stroll along Lake Geneva after a lovely dinner in a fancy French restaurant.

I feel glad too. So glad.

A business trip to England proves equally satisfying. I'm Jim's convivial companion during the company's social time and enjoy being a tourist during his business hours.

For me, the best part is the afternoon Jim and I rent a car and go looking for Wightwick Manor, a large half-timbered Victorian house and a National Trust landmark I'd discovered in planning for our trip. *I'm so lucky!* Here is my husband, willing to drive into the country on the "wrong side" of the road in order for me to see this place.

It takes us a while to find the manor, and we arrive late in the afternoon. Lady Mander, resident of the house and a descendent of the home's builder, meets us at the door. To our consternation, she tells us in a rather imperious British manner we are too late for the tour. Though we've arrived within touring hours, the actual time to begin is past. "Oh, please!" I beg, working up a mighty cry. "I came all the way from California to see your house!"

The Lady relents and leads us through the public rooms. Our tour ends in the kitchen where I have a chance to chat with her. I note that the artisans of her Wightwick Manor have highly influenced America's Arts and Crafts Movement led by Gustav Stickley.

She seems surprised by this information and quite interested.

"I'm lucky enough to have a Stickley Brothers oak table and chairs," I tell her.

"Indeed, you are!" she responds.

Dusk is upon us as we thread our way back to the city. "Thank you so much for this wonderful trip," I tell Jim, patting his leg.

Jim gives me a smile. "You were quite persuasive with Lady Mander. I'm glad she warmed to you. I know you've told me the table is special, but I didn't realize it was *that* special."

I nod. "I knew the original owners in Tigard. When they passed, I was able to acquire it with all four leaves and six chairs. I don't mind its wear and tear. It feels like a member of the family."

"I see what you mean, but right now we have a little problem—we're lost."

We drive and drive, getting hungrier by the hour. Finally, we spy the lights of a pub shining in the dark and stop to get something to eat. I choose a typical British dish of bangers and mash. Jim chooses lasagna.

"Lasagna in the middle of England's countryside?" I tease. "Seems odd, doesn't it?"

Jim shrugs. "Sounds good to me."

We pick up our meals at the bar and dig in. "Oh," I mutter. "I can't say I like this!"

"Here, taste mine," Jim offers, a smile teasing his lips.

I take a bite. "Wow, this is the best lasagna I've ever had. I think it must have fresh herbs in it. The laugh's on me!"

Back home, I begin my first journal, writing about our travels and how happy I am.

Journal Entry - January 12, 1989

Jim seems to be making an effort to leave most of his work worries at the office. My parents even noticed when they came to visit. I hope he can keep it up. We're finding time to have fun together again. Jim is helping Travis with his model rocketry hobby. I'm so glad.

Seven

On My Knees

*Let your compassion quickly meet our needs because we are on the
brink of despair.*

–Psalm 79:8

Jim and I have been married for over ten years, but neither of us has fully
recognized or talked about our different feelings concerning holidays.
During most of our time in New Mexico, we spent Christmases with
Jim's mother, sister, and cousin, as Jim's father had died shortly after
Travis' birth. Now that we're in California, and there are just the three of
us, Christmas traditions have become problematic.

As a child, I always loved Christmas—the decorations and lights,
the scented tree boughs brought into our home, the brightly wrapped
packages under the tree, and of course, the music! I try carrying on similar
practices with my own family, but I often feel as if I'm dragging Jim and
Travis behind me. Jim agrees to cut a tree in the forest, but there always
seems to be some problem that makes him miserable. Maybe the weather

is too cold. Or the roads are too snowy. Or snow slides down inside his collar while he saws at the tree. (I try not to laugh at that one.)

One Christmas, Jim sets up the movie camera in the living room and asks Travis to film us putting up our large, live tree. Jim gives me orders, and I'm cheerfully trying to follow them, while he complains about this and that. Exasperated, I take the empty plastic bucket I've put out to water the tree and place it ever so gently on his head. Travis and I exchange looks, both holding our breath, wondering how Jim will respond. He sits there for a few long minutes. Travis keeps filming. Finally, Jim takes off the bucket and gives us a rueful smile. Travis laughs and I breathe a sigh of relief.

Laughing at ourselves has always helped. So do pets. It is one thing Jim and I can agree upon, and their companionship and antics often serve to brighten the mood in our home. Yum Yum has passed away, and we adopt a young dog that friends have found abandoned in a park. She seems to be part Australian shepherd and part Border collie—a black and white ball of nervous energy. We name her Tillie, short for Matilda. Jim and Travis enjoy her tremendously, but I'm her alpha. She and I take daily walks around the neighborhood, to the nearby park, or through the gully. I can't convince my guys to go with me, but Tillie is always ready to be my companion and helps me walk off my growing frustrations at home.

Journal Entry – February 19, 1989

Jim came home from the dentist today in a foul mood. I took a walk around the block because there didn't seem to be anything I could do to help him. I wish his bad moods didn't upset me too, but when I gaze on the Santa Monica mountains, it helps soothe my soul.

On that occasion, I leave in a hurry without Tillie, and my walk has an unexpected surprise. As I near home, a young cat runs up to me. I ask the woman working in a yard nearby if it's hers. She says no, that it has been hanging around for the last few days.

I look at the cat—a pretty calico—and ask her if she wants to come home with me. To my surprise, she answers with a meow.

"Then follow me," I say, and she does. I open our front door, and she walks right in. Tillie and our cat Lucky inspect her. The calico hisses and stands her ground. We wonder if she'll decide to stay.

Eventually it becomes apparent the cat has adopted us as her family. We name her Rachel.

Our tightrope walk between good times and unhappy ones seems to be shifting more to the negative. Jim's prevailing mood casts a gloom over our family.

Journal Entry - March 29, 1989

Jim's work situation is not good. It seems someone is trying to get rid of him, just as they did his former boss. I'm sorry Jim couldn't tell me about it sooner; I might have been able to console him. I'm praying fervently he can withstand the slings and arrows coming his way, and that the Lord will guide him to a better situation.

Travis is also facing problems in eighth grade. His best friend Kevin becomes the leader of a small group of boys who begin bullying my son at school. Kevin has spent much time with our family, even going to Disneyland with us, and we have no clue as to what changed his attitude. Whatever the reason, I grieve for Travis and the hurt he feels, but I don't know what to do about it. I consider talking with Kevin but am afraid he'll label Travis a mama's boy. Travis' favorite teacher acknowledges the problem, but she doesn't seem to know what to do either. Kevin's betrayal has a profound impact on Travis, shaking his self-confidence and stealing his happiness. He begins to see himself as an outsider, different from the other kids.

My husband is being bullied at work. My son is being bullied at school. They're both hurting, and I hurt for them. What can I do but be available as a sounding board as they work out their problems? Prayer is the best answer I have.

Journal Entry - April 26, 1989

I'm feeling discouraged this morning. We must find a way to change our lives. Sometimes I think Jim and I hate each other. Sometimes he gets very angry with me and starts shouting obscenities. When that happens, I feel sad, angry, and trapped. I know he's under a lot of pressure, but it doesn't help either of us when he acts like this. There's a knot between my shoulder blades that never seems to go away. Something's got to give, and soon!

I pray for months, asking that Jim find a job near family, either in Oregon or back in New Mexico. I fall on my face before the Lord, sobbing and sharing my fears for our future. Even though Jim is a brilliant engineer and has a track record to attest to it, his lack of a college degree proves to be a tremendous handicap.

Jim comes home after going to a promising interview, and by his posture, I immediately know it hasn't gone well. "I sit down for the interview," he tells me, weariness in his voice, "and the guy has his head down, shuffling through my application as if he's looking for something. Finally, he raises his head and gives me a puzzled look, 'Now where did you get your degree? I'm not finding that information here,' he says."

"As you can see," I tell him, "I have extensive and successful experience in this field. I've never felt a need for a degree."

"'No degree, no job offer. Sorry!' he says, and escorts me out of the office, just like that!"

I give Jim a hug. "Oh, honey, that's terrible. I'm so sorry! You must be feeling pretty low."

"Yup," he says, squaring his shoulders. "Well, I'll be in my office."

My heart breaks for my husband, and I silently rail at businesses that insist on looking only at degrees and not real work experience.

Finally, on the ninth month of prayers, Jim's former boss calls and asks if he's interested in relocating to Central Oregon. Joe is working there for the subsidiary of a large company, and there is a position open that would be a good fit for Jim.

Perfect! Jim interviews and gets the job. We give God the glory and start packing. When I mention to strangers we're moving to Bend, they often ask why. I boldly reply, "The Lord is sending us," surprised and pleased their response is often positive.

Jim promises once he is out from under the pressure of his current work, he'll be happier and have more time for us.

Travis, then fourteen, doesn't want to leave California and fights the move. "Dad will never be happy," he predicts. "Moving won't change that."

Eight

Home to Oregon

1989

Although no one can go back and make a brand-new start, anyone can start from now and make a brand-new ending.
—Carl Bard

I'm ecstatic to be back in Oregon, and Bend is the perfect place to start fresh. I immediately take to the area—its mountains, trees, rivers, lakes, and friendly people. I look forward to cross-country skiing, hiking, and learning how to kayak at nearby lakes. Shortly after our move, I take Travis to one of Bend's two shopping malls. We both gasp when we spot a dead deer strapped to the roof of a parked SUV. Clearly, we aren't in SoCal anymore.

Feeling flush with Jim's nice salary, we buy a lot on Aubrey Butte with a view of a dozen snow-capped mountains where we plan to build a custom home. We also purchase an interim house in town where we will live until the new house is finished.

In the beginning, Jim spends more family time with us than he did in California. We invest in ski gear and take cross-country ski lessons on Mt.

Bachelor. After learning the fundamentals, we insist that Travis come with us. On a lovely day on the mountain, under a winter-blue sky dotted with fluffy white clouds, we ski as a family. At first, Travis complains, but finally settles down. Afterwards we picnic on a large rock on our lot. "Honey," I say to Jim at the end of the day, "this is the life I've always wanted for our family. Thank you."

Jim smiles and nods in agreement.

We continue to ski sporadically during the next couple of winters until Jim falls going down an icy slope. His left knee pains him terribly, and he can't stand. I frantically ski out to the parking lot and drive to the nearest phone to alert ski patrol. I return to the parking lot to meet the patrol and ride on the back of one of their snowmobiles in order to direct them to Jim. The hospital takes x-rays and confirms he has a broken kneecap that will require surgery. I'm sorry for him and his pain, and I don't blame him for not wanting to get back on skis. I must confess, though, I'm sad this is one more thing we won't be doing together.

Since I'd spent much time gathering information for the building of our new house, Jim suggests that, instead of getting a job, I look into what it would take to serve as our general contractor. I do some research but discover not being an experienced general contractor with a good reputation in the area would make it difficult to find good subcontractors.

We interview several builders, and Jim finds one he likes. He and the builder both pressure me to settle on one of the stock plans he shows us.

Jim tells me, "I like this guy, and we can save a bunch of money by using a stock plan."

"I've looked over those plans," I say. "I don't see anything that will work for us. For one thing, I thought we agreed we wanted a guest bedroom on the main floor so people like your mother wouldn't have to climb stairs."

"Well, yes, but if we have the master bedroom on the main, she can use that when she visits."

"I don't think she'd go for that. You know your mother, always sacrificing for everybody else. She'd feel guilty and uncomfortable. Besides, none of these plans gives the best views of the mountains. I think it would be a shame not to take advantage of all our lot has to offer."

"Well, I like a stock plan. You're too picky. We'll never get anything built."

"Oh, yeah? I'll tell you what; you build your house and I'll build mine!"

Jim and I can't agree. We put the project on hold.

The honeymoon period wears off at Jim's work, and, once again, he's unhappy with his job. From what he shares with me, he has plenty of reason.

Journal Entry - January 15, 1990

Jim's work situation has soured. The company is in a slump and they are cutting back people's hours and giving him lots of different jobs to do. Jim's new boss regularly tries to bait Jim into an argument. Why that would be, I can't imagine, but the man's behavior seems to be escalating.

Jim becomes even testier than he'd been in California. If Travis or I try to talk with him, we're greeted with, "Can't you see I'm busy?"

I tell my husband I don't need the home we planned to build. Since he's so miserable at work, I'm willing to go back to teaching so he can quit his job and finish his degree. He declines with a flat, "No." I'm secretly relieved, concerned that the stress of teaching might exacerbate my pain condition.

The issue of food comes up again in a new and unexpected way. I buy two cans of mixed nuts to bring to a church meeting. I put them in a serving dish and leave the empty cans on the kitchen counter.

Travis rushes up to me as soon as I get home, worry and shock on his face. "Mom, Dad called you a b****!"

"No! What?!"

"I'm not kidding. I guess he thought he'd help himself to some nuts from one of those cans, but when he discovered they were empty, he called you a selfish b****. He's never said anything like that before."

I put a shaky hand on my son's shoulder, feeling sick. "Wow! I don't know what to say. He shouldn't have said such a thing. I'm glad you told me. I'd better talk with him."

I climb the stairs to Jim's office, knock on his door, and go in. "Jim," I say, "Travis just told me you called me a selfish b****. He's very upset, and so am I."

Jim looks at me with a little frown on his face, his chin tilted up defiantly. "Well, you shouldn't have eaten all those nuts."

That sick feeling turns to anger. "For your information, I didn't eat any of them. They were for church. But that's beside the point. You called me a b***** in front of our son!"

"He's a tattletale. He shouldn't have told you."

"Of course he would tell me. He should have told me. He *needed* to tell me!"

Jim shrugs his shoulders and swivels around in his chair to face his computer screen.

"You're full of it!" I say, trying to keep my voice low so Travis won't hear me. I march out the door, slamming it behind me. *So much for keeping this quiet.*

I'm so hurt over Jim's attitude toward me and towards Travis, I can't sleep. I keep wondering what happened to the sweet man who had once said, "I wuv you, Linda" in his Donald Duck voice.

The next day, Travis tells me his dad gave him a bad time for telling me. I again confront Jim, and again he's unapologetic.

This incident involving food gets me thinking. Jim obviously has bigger issues than I'd realized. But I know from experience, talking with him about it won't prove to be productive.

I make Christmas preparations alone. Neither Jim nor Travis want to be involved, so I buy the tree from a lot (getting dog poop on my shoe), stuff it into the van, set it up, and decorate it. This isn't the kind of family I grew up with, and it isn't the kind of family I wanted or thought I'd signed on for. My anger, disappointment, and self-pity overshadow the season.

My folks are excited to have us "just over the mountains," and when they aren't traveling with their trailer, we visit back and forth every few months. Sometimes, I look at Mt. Hood and imagine my mom, who twice climbed the mountain as a Girl Scout, looking at it from her side. What a nice feeling.

Shortly before Mom and Dad leave for home from one of their visits, I come down with the flu. It's so nice having Mom taking care of me, but soon they have to go. Mom calls Jim at work to alert him I'm ill, and asks him to be sure to check up on me when he gets home.

Late that day, I awake to hear Jim come into the house. I desperately want water and meds. I wait to hear his footsteps on the stairs to our bedroom, but instead, there's the sound of the TV. I call and call, but he can't hear me.

What seems like hours later, he finally pokes his head into our bedroom.

"Why didn't you check up on me when you got home?" I croak.

He shrugs. "Oh, I didn't want to disturb you."

"But I needed you!" I say, near tears. "Didn't Mom ask you to check up on me?"

"Sorry."

His "sorry" feels insincere and I don't buy it. A familiar feeling of hurt and anger permeates my body, but I'm too sick to do anything but cry. Rex had physically left me, but at least he'd been honest. It seems that Jim has left me emotionally but can't, or won't, tell the truth. I guess I'm not ready to consider where that reality might lead.

Singing helps. When we first moved to Bend, Jim and I joined the local First Presbyterian Church, and I became a member of the folk choir. Four of us in the choir begin a tradition of going out for margaritas after practice. I so enjoy these women, all of whom are divorced, feeling more connected to them than to my few married girlfriends.

I often sit down at my piano, singing from a Twila Paris songbook. My voice chokes with tears as I sing, *Do I Trust You*. Proverbs 3:5-6 says, "Trust in the Lord with all your heart and lean not on your own understanding; in all your ways acknowledge him, and he will make your paths straight." I'm trying hard to trust the Lord.

Our interim home sits across from a two-acre field with a pile of rubble. I continue my habit of walking off my frustrations, and the field beckons me. Soon I discover I'm not alone, as I'm met with a shrill whistle. Looking around, I spy the head of an animal I don't recognize. It resembles a beaver, but since there is no water nearby, I'm puzzled.

After asking around, I learn it is a marmot. Marmots live in colonies and have scouts to warn other members of intruders, much like prairie dogs.

I climb on top of the rubble and look down at the paths the marmots have created in the field. Once, I spy a marmot studying me with his shoe-button eyes from a crack between the rocks. Almost every day, Tillie and I cross the road to the marmot field. One spring morning I follow the marmots' path to a smaller rock pile. The scrape of my boot elicits faint chirping noises from below. I've stumbled upon the marmot nursery. Being in touch with nature in moments like these always gives me a measure of peace.

Journal Entry - April 27, 1990

I'm getting so weary of Jim's moods. I tried to read Job just now, but finally gave up—it was so full of complaining! I wonder if we would both be happier apart. I'm glad we're going for family counseling this week.

Jim astounds me with his reply when I first approach him about counseling. "I don't believe in it!" he declares.

I feel the world tilt. "How could you forget what it did for us in the beginning? And Travis seems so unhappy. We have to go." I insist.

Jim expels an exasperated sigh. "All right."

In truth, we are all unhappy. Travis habitually shuts himself up in his room just like his father. I hope his behavior is a passing teenage thing. I know boys need to create some distance between themselves and their moms, but to have both my guys "absent" is nearly unbearable. Upset and depressed over the whole dynamic, I become uninterested in food and cooking (not like me!) and lose several pounds.

Our counselor observes I seem lonely at home. He also points out that we do a lot of conflict avoidance. I'm glad he understands our dynamic. Still, working with him doesn't help us solve our problems. Nothing changes.

Journal Entry - January 5, 1991

I'm probably going crazy. I keep expecting something to happen that will change my life dramatically. The telephone will ring, a letter will be delivered, there will be someone at the door to announce the news:

"Linda, from henceforth, your life will go in a new, wonderful direction! Here is the road map!"

I know better, of course. I know if I want my life to change, I must do it. I guess I feel I've been trying to do that all my adult life and it's like swimming upstream. Is there a time I'm going to hit my stride and flow with the river instead? I feel myself cracking.

I finally find an escape—or should I make that plural?

Nine

My Cheating Heart

*... the devil doesn't come dressed in a red cape and pointy horns. He
comes as everything you've ever wished for ...*
–Tucker Max, *A**holes Finish First*

Journal Entry – October 15, 1991
*I'm in the arms of another man. I tell him we shouldn't
be together. He says, "When love leaves one place, it finds
someplace else to go." I awaken, disturbed by the message of
my dream.*

I find someplace else to go at church in the person of Phil, a single
father—tall, intelligent, and kind—not unlike Jim when I first met
him.

I've quickly integrated myself into the life of our church. Besides
joining the folk choir, I volunteer to teach a class on spiritual gifts, a
subject I studied while living in Southern California. I haven't known
Phil, my co-leader, for long when he comes to our house to discuss the

particulars of the class. We sit at the oak table, brainstorming, and our planning proves productive. As he prepares to leave that day, he mentions being divorced and how his kids are going to help him paint his kitchen cabinets. *Pretty great for a man to be interested in doing something like that.*

I shut the front door behind him, and it hits me with an almost physical force—this is the man God means for me. The thought shocks me, and I almost laugh out loud. *How clever you are, Lord!* Then I stop myself. *What are you going to do with Jim? Bump him off?*

I look up the word "test" in the concordance of my Bible. "Do not conform any longer to the pattern of this world, but be transformed by the renewing of your mind. Then you will be able to test and approve what God's will is—His good, pleasing, and perfect will." (Romans 12:2). I know that "renewing of my mind" does not include fantasizing over someone other than my husband. Still, I keep being drawn to this man, even though it's a form of cheating.

I attend a meeting at Phil's house and discover he folds his laundry and likes to cook, unlike my husband who resists those chores whenever I ask him to help. Phil seems to be a real man, not like the grown child to whom I'm married.

One evening a few weeks later, Phil and I schedule a review of our plans for the class with our pastor. The pastor doesn't show, and we have no way into the church. For an hour, we talk in my van. We begin with the class, but then go on to share our faith and mutual love of singing to the Lord. Although an ordinary conversation, I feel a deep connection.

A few days later, Phil calls to tell me something of little consequence, and then proceeds to describe his first day at work on his new job. *That's something he'd do with a spouse.* It feels so intimate. I know he enjoys my company and appreciates my intellect. *I love this feeling and I want more of it.* It's been years since I've felt validation from someone I respect and find attractive. Although these feelings don't help my marriage, and qualify as a sin, I think of Phil way too much.

As much as I'm attracted to Phil, I don't put him in my new romance novel. The idea of writing the story began with a romantic dream—a subconscious means of escaping the pain of my marriage. The romance writer in my California church choir must have influenced me after all, as I make this decision unexpectedly. Perhaps it's my way of dodging an affair, but it's a curious choice, nevertheless. The only fiction I've ever written was in ninth grade for science class—a scintillating little tale about the unrequited love of Sid Squid and Cathy Cuttlefish.

The trouble is that my story has no plot. I get a few books on writing romance and plotting from the library, spend a couple of weeks reading dozens of romances, join a writer's group, and begin a new story—one with a plot.

I'd not been happy when Jim first brought an Altair computer home in Albuquerque—they already took up too much of my husband's time at work—but over the years I've become a computer convert. My office is in our kitchen nook, and thanks to Jim's tutoring, I become pretty good at basic word processing.

I soon become obsessed with writing. Every weekday morning, after sending my guys off for the day and finishing my chores, I hurry to my computer and write furiously. I write until noon and then pry myself away to clean up and eat. After lunch I take Tillie for a long walk, carrying a little tape recorder with me. As I walk, ideas for the story pop into my head and I get them down on tape. I love this process of writing, and discover I subconsciously leave hints of things to come in earlier chapters.

Fiction writers often start with a "what if" question. What if I had been born with long legs instead of short ones, and had been given red hair and green eyes like my dad instead of brown hair and eyes? What if I'd had the drive and confidence to pursue to the fullest my dream of being an interior designer? My heroine is someone I wish I'd been, and I'm able to incorporate some of the interior design experience I've had.

Unlike most romance novels, I give the hero of my story almost as much attention as the heroine. I want him to be a big proponent of living in Oregon to contrast with Meg's affinity for Los Angeles. Matt, named after my nephew, is self-confident, a lover of family and the outdoors, and, if pushed, open to self-examination. Since I've been enjoying Oregon Public Television's *Oregon Field Guide*, I give Matt the same job as the host of the show. I score an interview with the real host who shares some of his experiences, and weave those into the book as well.

At the end of the story, Meg is sad because her parents are selling the family home. Matt says to her, "We'll make our own home, Meggie—a home where we and our loved ones will always be welcome. A home of our hearts." Titling my novel *Home of the Heart* is a no-brainer.

It takes me nine months to finish. Jim helps me with the query letter, not only with the technical stuff, but also the composition. I submit it to six publishers and receive two rejections and nothing from the other four. Crestfallen, I file the manuscript away.

I begin looking for a job and find one with a small interior design shop, excited to get back into the business. Jessica, the owner of the firm, seems to be quite good and has a nice clientele. I like the two other women who work with her as well. The deal is for me to work on commission. Perhaps I should have known it would set me up for failure since I'm new to the community and don't know enough people to bring in clients. Similar to working for Polly, I do a lot to assist the owner. This time, however, I don't get paid. Whenever I bring up the issue, Jessica responds by saying, "Don't worry. I'm working on a plan."

Through the business, I meet Ann, a client who is a member of the American Association of University Women. We get to talking, and she learns that not only do we own a lot near her home on the butte, but that I've been an AAUW member in California. She invites me to a meeting and gives me a ride.

"How long have you been working for Jessica?" Ann asks.

"Six months."

"So, what do you do there—hold down the office while Jessica goes out on projects?"

"Yes, that's part of my job. I've also overseen an installation while she was on vacation. I had my own interior design business in California and I'm trying to establish a foothold in the business here."

"You're an interior designer?" she asks, incredulously. "I thought you were just office help."

I hate to admit to myself that's exactly what I am—an office worker in a cramped office with not enough to do, no respect, and no compensation.

"You're not doing any design work for Jessica?"

I shake my head, knowing it wouldn't be professional of me to complain to my boss's client. That night I have a dream.

> *I'm attending an AAUW meeting. I'm late. All the other women are already seated at tables and are being served their food. A waiter goes by with some delicious looking cake. I feel very awkward. I don't know anybody and I can't figure out where to sit. Then I realize that I'm not even dressed appropriately. I have on jeans and a turtleneck. On one foot is a boot; on the other, a sneaker. But it doesn't matter. No one notices me. I'm invisible!*

My new friend's revelation, and the dream, spurs me to quit working in the shop. I feel invisible there, rather like the situation at home when I sit at the oak table with my menfolk and feel myself shrinking without them noticing, what I call an "Alice-in-Wonderland syndrome." I leave Jessica's, disappointed she couldn't have had an honest conversation with me. But something big is about to focus all of my attention.

Ten

What-A-View

No one can drive us crazy unless we give them the keys.
—Douglas Horton

Journal Entry - April 23, 1992
Just a brief note to record current events on our house building. Yep, we are building our house thanks to a series of small miracles. We found a Christian builder with a can-do attitude, who in turn found a house designer. Together we came up with a good plan for 2800 square feet on the site.

We had a ceremony on the lot, dedicating our house to the Lord and giving Him credit for helping us find a way to build it.

Why do Jim and I decide to build our house on the butte when there are so many problems between us? Perhaps we both want it so badly we subconsciously decide to ignore them.

Or perhaps, our problems are so overwhelming we need the distraction. Frankly, I'm at a loss to account for the decision.

Since no one seems to be in charge when I visit the building site, I become the *de facto* foreman. Making sure the men are okay with my involvement in the project, my routine develops organically. Every morning, I bring a cooler of drinks and sit down with them to brainstorm the work for the day. Our contractor says he's never worked with a homeowner who knows as much about home building as I do. Good thing, because I catch some things that need changing.

Unfortunately for our contractor, he's figured his expenses incorrectly and is in the hole. Friends have given us many boxes of Mexican tile, which we plan to put in all three showers, the laundry, and the kitchen. To help out, Jim and I go to the house almost every night and most weekends to install tile. Our work is grueling, but we're excited about our future there.

When our house is finally finished, we throw a party for our friends and neighbors. We both love the iconic stone and timber of Timberline Lodge on nearby Mount Hood. We've captured a similar Northwest vibe with peeled logs at the entrance and anchoring the broad stairs, the intricate pattern of tongue-and-groove on the great-room ceiling, the river rock fireplace, and natural wood finishes.

I want our house to have a name like the Frank Lloyd Wright homes I'd visited in LA. Jim, Travis, and I have bandied about ideas without a reaching a decision. Guest after guest declare, "What a view!" as they're drawn across the room to the mountains beyond. "What-A-View"—the perfect name!

Among all these blessings, one stands out in particular. I'd shown our designer photos of the Elfery and he totally bought into the concept, creating a step-down courtyard of sorts. I've painted faux stone pavers on the floor and a welcome mat. Dad has crafted a half-pint arched door in front of the little room itself. One of the craftsmen has built a faux fireplace out of Zbricks with a mantel where the dolls can hang their Christmas stockings. I've found faux logs in a junk shop that have a light bulb and rotating motor, making them seem to flicker like a real fire. I've wallpapered the room in a petite floral and installed a chair rail. A string of Christmas lights softly illuminates the room.

Watching our guests' reaction to the Elfery tells me something about their personalities. Some poke their heads in, not sure what to think. Others ask permission to crawl inside. They remark on everything, especially the cooking corner, a cupboard with dishes and cooking utensils, and, of course, the tin-can stove. Their "Oohs!" and "Aahs!" make my heart glad.

The evening after our housewarming party, Jim and I clean up while sharing our guests' comments. "Ann said she loved our 'little brown house.' I could take her remark as condescending, but I believe she was sincere," I say.

Jim laughs. "I suppose some of our neighbors have chimney-envy."

"Chimney-envy?"

"You know, the need to compare sizes of homes and their chimneys. But I don't mind having a 'little brown house' and a smaller chimney than some of the massive ones here on the butte."

"I guess the neighbors at our party don't mind either, or they wouldn't have come," I reply.

Jim and I bundle up and walk out onto our upstairs bedroom balcony. "We did it!" I say. "Now let's be happy here."

"Agreed." My husband takes me in his arms and gives me a long kiss.

Unfortunately, and, I suppose, predictably, it doesn't take us long to resume our confrontations.

Journal Entry – September 28, 1992

I seem to be in the permanent role of "bad cop." Now that the house is finished, little details still need attending to. I don't mind following up on these, but I'd like a little backup from Jim.

Preparing for bed, I remember I need to tell Jim something. "I called Harold to ask him if he would come and fix the tub faucet," I say. "He didn't return my call, so I called again and left another message. He finally called back, and I couldn't believe it! He accused me of harassing him and his wife! All I did was ask when we could expect him to come." I'd been stung, and there were tears in my voice. "I've had to be the bad cop about getting everything fixed on this project, and that's been okay, but maybe you could call him this time."

"Are you letting him intimidate you?" Jim asks.

"What kind of question is that? I'm asking you to back me up on this."

"You don't have to get so huffy about it!" he retorts as he heads to his office.

"Never mind!" I call to his retreating back.

I don't notice or much care when he finally comes to bed.

During the construction of our house, Tillie and I had begun exploring the surrounding deer trails. Soon the resident red-tailed hawks in the big Douglas fir become accustomed to our presence. One day we round a corner and come upon a mother coyote feeding her kits from the deer she'd just brought down. As the coyote advances, my eyes meet Tillie's. Without a word, she follows my lead, backing away until the coyote finally relaxes and returns to her family. On another walk, we startle a great horned owl. We both need this time in nature to calm our spirits and keep us from going crazy.

Eleven

Our Dream Jobs

Some women choose to follow men, and some women choose to follow their dreams. If you're wondering which way to go, remember that your career will never wake up and tell you that it doesn't love you anymore.

–Lady Gaga

How can I object when, in 1993, Jim tells me he wants to borrow on our home equity to start his own business? He's been unhappy at work for some time, and is making plans to quit, partnering with a marketing friend at work. I'm uneasy with such a drastic move, but I tell myself I've had my business opportunities, and now it's my husband's turn.

In fact, I need a change too. I want work that will help us financially and also be fulfilling. If I have a good income, I'll be on a more equal footing with my husband, have some independence and a boost in confidence. I'd developed a passion for writing, but all I've managed is to write a silly romance stuck in a drawer. I desperately want direction.

Journal Entry – January 26, 1993

Dear Lord, I will do as you command—to praise you in all things. "Do not be anxious about anything, but in everything, by prayer and petition, with thanksgiving, present your requests to God." (Philippians 4:6).

Lord, I thank you for all the riches you have given me: a good intellect, imagination, ability to create with my head and my hands, a beautiful home and comfort, a husband who has supported me in many ways, loving and supportive family, friends, and church. I'm deeply touched by and grateful for all these blessings.

Lord, I petition you to make my way plain; to lead me in the direction of my life's work. It has been a long, hard struggle. I don't know how much longer I can wait without losing my faith, my sanity, my security. Lord, I ask and trust that you not stretch me beyond my breaking point. I ask that you strengthen my faith in you and in myself. Lord, if it be your will, bless my writing efforts. If this is not your will, please open the door to the direction you would have me take. I desire to serve you, Lord—to please you. Make my way plain.

I finally find my dream job as a kitchen and bath designer in a local business. Jerry has been in business for some time. Although he offers little formal training, he critiques everything I do, and I learn a great deal. I love the design part of the job and become proficient. I've avoided numbers all my life, but I find that at least I can retain the measurements of standard cabinets in my head.

I have a minimum-wage base salary plus a commission on the jobs I sell. Inexplicably, Jerry often insults me during my presentations, making it difficult for me to close those sales. I wonder if that's alcohol talking, as I discover a liquor bottle stashed in one of the display cabinets.

For weeks—maybe months—I keep thinking that if I can just figure out the key to dealing with Jerry, things will work out. I nearly drive myself crazy running different strategies in my head. I can't help wondering sometimes if the problem is me. After all, my experiences with my two previous bosses hadn't turned out well.

One day in town, I run into a woman for whom I'd made a presentation. "I want you to know," she tells me, "we really liked you and your design, but we were turned off by the owner and how he treated you."

I'm relieved, reassured that my struggles in the business are mostly not of my making. I do have a problem with Jerry and boundaries; I've allowed him to go beyond what is right and fair. Whenever I think about his behavior, my back muscles tense, my stomach becomes upset, I have trouble sleeping, and I'm not at peace. Some nights I cry myself to sleep, but I persist because I'm learning more about the business each week.

I finally have enough. Jerry's lack of respect for me as a person and as a designer won't change no matter how hard I work at it. Furthermore, I no longer respect him as a person or as a businessman. He becomes angry when I finally quit after thirteen months, blaming me for problems I haven't created. My experience there resembles a condensed version of my marriage, and I'm tremendously relieved leaving that situation.

Some good does comes out of my experience. I've received a year's worth of practice drawing up floor plans. Plus, through the shop, I've become acquainted with a few people who become my interior design clients. The best and biggest project is the interior of a new log home on a ranch just outside of Bend. I'm in accord with the homeowner's aesthetic, and she puts her complete trust in my suggestions—wallpaper and fabrics in bold Western colors and themes.

Designing the guest bedroom is especially fun. I dare to combine a sky-blue comforter sprinkled with gold stars with a red plaid dust ruffle for the log bed. The wainscoting portion of the wall is wallpapered. We both love the result, but when we stand back to survey the entire room, it doesn't seem quite complete. I make stencils, and my client and I use them to paint blue stars above the wainscoting and up onto the ceiling. We dance with glee when we finish, the effect perfect and our collaboration lots of fun. Still, my design work is only sporadic and seems more like a hobby than something sustainable.

Jim continues trying to get his business off the ground. To supplement the income from my infrequent design jobs, I decide to go back to substitute teaching—my default—and enroll in a few classes at Central Oregon Community College to update my certificate. I know its nearby campus, having joined the college choir shortly after moving to Bend. After the update, I generally substitute two or three times a week in the Bend and Redmond school districts.

Journal Entry - October 12, 1992

Yesterday, Travis and I did some acid cleaning of the decks. Jim said he couldn't help because he had other work to do. Nevertheless, he hung around observing our work and giving directions. I told him it made me nervous, but he didn't go away. Finally, Travis asked him why he wasn't helping, and why he needed Travis to help if he was going to hang around. Jim went off in a huff. Good for Travis for telling it like it is!

Journal Entry - October 20, 1992

Jim is continually giving me mixed messages about my working. "We're in deep trouble—you've got to get a regular job." And twice now, "What?! You have to substitute again? What about the deck work? Maybe you shouldn't get a job after all. Just kidding."
I'm so confused.

Travis graduates from high school. Despite his high intellect and our efforts to inspire him to live up to his potential, he's been an indifferent student and is unclear about what to do next. He half-heartedly considers going to the community college, but we tell him that unless he shows some motivation, we aren't interested in paying for it.

He gets a job as a dishwasher while still living at home, but he's snarky and discontented. When he mentions the possibility of joining the Army, I'm not pleased, wanting a safe and happy life for him. But as his bad attitude continues without any other plans, I begin to consider military service as an option for him. When the Army recruiter, with whom our son has been talking, calls and asks to speak with Jim and me, I invite him into our home. A few weeks later, Travis is headed for boot camp. Jim and I feel some relief to be free of our son's negativity, but, of course, we miss him and have concerns for him. Eventually, Travis becomes a Patriot missile operator and shortly after Desert Storm begins, he is sent to the Middle East. I pray every day for him.

I haven't lost my desire for sharing recreational activities with Jim, and I continue to solicit his involvement. I ask him if he has any interest in going to the Church's annual campout with me. "Too busy," is his predicable reply.

After dinner, I say to my husband, "You don't seem to want to do things with me anymore. What's going on?"

Jim's eyes grow hard. "If you're looking for someone to do physical activity with, I'm probably not your man."

His words strike me as a body blow. Thoughts whir in my head. Jim had enjoyed hiking and camping with me in the beginning of our relationship. We'd raised a son and built our beautiful home together. For God's sake, after taking a marriage class, we taught a similar one together at church. We'd used the metaphor of depositing plenty of good times in a couple's "bank account" to offset any bad times that might come our way. But it seems as if our own account balance diminishes almost daily.

Recovering from my husband's troubling words, I struggle to regain my composure. Though my heart beats a rapid tap dance, I say, with as much calm as possible, "You know I love to have you do those things with me, although right at this moment, I can't say why. But are you hinting we should divorce? Because if you are, we've got to think what that might do to Travis. How would the news of our breakup affect him?"

We'd received a rare letter from our son in Kuwait where he's been serving following Desert Storm: *"We are living in tents, and I have to put on protective gear when I go to the latrine. We could have a terrorist attack at any time."*

I imagine Travis reading our letter as dust and dirt swirls around his tent and a scorpion crawls onto his cot. *"Dear Travis, Your dad and I have decided to divorce. We are now in [insert different cities here]. You will have no familiar home to return to. Sorry about that."*

"Besides, you're under so much pressure with your work and you're involved in so many ministries," I continue, ticking them off in my head: a children's ministry at our church, a prison ministry, an interracial countywide ministry, plus mentoring a couple of troubled teenage boys. He's taken over Travis' room across the hall from his office, and spread out materials for each group with which he's involved. I survey the clutter and wonder if it resembles Jim's brain these days. "I don't think we should make any major decision right now. Have we done our best to make our marriage work? Isn't that what God wants us to do?" I ask.

Jim sighs. "I'll try to cut back on some of my outside responsibilities."

Though I feel a sliver of relief, I don't want to consider my most immediate fear—what would happen to me, a woman past fifty without good job prospects, if our marriage ended?

I make an appointment with Lorraine, one of our church pastors who serves as a spiritual advisor. She listens as I describe my struggles, and asks if I can define what's missing in my relationship with Jim.

"I've been trying to figure that out for a long time, and I feel I'm getting closer," I tell her. "Jim just told me he's not the man to do things with me. True, I want to feel connected to him in that way, but more importantly, I want to feel appreciated by him. I never know when he is going to get upset about something I say or do. I walk on eggshells, fearful of screwing up. He has trouble being consistent and realistic with his expectations about food, my making an income, use of money, my health, etc. For instance, he once suggested I check to see if I could qualify for disability insurance because of my chronic pain condition, yet he ignores the fact that too much of the wrong kind of work can hurt me. I guess what I'm trying to say is I don't completely trust him."

Lorraine shakes her head sadly. "Tell me what you'd like from Jim."

"Well, he frequently contradicts me, ignores what I say, and is impatient with me. I want him to quit it!" I laugh a little before growing serious again. "I wish he'd give me a reasonable level of encouragement, respect, and support, and be consistent about it."

"All that seems 'reasonable' to me," Lorraine reassures me. "It might help if you're clear with Jim that you need and deserve these things. Ask the Lord to soften both of your hearts. You need to be open to Jim's changing."

I leave Lorraine's, wondering if Jim would add my request to his list of things he isn't able or willing to engage in, proving he isn't the man for me.

Journal Entry – November 12, 1995

M. Scott Peck defines love, not as a feeling, but as the will to extend one's self for the purpose of nurturing one's own or another's spiritual growth. This usually happens after the process of falling in and out of love.[1]

Am I contributing to Jim's spiritual growth, or not? Is my own spiritual growth being nurtured, or not?

Twelve

Promise Keepers

*Promise Keepers is an Evangelical Christian organization for men,
built around the foundation of God's Word, committed to specific
promises about how men will commit to applying the Bible in their
lives. Their most widely publicized events tend to be mass rallies held
at football stadiums and similar venues.*

Promise Keepers

J im becomes involved in the Promise Keepers movement. It seems
so, well, promising. He spends more time with me and appears to
listen better. His angry outbursts become fewer. He brings me home a
T-shirt and a CD of a singer featured at the first rally he attends, someone
whose music he thinks I'd like. He even takes me dancing—once.

I ask him, "So what is it about PK that's caused this change in you?"

"Promise Keepers are committed to making their marriages stronger
through love, protection, and biblical values," he explains. "That makes
sense to me, and that's what I want to try to do."

Jim's efforts seem genuine, and I allow myself to relax and trust. Maybe PK will be the answer to our problems. I welcome my husband back to my side of the bed, and cry with sweet release as we make love.

As Jim becomes more involved with the local PK group, he begins holding meetings once a week in our home, and attends several large national rallies in football stadiums, including one in Washington, DC. He seems to thrive in his leadership roles, and I note his happiness even as I worry that all of these activities will add to the stress of trying to keep his business afloat. One day, he announces he's been chosen as leader of the entire PK organization in Bend. I feel a rock settle in my stomach. "Why didn't you talk this over with me first? How much time is this going to take?" I ask.

"Oh, I don't know. I can always quit if you don't want me to do this."

"That'd be just fine, wouldn't it? Then I'd be the bad guy!" I call Tillie and we go for a walk so I can calm down.

Jim tells me about John, a new friend he's made through PK. An intelligent man, John has strong opinions about faith and life. I can tell Jim feels flattered when John takes an interest in him, but I grow concerned over the man's influence. After one PK meeting, Jim tells me he doesn't want to "read any books not written from a Christian perspective, listen to any non-Christian music, or have any non-Christian friends." I am tempted to remind him that Christians are called to be salt and light in the world, but I hold my tongue, guessing my words would be wasted.

I read some of the materials Jim brings home, wanting to understand why he's found PK so appealing. According to the material, men are called to be leaders in their marriages, and women are to be subservient to their husbands. This stuns me. I have a different opinion from these writings, considering myself to be a good Christian wife, on equal footing with my husband, the same way my parents' strong Christian marriage functions.

Yes, the apostle Paul wrote, "Wives, submit to your husbands as to the Lord. For the husband is the head of the wife as Christ is the head of the church …" (Ephesians 5:22-23). Too many men have taken this to mean that they are the bosses of their wives, but they ignore the previous verse: "Submit to one another out of reverence for Christ." Paul was talking about mutual submission of husband and wife. I know this is a passage over which many Christian scholars and laypeople argue. I confront Jim. "What's this about wives being subservient to their husbands?"

"Oh, it just means that when there is a decision to be made, and the husband and wife can't agree, the husband should have the final decision."

"Is that what you think?" I ask.

"Well, decisions have to be made; otherwise there's a stalemate. God has given husbands the wisdom to be the final decider."

"I can't believe this! Remember when you gave all that money to Dr. Dobson's ministry without talking with me first? I only found out about it when his people phoned, thanking 'us' and offering prayers, which apparently they do for big donors. I called you on it, and you agreed to discuss important decisions with me. Isn't that the kind of thing we're discussing here?"

"I'm saying, in case of *critical* decisions, I should have the final word."

"You know I'm not going to let you have *'the final word'* on this issue," I declare.

While PK is a source of support for my husband, I'm losing the belief it can bring lasting good to our marriage.

A sliver of hope for a better future for me comes in the form of a phone call. A friend from my writers' critique group wants to know if I've had any luck selling my romance story.

"No," I tell her. "I received a couple of rejections from my submissions. That's it."

"I have just the place for you to send it," she says. "My daughter has written for this publisher, and I think, if you'd revise it just a little to fit their requirements, your story might get accepted."

I swing into action, shaping the romance to fit, and then hire an editor to make sure it's the best it can be. I send off the required three chapters, trying not to get my hopes up.

A month passes before I receive a response. Is it an acceptance or rejection? I hastily tear open the envelope. They like the chapters and want to see the rest of the story!

In September, I get the call that changes how I view myself. Avalon wants to publish my novel as a "Career Romance." The editor says they really like my style and hope I'll write some more. I'm ecstatic—a certified writer. I call Jim at his new business office. "Hey, that's great!"

I call my parents. "Wow! We're so proud of you!"

I tell the good news to practically everyone I know and receive a typical response. "Congrats! Now I know a real author."

When the contract arrives, I put on some thick red lipstick and kiss the envelope. I'm going to be an author of a published hardback book!

A few months later, a big heavy box arrives on our doorstep. I hurriedly open it and pull out one of the hot-off-the-press books. I wrap my arms around it, happiness flooding my body and soul.

The book-signing party at our house in February 1996 proves memorable. I clean and bake for two weeks, making special treats and decorations. Two friends help me set up vignettes from some of the book's scenes around the room, complete with banners of the appropriate text. My parents arrive the night before to help celebrate. The oak table covered with a white crochet tablecloth is loaded down with an assortment of cookies and other sweets. I've made the main character's favorite dessert, a chocolate raspberry cheesecake with raspberry sauce.

Jim warmly greets all my friends—forty-seven in all—at the door. Snow falls gently, giving a magical feeling to the world outside our big windows. The rooms fill with happiness and laughter. Jim takes pictures. The Elfery is decorated in hearts, and those who've not seen this little room before express their amazement. The day could not be more perfect. I sell all forty-two books, and take orders for more.

A couple of weeks later, Bend's Barnes & Noble throws a book signing party for me. People show up to enjoy chocolates and punch as I read scenes from the book. I happily note their swoons over the highly romantic scene in the log cabin on Mt. Hood. I feel like a real writer. Oh, happy day!

Thirteen

Guacamole

Ask not what you can do for your country. Ask what's for lunch.
–Orson Welles

Okay, so I can write, I tell myself, once the excitement dies down. *What's next?* The publisher has encouraged me to pen another book but I don't seem to have any romance left in me. Besides, I haven't made much money on the first one. Writing is in my blood, but it doesn't pay the bills. I decide to keep my subbing job and write when I can.

In April, Mom calls. "We've rented a cabin on the Oregon coast. Would you and Jim like to join us?"

"Thanks, but we can't, Jim is working," I reply.

"Maybe that's a good thing. You come anyway."

Staying with them feels strangely like it did when I was an adolescent under my parent's roof.

"Have you heard about the whale at the Oregon Coast Aquarium?" Dad asks after we settle in. "I think we should go see it. I'll pay."

"I'd love that," I reply. The animal Dad refers to has been all over the news—an orca named Keiko, star of the popular kid's movie, *Free Willy*. In the movie, Willy is rescued by a boy who recognizes his life is in danger at a deteriorating amusement park. Kids watching the movie discovered that Keiko's life in a Mexican theme park wasn't much better than Willy's, and organized a campaign to help rescue him.

The Oregon Coast Aquarium agreed to build a special pool for Keiko where he could be restored to health for possible release into the wild someday. Flying Keiko from Mexico City to Newport, Oregon, and lowering him into his new pool by crane proved to be quite an operation. I was one of thousands of people who followed the orca's journey in newspapers and on TV.

At the aquarium, I elbow my way through the crowd around the underground observation window. Keiko comes cruising by, a huge black and white bulk the size of a small school bus. He pauses, almost touching his "nose" to the glass, studying us. I get the sense he'd like to play. I stare, mesmerized, as are many around me.

After a few more days at the coast, I return home and resume my writing. I've become part of a children's writing critique group and discover I really enjoy writing nonfiction. I've begun working intently on a middle-grade book about sponges. They might seem an odd subject but I remembered Travis' third grade report on the animal. Their life as filter feeders intrigued him. I miss my son and writing about a favorite subject of his brings back good memories. I'm not a poet but I'm inspired to begin a little poem anyway:

> *I wish I was a simple sponge*
> *resting on the ocean floor*
> *loafing as the gentle tide*
> *passed through each waiting pore*

The more I read about sponges, the more fascinated I become. I request several scientific books about the animal through an interlibrary loan program. The information would have made my eyes cross in my college days, but I surprise myself by understanding much of the material.

I need no heart, nor lungs
nor head, nor hands or feet
for on that tide all kinds of treats
would drift on by for me to eat

I begin wondering about Oregon's native sponges. Where could I get that information? I think of the Oregon Coast Aquarium, and a lightbulb goes on. I've been writing about one of the lowest life-forms in the sea. But what about the most intelligent life in the sea? Whales! Has anyone written about Keiko, the most famous whale of all? Am I crazy for thinking I might be allowed to be the one? Probably crazy. Back to my sponge poem.

I would be quite handsome
My color'd win first prize
Physique declared superb
I'd never exercise

With beating heart, bracing for humiliation, I call the Free Willy-Keiko Foundation's spokesperson at the aquarium and get an answering machine. I stumble out my question and quickly hang up. One week. Two weeks. Christmas. Three, then four weeks. Really, really dumb question. Not worth answering. Just forget it.

You think a sponge's life
is boring as can be
but on this dreary morn
it sure appeals to me

I'm wrestling with my sponge poem when the call comes from Diane Hammond, spokesperson for the foundation. I introduce myself as a children's book writer and ask my question, sure she will laugh and tell me dozens of people are writing about the whale. But, no, they don't have a book on Keiko. Would I be interested in writing one? I try to stay calm when I answer in the affirmative. To my astonishment, she invites me to come to the aquarium and talk with her about it.

I can hardly believe it! I have to tell Jim my news! I wonder if I dare interrupt. Even if he gives me permission to speak, will he cut me off in mid sentence like he so often does these days?

Jim's business partner has quit after contributing little to their enterprise. My husband has moved his business back home to his upstairs office, determined to make it on his own. Under tremendous pressure trying to make his business profitable, he's been cranky and unapproachable for months.

I knock softly. "Do you have a minute?" I ask.

He swivels in his chair and shrugs. "I guess."

"Do you want to go to the Oregon Coast Aquarium with me sometime next week?" I ask with a hopeful smile. "I have a special invitation."

He frowns. "What are you talking about?"

I can't hold in my good news any longer. "I'm pretty sure I'm going to be writing a book about Keiko! The spokesperson for the Free Willy-Keiko Foundation has offered me the opportunity to meet him and his trainers!"

Jim's eyes widen with surprise. "The whale? Wow! That's great!"

"Do you have time to come with me? I don't want to take you away from your work and you've got all those ministries ..."

"No worries. It'll be good to take a break."

What a surprise! My husband seems to share my excitement. *Okay, I can live with this!*

"Maybe you'll be a famous writer yet," he adds.

At the Oregon Coast Aquarium, I interview Keiko's trainers and am introduced to Keiko himself. Jim listens and takes photos. I seem to have the blessing of the Foundation to write the book. I buzz with excitement, chatting with Jim on the way home, planning the writing of the story outline.

I dive into research on orcas. By February 1997, I have a manuscript of a children's book for ages eight to twelve and begin sending out queries. I receive an encouraging response from one publisher, saying my proposal will go to an acquisition meeting in March if the Keiko Foundation will send answers to a list of questions related to financial considerations. Unfortunately, the Foundation doesn't respond, and I don't get the contract. Other publishers decline, one explaining it never publishes anything concerning "celebrity animals." It looks as if all my hard work on this story won't pay off.

Despite Jim's claim he isn't interested in doing outdoor activities with me, he agrees to join me at our church's little canoe trip to the Sunriver area on the Deschutes River. I give Promise Keepers credit for his willingness to do this. We struggle to get into paddling rhythm, and he suggests I lay out, saying he can do better without my help. I sit on this bit of information for a while, knowing he thinks he's doing a great thing by letting me "rest." Instead, I feel diminished. Since Jim can always tell my mood even when I try to hide it, I decide I might as well talk with him about what I'm thinking.

"Gee," I say, "I'm feeling pretty worthless here. Telling me you can do better without me doesn't make me feel so wonderful." I smile, trying to let him know I'm not mad.

He stiffens, but I continue. "I thought the whole purpose of our trip was to learn how to do things together. Paddling as a team is pretty symbolic. I'd like to see if we can manage that. What do you say?"

He frowns and stops paddling for a moment. Then, brightening, he says, "Okay, I get it."

With some practice, we manage to do better. I hang onto that moment as a positive sign we just might be able to salvage our marriage.

Our long-simmering food issue pops up again. As I work on a new guacamole recipe in my spacious kitchen, Jim comes into the room.

"What are you making?" he asks.

My mood darkens and I bear down hard on the fork I'm using to mash the avocado. "Guacamole with cucumber." Tension creeps up my spine. *Ready for it.*

He grunts his disapproval.

My reaction is immediate. "Maybe you'd be happier eating out all the time so you wouldn't have to put up with my cooking!"

"Maybe so!" he shoots back.

I put down my fork, "Look, we've been having this same argument since we first lived together. We'd better find a way to put it to rest, because I'm sick to death of it!"

His mouth tightens. "I am too!"

Jim's food issues come into focus. He's told me more than once how, when as a boy, his grandmother harangued him during dinner times concerning his pickiness, his parents never coming to his rescue. He doesn't like trying new dishes in our home, but, when we go to ethnic restaurants, he enjoys choosing foods he's never had before. The issue isn't my cooking; Jim wants the power to reject my offerings!

"You know," I say in a quieter tone, "creative cooking is one of my outlets, but, just as often, I make familiar food I know you like. I've thought it reasonable to expect you to taste everything; I still think it had merit when Travis was young. But what if I give you the gift of never asking you to try any of my cooking again? In turn, you give me the gift of not making disparaging comments concerning what I make. If you do taste something and don't like it, you can tell me you don't care for it, but don't act as if I'm out of my mind for making it."

"All right," he says, tension draining from his face. "That works for me."

I hug him and tell him I want to love him, and I want us both to be happy. I say, "We can't sweep this kind of stuff under the rug anymore, because it never stays there."

Fourteen

Decision Time

1997–1998

Lift me up and take me back. Don't let me keep walking on broken glass.

—Annie Lennox, "Walking on Broken Glass"

Journal Entry - August 16, 1997
Jim was dashing around this morning, trying to leave for Tigard and losing stuff right and left and declaring he was going out of his mind and that he was going to drop everything and go hide. Maybe that helps him get out all his stress, but I somehow cannot avoid taking some of it on myself. It's really madness around here, and I want no part of it. Is there any way I can be on my own, make a living and be happy at my job?

Journal Entry - August 28, 1996
Maybe I suffer from pain because I feel I'm being pulled in two directions. On the one hand, I just want to escape the difficulties in my marriage—just run away. On the other

hand, I've got all these messages telling me I should be mature, to stay and work it out. It's not so much that I am on the fence; it's more as if I am being pulled to one side, then the other, across a giant and rather dull razor blade. I keep thinking "I can fix this problem," and when I work on it, the tugging sometimes subsides. But it always comes back.

I decide to talk about our marriage difficulties with Patti, our church's co-pastor. She listens intently and tells me she understands my pain. "It's important Jim changes his attitude toward you and toward life in order for your marriage to heal," she says.

I feel relieved she understands my difficulties, and glad she'll be praying for us.

By December, Jim confesses to being depressed and tired, sick of all the work and worry. He contacts a headhunter, hoping to find a job. I know that means we'll have to sell What-A-View and move to who-knows-where, but it seems the only way out of our madness.

I tell myself I'll give my husband six months after he finds a new job to change back to the loving, attentive man I'd fallen in love with so long ago—or at least for him to show a genuine effort in that direction. If that doesn't happen, I'll have to pull the plug on our marriage for my own sanity.

Journal Entry – September 14, 1997

A lot of the time, when I am with Jim or thinking about him, I have a sick feeling. It doesn't seem right because I know he loves me and I know he does a lot of things for me. So then I feel guilty. Would God be able to fulfill His plan for my life if I left Jim?

Almost every day, as I drive up the hill to our house, my eyes seek out a small cottage not far from the road. I begin to fantasize about making it my own. *I'd paint it a vanilla-cream color with cherry-red trim and expand the tiny stoop to a porch that spans the front of the house where I'd assemble large pots holding wonderful plants.* I visualize being cocooned in a new red velour overstuffed couch—much comfier than our cold leather one shredded by Jim's cat, JazzPurr. Jim can have that couch and the cat too. Although the house might be small, there'll be room to add all four leaves to my oak dining table when I decide to entertain. And as much as I've loved our lodge-style décor, my bedroom will be lighter and more feminine, though not frilly. The yard will have a few trees and a sunny spot for a garden. Maybe there'll even be a little writing studio out back.

Talk about fantasy! In reality, if I leave my husband, my life will be up for grabs. I'd probably have to find a "real" job. Who knows what that might be or if I could handle it; I have such a miserable track record with the jobs I've had. Then there is my health—always a factor. And where would I live? Some of my divorced friends live in little cottages they've fixed up. I should be so lucky. One friend lives in a tiny apartment. I know that isn't for me!

February 3, 1998

No word from the headhunter yet. Jim asked if it was all right to speak to a Promise Keepers dinner Friday night. He had already told them he would, but he could "back out of it." He has always been too busy on Friday nights to spend with me, so I had no idea I had a choice. What could I say, but "Go." He went and we had our "date" Saturday night, but he was so stressed out, it was a disaster. Because we had sex, he thinks we're okay.

February 14, 1998

I stood in front of all the lovely valentines at the store yesterday and cried inside. Giving Jim one of those cards would have been a lie. For the past few years I've chosen a jokey one. I'm sure he isn't fooled.

Jim is changing in ways I haven't anticipated. Sunday morning, as I'm getting ready for church, he tells me he has a stomachache, a regular Sunday occurrence these days. He says he's decided to stay home. I don't understand what's going on. *Is he uncomfortable because I'm clearly visible on the platform during the worship service? Is he's bothered that I shine a little bit?*

The next Sunday, he tells me he's going church shopping. This is another punch to my gut. This church is my family, a place where I feel I belong, where I thought *we* belonged. But I tell him when he finds a church he likes, I'll go see for myself. Eventually, he finds a charismatic church. I go with him once and he introduces me to Pastor Susan. "I'm sorry, this is not the church for me," I tell him.

Journal Entry - May 25, 1997

I'm trying not to be scared and to stay calm. Jim finally did his financials and discovered his company is broke. I'm having a difficult time not being angry with him. He has some big issues in his business that he keeps putting off. I find this all very scary. I know he feels bad, so I don't say much, but I'm at the mercy of his bad decisions.

Jim has been half-heartedly looking for a job, but now he must find one, and soon. He finally receives an offer in Beaverton, a city adjacent to my hometown of Tigard. This position is for an application engineer. Jim is a hardware guy, and this job does not capture his creative interest.

"I can't say I'm excited about this job," he explains to me as we sit at the oak table. "But it should be a lot less stressful than the ones I've had in the past. You'll see how I've changed. I want to be a better husband. Work is no longer my focus."

Reaching out, I place my hand on top of my husband's and search his face. "You know, Jim, I've heard this before. We're at a crossroads here, not just with your work but with our marriage. It hasn't been good for a long time. Do you even want me to stay?"

He nods, not seeming to be at all surprised at my question. "Yes. If you haven't made up your mind to leave, you might as well come with me and see if we can work things out."

No "please don't go," or mentions of loving me. "By 'working things out,'" I say, "I hope you mean counseling. I'll give us one more shot, but this is it."

"I understand," he mumbles, looking downcast. "I've already made an appointment for myself this week with Pastor Susan who also does counseling," he says. "What would you like me to tell her?"

I blink. I guess my husband has gotten at least part of my message. "Tell Susan this: if you don't acknowledge you could have made wiser choices over the last several years, I can't have any faith in the future of our marriage."

"What do you mean by wiser choices?"

"How about starting with how you spend so much of your time with other people and things while ignoring me?"

He stares at me for a brief moment and sighs. "Okay." Without another word, he gets up from his chair and leaves the room.

Guilt washes over me for hurting him, for being so stubborn, inflexible, unforgiving, etc., etc. But then I remind myself our marriage will continue to be an unhappy one if this issue doesn't get resolved. *I'm practicing tough love, and it's tough on both of us. This is like a staring contest. If I blink, I lose. But if I stand my ground, I'll probably lose anyway—a classic lose-lose situation.* I lean on the table, my head in my hands, my chest tight with unshed tears. *Lord, please help good come out of this mess we've made.*

Fifteen

For Sale

Sometimes we have to let go of something precious before something better comes into our lives.

—A friend

It's time to put What-A-View up for sale. Friends ask how I can leave such a beautiful place. I don't have a choice, and though I know it will be hard, I realize happiness can't be found in a house, no matter how wonderful. Even a beautiful home into which one has poured heart and soul can become an albatross. I need to leave Bend behind, and all the things it's meant to me in order to find a better life. Realistically, I know that the Portland area will have more opportunities for me in all areas of my life. Being closer to my family will probably be a good thing too. But leaving behind my friends, my church, my house, and the mountains—these are all losses. This may mark the loss of my marriage as well, but I must be resolute and put one foot in front of the other.

At the last PK meeting at our house, I overhear a conversation that reminds me of how crafty Jim is at manipulating facts to put himself in a better light. The men ask what happened to the speakers missing from our living room ceiling.

"Oh," Jim replies, "Linda didn't like them up there, so I took them down."

Liar!

I'd protested Jim's installation of the speakers to no avail. When we had a new entertainment cabinet built a few years later, Jim agreed to put smaller, better speakers in it, leading me to believe the big speakers would go away. But it wasn't until we began making preparations for selling the house that he finally removed them. Because I don't want to ruin Jim's relations with these men, I keep quiet.

Is this a mistake? I don't know!

Our house is about to go on the market when Jim tells me he has business in Portland and will be gone for the weekend. My parents, still living in the home where I grew up, have given Jim my old bedroom so he can have a place to stay near his new job while we wait for our house to sell. I will stay behind to show our home, just as I did in Albuquerque.

I've worked hard, keeping our house looking good inside and out, but there's always more to do when motivated to sell. I toil frantically getting it ready for showing while also working on our big garage sale, hoping Jim will help. But, I reason, I shouldn't interfere with his business in Portland.

When my husband returns, I discover his "business" was a Promise Keeper's rally. I feel totally betrayed. He's deceived me, even involving my innocent parents in his duplicity. Lucky for him, I've given up throwing things long ago, because it wouldn't be a harmless salad I'd toss at him this time.

"What were you thinking?" I demand. "You left me here to take care of *everything*! You know all this hard work makes my pain so much worse. Some Promise Keeper you are!"

"I'm surprised," he replies, looking injured. "I haven't broken any promises to you."

Anger toward him burrows deep into my body and soul. My feet hurt too much to take a walk to cool off.

That night I have a dream. In it, Jim comes into the room carrying a basket with a deadly snake inside. Its large, articulated scales in shades of gold are beautiful in the serpent's deadliness. There are children and animals around, and I'm afraid the snake might attack them. At first, the reptile stays coiled in its basket. Eventually, though, it begins to inch its way out. I grab all the children and animals and pull them to safety. I yell at Jim to get rid of the snake. He studies the slithering presence. Finally, he picks up an iron rod and strikes the thing, killing it.

I awake with a start. What does the dream mean? Is Jim on a dangerous path, bringing poison into our marriage? What about the role of the children and animals who were obviously innocents? I don't think it's our son, now twenty-three years old, and not living at home. Am I the innocent? No more. The snake is out of the basket.

Jim suggests that, while I'm still in Bend, I also do some counseling with his pastor, Susan. I agree, and at our session, describe how Jim has promised to change over and over again, and yet he hasn't. "I'm having difficulty believing him anymore," I tell her. "I don't think he has any chance of changing until he understands his past behavior has been unacceptable. He tells me one thing one day, then the opposite the next. I try calling him on it, but he never acknowledges the difference."

I give her several examples: "The finish on our beautiful front door with a laser-cut tree was deteriorating and needed refinishing. I got an estimate from a professional, but when I showed it to Jim, he said, 'Wow! That's really expensive. Can't you do it?' I took that to mean we didn't have the money. So, despite the fact that I knew it would be hard on my body, I tackled it. It took several days, and, as predicted, it was painful work. Do you know what Jim said when I showed him how much I'd saved us? 'Good job! What will we do with that extra money?'"

"How did you feel about that?" Susan asks.

"I'd been played. I was so mad—at Jim, of course, but also at myself for believing he was right to urge me to do it. I told him he owed me a year of professional massages."

"What you're describing is called 'crazymaking,'" Susan declares, and explains what she means. Crazymakers want their victims to feel confusion and shame, making them believe they're the bad or crazy ones. All these things you've told me about Jim: saying one thing, and then later, the opposite, without acknowledging the difference, his lack of empathy for your physical and emotional state, making you the bad one in the relationship, encouraging you to doubt your feelings—they convince me he's a crazymaker. I'm not optimistic he'll own up to his behavior."

"You are the strong one," she reassures me, "and Jim resents it. That's why he takes jabs at you to cut you down to his size. He has to appreciate the strength in you rather than trying to compete."

For the first time in all of the counseling I've had, I've received a definitive assessment of my situation. It isn't pretty, and I'm not sure I want to face it.

Something else has been gnawing at me, and this seems like a good time to address it. I briefly describe my work for the three interior design businesses at which I'd been employed. "Since there seems to be a pattern, I can't help wondering if some of the difficulties were my own fault," I tell her.

Susan shakes her head no. "I believe you didn't do well because you were smarter and could see further and better than your bosses. They probably resented you because you couldn't hide your light under a bushel and they were threatened, just as Jim has been."

I hope this is true, and I feel a little better about my lack of success with these people.

At the end of our session, Susan makes me promise to see a counselor with Jim after we settle in the valley, even though she says she isn't optimistic Jim will change. "Don't buy another house with Jim until and unless you've worked out your issues with him."

Journal Entry - April 26, 1998

No wonder I've been struggling so much. I haven't even been aware of the double bind I let Jim put me in. I'm beginning

*to think Sandy [my sister-in-law] had it right when she
questioned if my neck and shoulder aches were a result of living
with him. When I think about it, I realize he's supported me
financially and physically (like helping me with my interior
design books, etc.) but not verbally or emotionally. I guess I'm
just foolish enough to want it all.*

Jim and I talk regularly on the phone during his days in Tigard and
he comes home most weekends. One evening, he calls to tell me about his
car, which had been parked in my parent's driveway. "Somebody broke
into it and stole all my praise CDs. I don't want to live in Tigard anymore,
and I don't want this job!"

Another worry! "I'm so sorry you're having such a rough time. I hope
things won't seem so bleak in a few more days," I tell him. I wonder what
I'd do if my husband fell apart. I'm sure his knowing our marriage is on
the brink has contributed to his emotional state.

In another call, he asks me how my session with Susan has gone.
"Pretty interesting," I say. I don't elaborate, and he doesn't press.

As I plan a trip to Tigard for the weekend, Jim calls and asks me to
bring a copy of *Home of the Heart*. "Since I've been telling our secretary
about your book, I thought it was time I read it," he explains.

*So, you want to impress this woman, but you didn't bother to read it when
it was published two years ago, even though you helped with my book party.
Who were you trying to impress then?*

In another one of our calls, my husband informs me he's quit going to
his new counselor. "I don't need him right now," he explains. "I have the
antidepressants he prescribed. Besides, I've found a Christian counselor
with a great reputation we can both go to when we're settled in here."

I chalk it up as just another one of his bad decisions. I'm too immune
to feel much disappointment.

Memorial Day weekend comes and goes. Jim is home, and we're doing
pretty well together, but I feel we're in a holding pattern until the move.

As an early Father's Day present, I give him a Pooh bear to keep him company. He seems to like it.

I throw a Farewell-To-The Elfery party, my house filled with friends. I serve miniature elf cookies as well as cake and punch. Friends bring goodies too. They express their sadness at saying goodbye to me and my little playhouse. I remind myself that the warmth of their friendship will linger with me for a long time to come.

I still have fantasies concerning my romantic interest at church. I dream up several ways of saying goodbye:

I've always admired you.
You'll always be my one true love.
I wish I'd never met you!
I'll never forget you—unless I become senile!
You know I've had a crush on you for a long time.
I wish we could have …

What do I really say? Nothing.

June 12, 1998

Last night was my last Building Committee meeting. The other members presented me with a certificate of appreciation for the five-and-a-half years of service—first on the Master Plan Committee, and then on the Building Committee. In response, I made a little speech about how much serving the church has helped me grow. I explained that working with church members in various capacities and situations taught me how each person has something to contribute, even though it isn't always obvious at the moment. I'd learned that God takes all our contributions and creates something wonderful. As I spoke, my tears splashed on the table in front of me.

Sixteen

Farewell Bend

Saying goodbye is the hardest solution of any problem. But sometimes it's the only choice we have.

—Anurag Prakash Ray

From our bedroom balcony, I watch as fantastic-shaped clouds rise behind Mt. Bachelor and become lined with glowing gold. The nighthawks will soon whir and soar, producing strange groaning sounds as air rushes through their outstretched wings. I will not be here to enjoy the spectacle. Those moments are already in my past. Under piercing blue skies and surrounded by scrub juniper and tall pines, our dream home has been the one thing that kept Jim and me together the last several years. My heart is heavy over leaving this wonderful place.

The movers arrived early this morning. They packed and packed and packed, finally leaving a short time ago. With Tillie at my heels, I go from room to room saying goodbye. My feet throb from organizing our giant garage sale and my work in the days that followed—cleaning, wiping out cabinets, and patching and painting blemishes. I'd run my paintbrush one last time over the marks in the hallway left by the luggage Jim habitually banged against the walls as he hurried, cursing, to load up his car and begin yet another business trip.

I pause at Travis' old bedroom. I'm relieved he is safely out of the Army and living in Seattle, but sad I'm not able to see him more often.

Descending to the main floor, I embrace the fifteen-foot peeled log that anchors the broad staircase, pressing my cheek against the cool, smooth wood. Next, I say my final goodbye to the Elfery, remembering the little room's many visitors, both young and old, from near and far. I picture the time Dad invited a visiting buddy to go inside with him. There they were, two old men sitting on the floor, grinning like little children. I'm told this creation of mine will become a resting place for the new owner's two big dogs, information I try hard not to picture. I've been writing about the elves, and vow to continue so they can live on in children's imaginations, even if not in the Elfery.

Tillie plops down next to me as I lie on my back on the living room floor. Trying to drink in every detail of my home, I shift my gaze from the pattern of the ceiling to the broad, west-facing windows framing the dozen snow-capped mountains turning rosy in the setting sun. The memory of my book signing on that magical snowy February day comes alive again.

I wonder what life will be like in the suburbs. A friend once told me sometimes we have to let go of something precious before something better comes into our lives. I desperately hope that's true.

One last glance—the house's empty windows stare blankly back. Tillie and I climb into the Voyager stuffed with houseplants and other fragile items and head for our new life. As I drive down the hill, a rainbow shimmers against the darkening sky. *This is God's promise of better things to come*, I tell myself. "'I know the plans I have for you,' declares the Lord, 'plans to prosper you and not to harm you, plans to give you hope and a future.'" (Jeremiah 29:11).

I cruise down Highway 20 through the darkening night, flashing back to that long-ago day in Albuquerque when I left my first house for the last time, Yum Yum at my side. Now at the age of fifty-four, I've left another house, this time with Tillie. Although I haven't lost my current spouse, the possibility looms.

Driving through the quiet town of Sisters, I reject the idea that this move back to the bosom of my family is a coincidence. I've come full circle, from growing up in Tigard, to moving to Albuquerque as a young bride, to being transferred to Southern California with Jim, to my life in Bend, and now, back to the Tigard area—all through no effort of my own. Just as God sent us to Bend after Jim's work went sour in California, the Almighty must have something up His big sleeve this time around.

My headlights pick up the green highway sign pointing to the Metolius River. Although I've traveled a bit, it remains my favorite river in the world. A few more miles down the road I pass Suttle Lake, where I attended church camp as a kid, and begin the climb to Santiam Pass. I've driven this route solo in a snowstorm, praying for safety, and I'm grateful tonight just a few raindrops are hitting the van's windshield and the pavement is mostly dry. Soon I reach the summit—elevation 4,816 feet—and a few miles later, branch off to Highway 22 to start the long descent toward the valley.

I slow, winding my way in the dark, close to the sheer drop-off above Detroit Lake. Even though I'm dead tired, I must stay alert. I round a corner and blink at the bright lights of Detroit Dam blazing against the night.

It's all downhill from here. The pressure on my bladder has been building, but I've refrained from stopping, knowing that Maples, my favorite rest area on the route, is not far. I finally pull into the deserted parking area and run to the restroom. I return to let Tillie out, and, while she does her business, I stretch to relieve the tightness in my back. Cold night air prickles my arms and wakes me up. The metal-halide lights on their tall poles cast a harsh glare reminiscent of a bad horror movie, but in the stillness, I hear the faint rushing of the North Santiam River—a soothing antidote. Back in the van, I head out on the last leg of our journey through the fertile Willamette Valley.

Tigard and Tualatin were small towns when I left the area at age twenty. I remember, as a small child, shopping in my grandfather's grocery store in "old" downtown Tigard. Now the building houses an antique store. The bank building next door that gave out cardboard Santas complete with a metal strip that squeaked out "Ho, ho, ho" when you ran your finger along it, now houses a picture-framing business. A big Costco Warehouse occupies the site where the outdoor movie theater once entertained us. Dad has closed his small jewelry store and moved his watch repair business to their home. Mom and Dad were married in the town's Methodist church, as was I the first time around. Our big Moore family Thanksgiving potlucks have shrunk, but still continue with several cousins who remain in the area, and a few remaining elders who have all retired from their family farms.

I tell myself it will be good to be closer to my aging but still active parents. Most of all, I look forward to spending more time with my cousin, Ros, who lives not far from our rental. She is just a month older than I am, and I feel as if we've known each other before we were even born, our pregnant mothers having spent so much time together. I've always looked up to Ros and consider her my "sister-cousin."

The lights of Salem confirm I've left the Cascades behind. Just past midnight, exhausted, I pull into the driveway of our Tualatin rental house. Jim greets me at the door with open arms and I relax into him. "It's so late. I worried for your safety," he says. Tillie, stiff from following me around for days, paws at him. He laughs, kneels down, and hugs her too. The cats, Rachel and JazzPurr, poke their noses into the entry to inspect the commotion. I hold Rachel in my arms, talking kitty talk to her and she begins to purr.

"These two kept wandering the house as if looking for you," he says. My worries subside and my heart warms at being back with my little family—my family who is concerned for me and happy for me to be "home."

The movers arrive the next morning. One of the men wonders how I could leave such a beautiful house for this ordinary one. I don't tell him the emotional toll I've paid to stay in our Bend home.

Once again, I'm on my feet, trying to organize all of our belongings. Despite the mover's comment, this house isn't half bad. There's plenty of space for the two of us. I will set up my office in one end of the family room. Jim will have his office in a bedroom upstairs, and we'll still have a guest bedroom. The kitchen is dated but workable, with an island and pantry shelves.

That night my feet are screaming, or as I like to say when in a better mood, "My dogs are barking." Jim, already in bed, laughs as I crawl to the bathroom. *He thinks I'm faking. He doesn't have a clue as to how I'm feeling. Typical.* I imagine my reaction is typical too. I shoot him a dirty look. He covers his mouth, knowing he's screwed up. I climb in next to him and we're back-to-back. With the background noise of the distant freeway, a familiar heaviness weighs me down as I toss and turn.

Seventeen

All Over the Map

1998–1999

Give me one reason to stay here and I'll turn right back around.
—Tracy Chapman, "Give Me One Reason"

The third morning after our move, Jim asks me to go with him to an evening service at a church he's eager to check out. I agree, but by the time he gets home from work, my feet are throbbing. I try begging off. "Honey, I've been on my feet all day." I wave my hand at the empty boxes littering the kitchen. "I'm hurting like crazy, and I haven't even made dinner or changed my clothes. Can't we put it off until next week?"

He gets his familiar little-boy pout and hunches his shoulders. "You said you would. I don't want to wait. We'll make PB & J sandwiches and then we'll go. Come on."

I'm too tired to argue. I have a bite to eat, change my clothes, and hobble off with him. The evening service we attend includes a dedication of elders. Having been an elder in my church in Bend, I notice no women are included. After the service, I introduce myself to the pastor and ask, "Are there any women elders in your church?"

"No, of course not! It says in the Bible that only men are to be elders. There's no mention of women, but," he continues, "these men's wives are all involved in ministry."

"This isn't the church for me," I tell Jim on the way home. "I'm sure the Lord ordained and blessed me as an elder, and I don't want to be part of a congregation that believes women shouldn't be."

"Well, I like it!" he declares, staring at the road ahead.

My shoulder muscles tighten. *Here we go again.* "Are we considering going to different churches like we eventually did in Bend?" My voice begins to rise.

He doesn't answer.

"Okay, then," I say, trying to lower the tension. "Let's discuss what we want in a church. I'd like one where I can sing again on a praise team."

"I don't want you to do that anymore. I want you to sit beside me throughout the service."

"Who are you?!" My head feels as if it will explode. Any patience I have with my husband evaporates and much of the remaining trust and respect I have for him crumbles. Jim knows that singing to the Lord is my passion. My thoughts whirl and then congeal in an "*Aha!*" moment. "Is that why you claimed to have a headache and stayed home so many Sunday mornings? You didn't want me in front singing? Is that why you began looking for a different church?" My voice shakes, suppressing anger as best I can.

"No. *Your* church didn't have the spirit of Christ."

I open my mouth to respond but shut it instead. *Promise Keepers,* I think, my heart rate rising. *It's all because of Promise Keepers!*

A month into our new life in Tualatin, Jim announces, "That Christian counselor I mentioned, the one with a great reputation for saving marriages no one else can, has an opening for us."

An ironic laugh escapes my lips. "That would be our marriage." Skepticism around this issue is my default these days.

We meet Norma for the first time in her office in the church without women elders. She's a stocky woman with short, graying hair who claims the Holy Spirit has given her extraordinary discernment about people. Since she doesn't have a wedding ring, I wonder what she knows about marriage. *We'll see how her discernment works for us.*

"You can be assured we will get to the heart of your problems in a short amount of time," she says. "And then you can get on with your healing." As first steps in this process, we make individual and joint appointments to see her in the coming weeks.

Journal Entry - July 9, 1998

A red-letter day. Mom and Dad called to say they were back home from their trailer trip, and I invited them for grilled salmon. I was snapping green beans when Jodie, my new literary agent, called to tell me that 21ˢᵗ Century wants to publish my Keiko book. She said, "Now we've got to talk about your next book." Yippee!

A couple of days later, I have a little party with Mom and Dad, Ros, and an old friend who's recently moved from Bend, to celebrate my book contract. Jim is sweet to bring home dinner, plus flowers, and sparkling cider. Earlier in the day I'd gone to my first counseling session with Norma, and come away thinking very sad and dark thoughts about my marriage. My emotions are all over the map.

I receive the news that the foundation is moving Keiko to Iceland in the Atlantic near the spot where he'd been captured as a two-year old. He's been rehabilitated as much as possible at the aquarium and is obviously bored. The world's largest sea pen is being built specifically for him where his trainers will continue to work with him until they judge him ready to be released to the open sea.

"You've got to go to Iceland," Jim tells me.

I'm surprised and pleased at my husband's enthusiasm.

I want a good camera for the trip, and Jim drives me to Portland to buy one with a telescopic lens. "Maybe I'll go to Iceland with you. I think I might be able to get the time off," he says.

I'm touched by all his support concerning this venture, but I want to prove to myself I can navigate on my own. *How do I tell him?* "Uh, that might be good, but I've been thinking of spending a couple of extra days sightseeing."

His face droops. "Oh."

I feel a stab of guilt, but I'm determined to go alone.

Jim volunteers to drive me to McChord Air Force Base to watch the airmen practice transferring Keiko's carrier from a flatbed truck to the cargo bay of a C-17. With a mention that I write for children, I'm able to wrangle a couple of press passes.

I've been reading Katy Muldoon's articles about Keiko in *The Oregonian* and am happy to meet her there. I talk to the pilots and the loadmaster, fascinated by the plane and the logistics. A new book idea comes to me: *How Do You Mail a Whale? Strange Airborne Cargo.*

As I begin my trip, I find myself wishing Jim had come with me, but then I remember other times in other airports when I had to run to keep from losing him in the crowd as he forged ahead on his long legs, never looking back to make sure I was still behind him. Nevertheless, I'm scared spitless. I fret over everything: getting up in time to catch the taxi to the airport (Jim is on a business trip); getting to the plane on time; staying overnight in Baltimore—you name it, my insides are churning.

Journal Entry - September 9, 1998

I'm on the plane for my overnight stay in Baltimore. My polyester pants are making me hot and sticky, and my stomach feels as if rats are gnawing at it, but I'm doing my best to project good cheer to those I meet. One of my gentlemen seatmates has helped me decipher my itinerary and reset my new digital watch. I'm sure I come across as a helpless woman, but I don't mind a little aid.

The flight gives me plenty of time to think about my hopes for a writing career. Keiko is a big star, and I can envision my book being big too. Not only might I earn a substantial royalty, it could give me the momentum I need to get more contracts. I don't expect to support myself with writing—that would be a fantasy—but it could be a wonderful part of my financial independence. My entire being is infused with a fierce desire for it to be so.

My decision to travel alone begins to pay off once I reach the Westman Islands. After I settle in at the guesthouse of a lovely woman artist, I venture out into the small seaport of Heimaey. First, I inspect a crumpled house on the edge of a lava flow only yards from where I'm staying; Icelanders have had to deal with volcanoes ever since settling there generations ago. A mother cat and her kittens now inhabit the ruin.

Then, it's off to a press conference announcing Keiko's arrival the next morning. Nervous from being on my own in a foreign country, I'm relieved to see the familiar faces of the staff people from the aquarium, and Katy Muldoon, and to shake hands with Jacques Cousteau, among other dignitaries.

A well-dressed attractive woman close to my age overhears our conversation and introduces herself as Peggy Walton-Walker, actress and widow of Keith Walker, author of the screenplay for *Free Willy*. With tears in her eyes, she tells me this is a spiritual journey, and how her husband seems to be here with her.

I realize I have a connection to her, having read an article featuring Keith Walker in a writers' newsletter. "I've taped a note to my computer," I tell her. "It says, 'Trust God and do the next thing.' I put it there after reading this was your husband's mantra. Now it's mine too."

Peggy is speechless, but her eyes say it all. She hugs me. We compose ourselves and exchange business cards. *I am meant to be here.*

Afterwards, I look for something to eat and find a pizza parlor. I see a young woman sitting alone and despite my nervousness at being a stranger, I ask to join her. She introduces herself and says she has her own children's TV show in Reykjavik. We have a lively and simpatico discussion regarding Keiko and whales. She'd seen him in Newport but made the mistake of mentioning on the air that he used an inner tube as a sex toy. The media picked it up, quoted her, and made much of it. She's embarrassed but amused at the same time. I've seen Keiko's "sea snake" too, and it's not a sight to forget. We laugh uproariously.

We join a table of journalists from all over the world who are here for this big event. Because I've been studying Keiko and wild orcas for some time now, I find myself sharing my knowledge with them. They treat me with respect, as an equal. *How good and right this feels.*

Early in the morning, I join a growing crowd at the airport, waiting in a cold, stiff wind for the C-17 to land. A friend who works at REI has made sure I'm dressed for the Icelandic weather. I'm feeling comfortable in my layers of fleece and yellow waterproof jacket. Jim is on a business trip in Ottawa and will tell me later he saw me in the crowd on TV. A Japanese journalist tells me Keiko is a Japanese girl's name. A photographer from the *Seattle Times* shows me how to change lenses. "It's like doing surgery," he cautions. Being on my own no longer feels so scary. *I believe I can trust there will always be people willing to come alongside me as I step out of my comfort zone.*

After Keiko is unloaded from the plane, we pile into buses following him in a little parade to the barge that is taking him to the sea pen. The villagers line the route, waving signs of welcome.

We reach the harbor and crowd onto boats. I jostle into position, standing on my tiptoes, holding my camera as high as my arms will reach above the other photographers to get my shots. I hold my breath as a large crane lowers Keiko's sling inch by inch toward the water below. He doesn't move a muscle. He'd been taken from his family as a baby. Does the scent of the sea bring back nascent memories?

Lower and lower he goes. Someone whispers, "Is he dead?" Lower, into the medical pool part of the pen. Cables are removed from the sling. He eases out. He's alive! He's made it! We all clap and shout, warm tears running down our cold cheeks. Keiko has made a remarkable journey home and I'm there as witness. I'm filled with joy. *This is a great ending for my book.*

After the next day sightseeing with my new *Seattle Times* friends, I fly back home. This trip has given me a boost in confidence, as I've been able to navigate on my own with help and encouragement of others. Like Keiko, I have returned to my home waters, my future yet to be revealed.

Eighteen

Dish Detail

The opposite of Loneliness is not Togetherness. It's Intimacy.
–Richard Bach

Journal Entry - October 1, 1998
I dreamt I'd decided to leave Jim, and I had the most wonderful, clear, cleansed feeling inside me, as if my insides had been washed with Dr. Bronner's Peppermint Soap.

"Y ou are a twelve-year-old boy, and you need to grow up!" our new counselor, Norma, declares, pointing at Jim during our second joint visit.

We're both startled. His rueful grin gives the impression he thinks her assessment is funny and maybe a little true. I try to hide a smile, mentally nodding my head. *Now maybe we'll get somewhere.*

Norma asks us to discuss what we want in our marriage and what's missing. Four years ago, I wrote in my journal, "If Jim desired to save our marriage, he'd do the dishes with me." I'd told him time and time again I

109

missed the intimacy we once had, doing things together. "Honey," I'd say, "lovemaking starts in the kitchen, cooking together or doing the dishes." Or, "Come talk to me while we do the dishes." Or, "Do you remember how we used to sing faux opera together when we did the dishes?" Once he suggested I let Tillie lick the dishes clean (I didn't find that amusing), but his answers always concluded with, "I have work to do."

One evening, after I'd once again finished the dishes alone, I walked by his office and found him playing a computer game. Anger bubbled up inside me. He didn't have time for me, but he had time to play a game. Maybe he needed a break, but at my expense? In order to avoid escalating our cold war, I said nothing and walked away. The erosion of trust that I'd once had for my husband had become a landslide.

When Norma asks me "What's missing," I answer, "I know I'm going to sound like a broken record, but I'd love for Jim to help me with the dishes. It doesn't have to be every day if he has a deadline or something, but I'd like it to be on a regular basis. I used to ask him, but I've given up because he's always too busy."

Jim snaps erect in his chair, his face growing red. "That's it?" he fumes. "You're mad because you wanted me to do the dishes? You've had this secret expectation of me all this time?"

I cross my arms and hold myself tight. It's all I can do to keep from slapping him.

"And what do you want from Linda, Jim?" asks Norma. *She's doing her best to keep her professional calm.*

I'm remembering a request he'd made a couple of years ago: "I'd like you to stay home at night instead of going to choir practice or church meetings," he'd told me.

"Really?" I'd replied. "What would that accomplish? When I'm home, you ignore me and stay in your office. Besides, you know how much I enjoy being in the choir."

Now that we've moved away from Bend, he has what he wanted, but he's still in his office instead of spending time with me. Norma and I wait while Jim mulls over her question. "I wish she'd grow her hair long like when we first met," he says. "And I know it's way too late, but I wish she would have agreed to have another child."

I want to pummel him. I don't wait for Norma to ask me how I feel about this. "We discussed it, and you approved my getting a tubal ligation!" I blurt, feeling my blood boil. "You said I should decide!" *Is he making it up now just to get to me? Or is he losing his mind and memory?*

"I see," says Norma. *She's seeing what a challenge is ahead of her.* She changes the subject. "Here's some homework for you both. Think of something good you'd like for your mate."

For my part, I don't have to think hard. I've known for years what I want for Jim, and I've tried telling him more than once. Maybe now, with Norma's help, he'll hear me. What does he want for me? He's been so supportive toward my Keiko book efforts, I imagine he'd like me to make money with my writing. Beyond that, his thinking remains a mystery.

At our next session, I hold my husband's hands. "Honey," I say, "I'd like you to show more caring behavior toward yourself by getting regular exercise. I believe it could make a world of difference in your physical and mental health." Tears are in my eyes and my heart is full, wanting him to feel relief from the dark cloud following him for years.

Jim doesn't move a muscle.

"How do you feel about what Linda just said, Jim?" Norma asks.

He shrugs. "She's been trying to get me to exercise for a long time."

I withdraw my hands and sigh. I promised myself early on I'd be careful about bringing up sensitive issues like this one. But in our long marriage, I probably did suggest more than once that exercise would improve his health and overall attitude. I'm quite sure I didn't harp on it.

"So, what do you want for Linda?"

Jim takes my hands. "I'd like you to find a good job," he says. "I mean one you'll like," he adds.

His words touch my suspicions, not my heart. He's been pushing me to find a steady job ever since we've moved to Tualatin. Is he hoping he won't have to pay alimony if we split? My trust in him has vanished. We ride home in silence. *I'm afraid we'll get into another fight if I try to discuss any of this outside Norma's office.*

While browsing in a thrift shop, I have another moment of mental cheating. I see a microwave popcorn popper like Jim's. I consider it, thinking how, in the middle of a movie, Jim used to put it on pause and make us popcorn. If we should divorce, no doubt he'll take his popper. A rush of heat and a mix of guilt and excitement flood my body. I will buy my own popper. I'm no longer fantasizing over the single life I'd have without my husband. I'm buying something for that life. Although I don't know how often I'll make popcorn, I want to have a popper when I do. I take it home and hide it away. I have a foot-and-a-half out the door.

It's October, and I wonder at the timing of Lorraine, my friend and spiritual counselor from Bend. I've been keeping her informed on the state of our marriage. There's a conference in Portland, and she asks if she can stay overnight with us. It's our twenty-fifth wedding anniversary, but we have no plans. I tell her she's welcome.

Jim and I let her take us out for dinner. He suggests I drive because he's tired. He's always tired, and I drive us a lot, but I'm disappointed he doesn't take this opportunity to be more chivalrous this evening. Lorraine seems to understand her role is to help us pretend, for one night at least, everything is fine. We chat about this and that, never mentioning the milestone occasion. Jim takes the last of the shrimp, and after consuming it, says, "Oh, I hope neither of you wanted that."

Lorraine collects the check, and she and I struggle with our coats while Jim waits for us in the lobby. *Is he feeling ashamed? Is that why he's off by himself? I don't know what to do here.* We drive back to our house in silence. I want to cry. Maybe he feels the same. Neither of us cries.

Nineteen

Will Satan Win?

Satan is a figure appearing in the texts of the Abrahamic religions who brings evil and temptation, and is known as the deceiver who leads humanity astray. See Psalm 23:4

—Wikipedia

We've been seeing Norma once a week—both as individuals and as a couple—when I realize I'm in the middle of a religious debate much larger than myself.

By now, I'm sure Jim has told her of his hurtful family dynamics. Since, in previous counseling, he had complained how "out-of-the-blue angry" I get with him sometimes, I imagine he's told her that too. I doubt he mentioned he provoked most of those outbursts.

In my own sessions I say, "I believe Jim has put me in the role of his grandmother, acting out against me in her place. After many attempts, we managed a détente on the issue of my cooking, but he still acts as if I'm punishing him when I ask for his help with a little bit of housework."

"I've tried to change in various ways to get along with him. I tried being extra attentive. I tried emotional separation. At one point I attempted to get his attention by refusing to make love with him, trying to get him to understand the brokenness of our marriage. That strategy didn't work, and I discontinued it, but these days I'm just going through the motions."

"Maybe you have some anger too?" she suggests.

"Yes, I do," I admit. "Anyway, I decided that just because he's unhappy and doesn't care to participate in fun activities with me, I'd find ways to be happy on my own and not feel guilty. I developed a friendship with a few single women in our church in Bend, and we went camping and hiking together. Maybe Jim has felt abandoned, but, then again, maybe he hasn't even noticed. Having those friends has been good, but they couldn't take the place of a loving husband."

Norma tosses me a hard one. "What do you see as your part in this struggle with your husband?"

The silence stretches as I process her question. "I've asked Jim what I do to upset him, but he refuses to dig deep and tell me the truth. I guess my part is that I have trouble changing my reaction when he purposely provokes me. Even when I try not to show he's gotten to me, he can tell I'm ticked. I've never learned how to handle those moments in a more positive way."

Journal Entry – October 24, 1998

Jim has had extreme ups and downs. He's been exceptionally contrary these days. Norma claims the devil is making him do it. Whatever is going on, our troubles seem to be coming to a head. Like cysts, they've been under our skin, poisoning our relationship. They'll erupt soon. Then we can decide what to do with the mess.

After several sessions with Norma, little has changed between Jim and me. Disheartened, I bring up the subject of divorce. "I can't stay with Jim if he keeps pushing me away. Whenever we've been to counseling, he seems to understand how his behavior impacts our relationship. However, the gains are soon lost, and he's more contrary and distant than before."

"We don't talk divorce here," she declares, and quotes Matthew 19:6. "So they [husband and wife] are no longer two, but one flesh. Therefore what God has joined together, let no one separate."

"Jesus said divorce is only permitted if there is marital unfaithfulness. If you divorce Jim, Satan wins," Norma adds.

I feel heat rising in me. Norma's refusal to discuss divorce is too much. I blurt out my truth. "Satan has already won. Satan won when Jim broke our marriage covenant by not loving or honoring me. He's addicted to his work and his religious pursuits. To me, that's being unfaithful. And he refuses to acknowledge those actions that have driven us apart and to ask for forgiveness. He's unrepentant, and I've lost all hope for reconciliation."

Norma shakes her head with sadness. "You will be making a huge mistake if you leave the covering and protection of your husband."

I reject her words. What covering and protection has my husband given me? I don't see it. This is hierarchy talk—the same kind of reasoning I read in the PK material. This dogma says I will be vulnerable to demonic influence because I have not given control of my life over to my husband.

Clearly, if I choose divorce, I will experience condemnation from certain Christian sectors. I'm no biblical scholar, but everything I know about God tells me He will not abandon me if I choose to take a healthier, more peaceful path than the one I've been on. I believe God wants peace for me and for Jim, and it's obvious we cannot regain that in our marriage.

I go home and look up *covering* in the Bible. "Oh God the Lord, the strength of my salvation, You have covered my head in the day of battle." (Psalm 140:7 NKJV). God is my covering. Not a mortal man.

I email Lorraine and share Norma's statement. She writes back. "This 'Satan winning' stuff is too simplistic. Yes, God is saddened by divorce, but He never turns away from people having to choose the best of several not-very-great options."

I'm grateful for her words. How can it be that all Christians sin and "let Satan win" when deciding on divorce for reasons other than adultery?

I think back to a friend's marriage. I'd met Sheila and her husband Rob through a small independent Bible study while living in Southern California. Sheila, a slight, quiet woman, seemed likable enough, but my intuition warned me of some kind of problem with Rob. Still, I did my best to suspend judgment.

During the group's time together, Sheila became pregnant with their third child. After the birth of their healthy baby, Rob made a confession. He had hit Sheila in her third month, and she had fallen down the stairs. Raised in a family of hitters, this wasn't the first time he'd struck her. However, this recent birth had changed him. He claimed to have sought the Lord's forgiveness and vowed he would never hit Sheila again. We commended him and prayed for continued healing in their marriage.

A year or two later, Sheila had a breakdown and spent time in a mental health facility. We group members did our best to support her during that time, praying for her healing and bringing meals to the family.

Sheila returned home after a month and began keeping a private journal, as recommended by her mental health counselor. The counselor admonished Rob not to read it, but he did, finding something in the journal that set him off. He attacked Sheila, breaking her arm before she managed to wrestle free. She ran out into the front yard, calling for help. A passerby picked her up and drove her to the hospital. I learned that Rob's abuse centered on wanting complete control over Sheila.

These events, although not surprising, saddened me. I applauded her when she sued for divorce and got custody of her children. A few weeks after the divorce, I took her to lunch. She knew she couldn't live with Rob anymore, but, at the same time, she expressed fear she had sinned by leaving her husband. I told her I believed God did not want her and her children to be exposed to Rob's violent behavior. "I'm quite sure that is not God's plan for you," I said. "The Lord wants you to have a safe and peaceful life." I'm sorry I didn't think to ask why she wondered if she had sinned, or how her church had responded to the divorce.

We all know of other kinds of abuse that exist in dysfunctional marriages. What if the wife emotionally abuses their children? What if she's addicted to gambling and refuses to get help? What if he's addicted to drugs and refuses to get help? What if she can't stop spending their money? What if the husband beats their children? What if there is physical or emotional abandonment? Conversion to a cult? I could think of multiple scenarios that seem to justify divorce, but do my own circumstances qualify? Despite my declaration to Norma, would God find crazymaking and emotional distancing a valid enough reason?

It might seem as if I've made up my mind about leaving, but apparently, I can't stop getting advice from various people. I make an appointment with Barbara, the women's pastor of our Presbyterian church in Beaverton.

"Your decision should be based on what God wants you to do or to not do. It is not about whether you're happy or unhappy," she tells me. "God wants obedience. You should be asking Him what He wants from you in your marriage."

As if I haven't been doing that for years!

"If you're leaving to escape the pain, you'll only find more pain."

I don't get it. I've given Jim my best for twenty-five years and have been mostly miserable with him for the last twelve. It seems to me that God wants me to use my mind, my instincts, and my will to take charge of my life—not out of anger, but out of love for myself and for Jim—and stop waiting for things to get better.

Barbara tells me a little story.

A woman in the church had been in a difficult marriage, but she believed God's will required her to stick with it. She obeyed and grew as a Godly woman. Then the husband died, relieving her of the burden of being married to him.

Barbara sees the man's death as God's blessing! Is she saying I should stay with Jim and trust that God will kill him off one day? *Weird. I wonder how many other women have come to Barbara with this exact question and been given this story.* Perhaps I'd wanted a stamp of approval from Barbara, but I'm obviously not going to get a definitive opinion from her one way or the other.

I read in Richard Foster's *Money, Sex and Power: The Challenge of a Disciplined Life*:

> Christian marriage is a "one flesh" union ... We split it open when no other option is open to us ... But we live in a fallen world, and there are times when, despite all our efforts, the marriage enters the valley of the shadow of death. Every resource has been used. Every possible way to bring healing and wholeness has been tried. Still the marriage is immersed in destruction and bitterness. When such is the case, the law of love (agape) dictates that there should be a divorce.[2]

This seems to make sense, but is this the world speaking, or a message of mercy from above for a couple who can no longer live peaceably as man and wife? I'm leaning toward mercy.

Although M. Scott Peck's words are not biblical, they resonate with me.

> "The unconscious is always one step ahead of the conscious mind, and it is therefore impossible ever to *know* that you are doing the right thing ... However, if your will is steadfastly to the good, and if you are willing to suffer *fully* when the good seems ambiguous, your unconscious will always be one step ahead of your conscious mind in the right direction. In other words, you will do the right thing, even though you will not have the consolation of knowing at the time that it is the right thing."[3]

Ros has recently been transferred to a new clinic in Tualatin. She suggests we meet for lunch once a week at Carl's Jr., an arrangement that helps keep me grounded.

I tell her, "I've given Jim the best I have, and yet I've been unhappy for a long time. I'm not saying I've been perfect. I have a temper. I've made mistakes, but I sure have tried. Yet all that trying hasn't moved us to a better place."

"I know," she says, compassion in her eyes. "It takes two. So have you decided what you're going to do?"

"I think so. It's obvious that our marriage will just keep getting worse. It seems that God wants me to use my mind, my instincts, and my will to take charge of my life instead of spending more years in pain. I don't want to leave out of anger. I still love Jim in a way, and his awful childhood breaks my heart, but I think a separation might be better for both of us. Maybe my leaving will open his eyes and cause him to do some soul-searching."

A flash of impatience passes across my cousin's usually sympathetic countenance. "Jim's childhood is no excuse for how he's treated you. He's made conscious choices and now he's reaping the results." Ros is the perfect person to speak to this subject, having survived a hellish childhood with an alcoholic father.

I nod my understanding. "I've been thinking what Norma said about Satan winning," I say. "Satan can win whether I stay or go. Thank goodness God is bigger than Satan and full of mercy because I'm sinking and I have to save myself."

I lie in bed that night, my back to my sleeping husband. I'm in agony, wrestling over my spiritual beliefs, my human condition, and my intuition. I tell God I'm sorry I've not always fulfilled my part of our marriage, and I hope He'll forgive me. I feel God telling me He does forgive me, He understands my pain, and He'll be with me no matter what. I cry in silent relief, sensing God's permission to choose.

Twenty

Breaking Up Is Hard to Do

A breakup is like a broken mirror. It is better to leave than risk hurting yourself trying to pick up all of the broken pieces.
—Linda Randall Wisdom

Journal Entry - October 30, 1998
Sometimes I wonder if the Jim and Linda Saga of Troubles is a creation of my need for drama. The cost is high and will climb higher if I continue on this course. I know my troubled marriage has been an enduring topic of conversation with my friends the past several years. What else is there to discuss? Can I be as compelling? Will my friends be as compassionate without hearing my problems? How many of my Christian friends will understand if I choose divorce?

What makes my marriage so confusing is that Jim will send me to Iceland, go miles out of his way to buy me a Keiko radio (yes, he did that), remember my birthday and all our wedding anniversaries, but ask him to help a little around the house, and he's a small boy, throwing a tantrum. I'm tired of being the mean old grandmother. I want a partner who is a partner, an adult.

A friend once told me she was waiting for her husband to make a wrong move so she could leave him. I said to myself, "What's she waiting for? She's already made up her mind." Now I see myself in the same situation. I've been waiting for some clear evidence that Jim has changed or will not.

Journal Entry -November 12, 1998

Last night, when Jim once again refused to help with the dishes, was the clear-cut answer I've been waiting for. Of course, it's not about the dishes; it's about working together, being connected enough that most of the time we're considering our mate as well as ourselves. In the beginning of our marriage, Jim and I had that connection, but it's been missing for far too long and will never be regained. I must accept this reality.

"I think we should separate," I tell Jim as my fifty-fifth birthday nears. I'm feeling shaky, knowing this is a momentous landmark in our marriage. "The counseling's not working—nothing's changed. You're not happy, and I'm not happy. Maybe if we get some distance from each other, our thinking will be clearer. We might discover we miss one another."

Jim nods as if he's been expecting it. "I won't try to stop you," he says, "but I'm not giving up on our marriage." Then he adds, "So I guess you'll be moving out for a while."

His words hit me with hard reality. *He says he's not giving up, but what does that mean? He expects me to move out without even talking about how that might work. Maybe I'm off here, but this feels like retribution.* "Uh, I haven't figured that out. But now that you've brought it up, it makes more sense for *you* to move out. Since you're traveling quite a bit, I'm left to take care of the animals. I can't imagine taking them with me to an apartment."

Jim squares his shoulders. "Well, I'm not moving out!"

"Well, neither am I!"

We conclude that we will stay in the house together until the end of January. "That will give you time to figure out what you want to do, job-wise," Jim says.

I move into the guest bedroom, sick at heart but resolute, as I transfer a few essentials. That night I toss and turn, trying to adjust to the single bed and wrestling with God and myself over my decision. Am I doing the right thing? How will I support myself? What if I don't figure out what "I want to do, job-wise"?

I have no idea what kind of spousal support I will get if I go through with a divorce. We are not rich. Besides, I hate the idea of depending on Jim for my financial well-being. I begin reading help wanted ads and attending career classes. I try to imagine myself confidently going through a five-day workweek. Will my pain condition allow me to handle the pace? I wish I knew.

Except for us sleeping apart, not much has changed between us except I no longer ask Jim to help me with the dishes and other domestic work. I will no longer set myself up for disappointment around this issue.

Jim urges me to take some computer classes held in downtown Portland. I have a panic attack the first day as I steer my way through the parking garage. I fear my van is too tall for the ceiling and I'm going to crash. Each time I drive under a beam, I can't restrain myself from ducking. I know I'm being illogical, but it's all I can do to find a parking space. I arrive at the classroom late, sweaty, and out of breath. I manage to get through the lesson, but I feel this is too much for my poor brain.

Over time, with a lot of help and effort, I overcome my anxiety and learn a bit of Internet software: HTML, Front Page, and Netscape. I may never be at ease with technology, but I lose some of my fear and my self-confidence inches up a bit.

I've seen doctors over the years, and had multiple pain medications prescribed as well as various physical therapies. Because I'm concerned about my ability to work full time, I hope new treatments are available. I see a rheumatologist at Oregon Health and Science University to get an update. His assessment and advice contain no new information. He cautions me to avoid stress, gives me some stretches and exercises to do, and recommends regular massage. Since I have heard these same things before, I'm not optimistic about reducing my pain. I do take his advice and begin going to a massage therapist I find in the Yellow Pages.

To add to my discomfort, I get a bit of something between my eye and my contact lens. Because my cornea feels like it might be scratched, I call my ophthalmologist. He's not in, but his partner can see me. The first thing the doctor asks is, "Besides your eye problem, how are you?"

I'm surprised at his question, not expecting him to have any interest in my health beyond my eyes. I give him my standard answer. "Well, except for my chronic pain, I'm just fine."

"Chronic pain? Tell me more."

Still surprised, I describe it to him.

"You need to go see David Allen at Progressive Fitness in Sherwood," he says. "He owns the studio, and I'm sure he can help you."

Since it's not often that an ophthalmologist tells his patient to go work out, I obey. I'm about twenty pounds overweight and out of shape. It seems as if each time I do any kind of fitness routine, I hurt myself. But, I'm ready to try something new. I know if I stay inactive for long, I'll become bedridden.

These days, most things make me nervous, and I'm feeling that way as I approach the studio in a business park. I expect it to be filled with hard bodies, but I'm relieved when I enter. I see several impressive physiques but just as many people with ordinary builds.

David is muscular and straightforward. He runs me through a series of physical tests before showing me a few stretches. One has me on my back with my legs up on a wall, easing my back muscles. I try a wall sit, standing with my knees bent and the wall supporting my back. I manage all of thirty seconds, my legs shaking.

David directs me to lie face down on the mat, spread eagle, and props my arms and legs with foam blocks. It seems as if I've been holding my breath during these last few years, keeping in the emotional pain of my marriage, trying to bury my hurt, frustration, and confusion in my muscles and the bottom of my lungs. Now I'm forced to breathe deeply. All the pain and ugliness come rushing out, and I'm racked with sobs. I'm prostrate, vulnerable and bawling in front of strangers, but I can't stop myself. The genie is out of the bottle, and there's no way I can put her back.

I hear the woman next to me asking if I'm all right. "She's good," David replies. "Her body is filled with tension and she's letting it out."

I silently thank David for understanding and being my advocate. I feel weak, yet cleansed, as I leave the studio.

Jim and I keep the status quo through the holidays, letting only our parents and siblings know of the separation. Travis is busy with his own life and doesn't need to know what's going on with us. At least, not yet. Other than sleeping in separate bedrooms, our relationship hasn't changed much. I take care of the household duties, and Jim works. We decorate a Christmas tree, and Jim fashions a cross out of a light string and attaches it to our big front window. We spend Christmas day with my family at my folks' house. My sister-in-law Sandy asks what's going on with us. "Aren't you separated?"

We shrug. We don't know what we are.

In January I have to "grub to Jim" for enough money to buy groceries. Yet he buys himself a thirty-five-dollar screen saver for his computer. He also refuses to do his job of picking up the dog poop because it's "too wet outside." We're living in the wet Willamette Valley for goodness sake! In contrast, I'm still doing the housework, the laundry, fixing our meals— taking care of everything I've always taken care of.

Twenty-one

Pushed Off the Fence

*Even though I walk through the valley of the shadow of death, I will
fear no evil, for You are with me.*
—Psalm 23:4

"We need to talk," Jim says in early April. "As long as you
can't forgive me for things in the past, there doesn't seem
to be much hope for us. I'm tired of waiting for you to
make up your mind. You need to get off the fence and move on."

We both know our marriage is over, but his harsh words feel like a slap.
I'm stuck, not knowing what my next move should be. Since Jim's emphasis
has been my getting a job before I move out, this is a new development.
Yet, I understand we can't remain in our state of uncertainty for much
longer. "How can I move on without your financial support?" I ask. "You
know I've been trying to find a job, but I haven't been successful."

"You'd better find something soon," he warns.

I'm depressed and stuck. I lie in the tub and cry out to God, my tears plopping into the water. "What am I going to do?" I wail. "Where will I go? How can I live on my own?"

"Be of good cheer," comes an inner voice. "Trust me and have hope."

I get out of the tub and dry myself off. I will do my best to trust God and do the next thing, whatever that might be. Being of good cheer is a bigger challenge.

I tell my parents it looks as if we're headed toward divorce. I'm relieved they don't bring up the subject of divorce in the Good Book. Dad focuses on the practical. "You've spent a lot of years with Jim. How can you leave now? How are you going to support yourself?"

"I don't know, Dad. All I know is that if I stay with him, I'm going to go crazy."

He shakes his head. "You have a lot to lose."

That's Dad, being his practical self. I wish he understood my emotional health is in jeopardy.

Mom does not disappoint. "I understand, honey. Your dad and I love Jim, but he can be difficult. Whenever he's stayed with us, I've been a nervous wreck, wondering if my cooking will please him, or if he'll be in one of his dark moods. He can be warm and funny, but I never know which Jim will show up. I know you've struggled to save your marriage, and I believe you if you say you have to leave."

That's Mom, my champion, the best kind of mom, who trusts in her children.

Since I've been through enough counseling to recognize my parents' patterns and my responses, their reactions don't surprise me. Although I have a history of receiving Dad's "helpful" suggestions as criticism, we are evolving. In the last few years, he's learned to show his appreciation for my abilities, and I'm able to receive his concern as an expression of love. I know both he and Mom will be by my side, whatever the fallout from my decision.

I'm busy in the garage, separating some of our stuff, when Jim comes in and says, "I'd like us to try more counseling. What do you think?"

I'm astounded. *Is he sincere or is this more crazymaking? If I refuse, he's going to blame me for not wanting to fix our marriage.* I pause before I answer. "I think you should work on yourself," I finally tell him. "In all these years of counseling, the only changes I've seen in you have been for the worse. If you think counseling will help you now, I'm all for it, but I've had my quota."

He shakes his head and stomps off.

Not long after that conversation, I overhear him talking with his sister on the phone. "Linda wants a divorce," he says. "I asked her to do more counseling, but she won't."

Always the half-truths with my husband. I'm no longer outraged or the least bit surprised.

I have to tell Travis I'm divorcing his dad. The four-hour drive north on I-5 gives me plenty of time to think. My son has kept his emotional distance from us since his discharge from the Army. I wish we could have given him a happier family childhood like my own. He and I had such a great connection when he was younger. I yearn for us to be able to have something like that again someday.

I need to be careful with how I communicate with Travis, and that hurts. What will be his reaction to my news? I'd been advised by a divorced friend to say only positive things concerning my child's father. "Don't share the hurtful stuff. Even though he may know, even though he may understand, he will personalize it, internalize it." I know this to be true.

I'm in such a state processing all this, I become lost in Tacoma before I realize I haven't reached Seattle yet. *Oh, crap!*

Travis and I sit on his apartment couch as I struggle to give him my news. "Maybe you've guessed why I'm here. You know your dad and I have had our problems." I begin to cry. "I can't stay with him anymore and I've asked him for a divorce."

He puts his arm around me. "I'm not surprised. You guys haven't gotten along well for a long time. Of course, I'm sad; I love you both. You've been good parents and I'm grateful."

"I love you so much. This must hurt, and I'm so sorry," I say, hugging him.

"I understand this is something you have to do. We'll both be all right, Mom."

His words take a bit of the weight off.

"I hope someday I'll find someone who truly loves me," I tell him. "But I have a lot of adjustments to make before that can happen."

There's not much more we can say to one another. I offer to take him out to an early dinner, but he declines, so I leave him to process my news. This feels too abrupt, and I wish I had more time with him, but it's not to be.

Relieved our conversation went as well as it did, I search out a little retail therapy. I go to Nordstrom's Rack and buy myself a beautiful pair of trousers—a great bargain—to help build my professional wardrobe.

I stay alone in a motel because it's such a long drive home. *This feels strange and uncomfortable.* The next morning, when I go to pay the bill with my credit card, I discover it's expired. Jim has always renewed it, but not this time. He hadn't even bothered to alert me. It seems he's upping his underground war against me. *Rat! Why should I be surprised?* I write a check, praying I have enough money in my account to cover the bill.

When I get back to Tualatin, Jim has news. He's talked with a Realtor and might be buying a house.

"Oh, that sounds like a good idea," I say. "I suppose I should consider doing that myself."

"You'd better get a good job then, 'cause otherwise, you won't be able to afford one."

I'm speechless, but I'm sure my face betrays my shock and anger. I've been a faithful wife all these years, taking care of our son, keeping up our homes, working at outside jobs at least part of the time, not to mention putting up with him. I can't have a house, but he can?

"Oh, and by the way, you'd better sell the van and find something cheaper," he adds.

Something cheaper than my four-year-old Plymouth Voyager? Come on! Does he mean to strip me of everything?

Les, my brother with whom I've always been close, is the one in my family who raises the religious question. I'm surprised and disappointed when I visit him and Sandy in Eugene and we go out to dinner. "You know the Bible is against divorce," he says. "I don't think you're doing the right thing. Besides, I like Jim. I'll never forget his kindness by donating money to Boys Town in Matt's name when he died."

Sandy extends a hand across the table. "We're both sad that you and Jim are breaking up, but I know you've struggled for a long time. I wish you well as you go forward."

I leave the next day, their sadness weighing on me.

Acquaintances have various takes on my decision to divorce too. I'm astounded when I receive an email from someone on a children writers' listserv: "I know nothing about your situation, but your post on the listserv telling of your separation from your husband saddened me greatly. From previous posts, you talked of singing in a praise group at church. You know—I'm sure—that God does not want separation/divorce for you. When Christians, especially, go through this it really makes me sad. It is not only a personal tragedy, but also a poor witness to God's power to transform lives. I'm sure I'm not telling you anything you don't know— but pray about this and seek counseling!"

Amazing! We are acquainted through only the listserv, and she thinks she has the answer to my situation. I'm in the middle of a Christian conflict over marriage and divorce just as I predicted. I send her a reply.

"I know you meant well, but your message felt like a dagger to my heart. Being misunderstood by a fellow Christian hurts more than any slings and arrows the world may throw my way. You have no idea what my struggles have been, the condition of my heart, or what kind of help I've sought. God knows, and only He can judge me. Until you've walked in my shoes and talked over the situation with God for years, done all you know to do to make it better, you cannot say what He wants for me. And if you think I'm taking the easy way out, think again. I'm taking the sane way out. Believe me when I say this has not been an easy decision."

My nurse practitioner shares her story. After years of emotional abuse, she left her husband. He turned their children against her, and it brought her deep sorrow. After a year had passed, she went to a Chinese restaurant she and her husband had patronized. Two of the women there rushed to her, welcoming her back. "You look so good. You've lost weight," one said. The nurse explained that she had divorced her husband. "Oh," cried the other woman, raising her hands in the air, a big smile on her face, "Freedom!"

I laugh, believing I too will eventually rejoice in freedom. Losing weight might be an added benefit.

I tell my massage therapist of my decision. She stops working on me. "Yes!" she shouts. "Good for you! I've known you should do it since we first met, but I also knew you needed to figure it out for yourself." She then astounds me by saying, "If you'd stayed in that marriage, you would have died of cancer within the next couple of years."

I'm having difficulty getting to sleep. After I do fall asleep, I often wake from nightmares, tormented by my new reality, and have trouble going back to sleep. I see my doctor for some sleeping pills, explaining my situation. I'm surprised when he says with great emotion, "Oh, no! I'm so sorry!" While mulling over his reaction on my way home, I run a stop sign and get a traffic ticket. *Just what I don't need!*

One last trip to share my news, this time to Bend. I stay with Lorraine and see other friends as well. They're all supportive and don't seem surprised. "You struck me as an unlikely couple," one of them remarks. "You've always seemed so alive, and Jim—well, he appeared to be ill at ease much of the time."

I guess I hadn't wanted to see that in Jim, but I realize her observation is true. I'm glad I've remained "alive" even during our difficult times.

While there, I arrange a tour of the new addition of my former church with Bruce—a gentleman who served with me on the Building Committee. I'd challenged the architects to figure out a way to create a sloped floor in the sanctuary with pews for better viewing of the platform, as well as a flat area down front for chairs or other flexible uses. They devised a brilliant solution, and, since then, other churches have copied the idea, and the space is in demand for community events. Since I'd moved away before the completion of the addition, I'm glad to see how well it turned out.

"We did good," Bruce says, giving me a warm smile.

"Yes, we did." I give him a high-five. Although I'd had problems at home and sometimes at work, I'd accomplished good things.

I recall my last Sunday of attendance when Pastor Tom thanked me for my service. The knowledge that I'd used my gifts of organization and artistic vision for the good of the church community and beyond buoyed my spirit. My church's recognition kept my ego from taking a deep dive.

I don't have the heart to drive by my beautiful home on the hill. I think of all the hours Jim spent there in his office in front of his computer while I tried my best to live my own life. I drive back over the mountains in slush and rain.

When I return to Tualatin, Jim greets me with startling news. "I've received a job offer in San Diego and I'm considering it. I've found a lawyer who suggested that I make a cash settlement with you after two years of spousal support."

His news hits hard. "That doesn't sound very good. I'll get my own attorney and see what he says."

The divorce is happening. After all this time contemplating the possibilities and repercussions, I don't feel prepared. I'm facing a leap into the unknown.

Twenty-two

Job Hunting

I'm gonna harden my heart, I'm gonna swallow my tears.
—Marvin Ross

I take my dad for a ride in the country to visit Colton, a little town in which he'd lived as a young boy. Our little trip reminds me of when our family used to take Sunday drives through the countryside. We stop in the yard of the old church his father helped build. "How's the job hunting going?" he asks.

I discern he's trying to be supportive. "Not good," I answer.

"Have you considered going back to teaching?"

I sigh. "You know, Dad, I did okay teaching art those four years in Albuquerque, but I never wanted that as my career. I'm good at ceramics, jewelry making, and weaving—but I'm not good at drawing and painting, and I didn't feel comfortable teaching it. Wouldn't it be ironic if I'm forced to repeat my history? Besides, I was a lot younger then. To be honest, I don't know if I have the physical and mental strength to handle the stress of full-time teaching."

"I'm sorry you have to go through this, kiddo," he says.

"Thanks, Dad. You know, growing up, I thought I'd have a good marriage like you and Mom. It worked out so great that you had your little jewelry and watchmaking business with Mom helping out. You were great partners. And you always seemed to have time to enjoy life as a family."

Dad pats me on my shoulder. "We were blessed in lots of ways, including having two great kids. You're smart and capable, and things will work out for you."

A couple of days after my trip with Dad, I'm excited to find a notice in the classifieds for a part-time interior design instructor position at a nearby community college. Maybe there's still an opportunity for me in the design field. I need a letter of reference. I call Phil, who is an educator, to ask if he's willing to write me one. My feelings for him have not abated, and my heart rate increases as I anticipate our conversation.

"I'd be happy to write you a reference," he says, his familiar voice sending pleasant shivers through me.

"It's been a while since we'd worked together. Do you need a reminder of my work style?" I ask.

"Not necessary. I still remember that meeting we had in your van concerning our class when we found ourselves locked out of the church. We worked well together."

"I remember it too, and yes, we did." My heart beats a little faster, affirming my belief in our special connection. I can still feel it.

A pregnant pause and then he says, as if worried he's showing too much pleasure at my call, "Well, give Big Jim a hug for me."

Don't hang up! Jim and I are divorcing. I'll soon be free! Are you interested? Way too awkward. Why couldn't I have simply said I was sorry to report that Jim and I are getting a divorce? Once again, I say nothing.

Two days later I receive Phil's recommendation, noting I am "extremely organized," have a "nice teaching delivery," and he found me "a pleasure to work with" among other nice attributes. I have other good teaching recommendations too. *How could the college not want me?*

A week later, I receive a call telling me the college would like to interview me for the position. I'm happy and panicked all at once. It's been a while since I've practiced interior design on a regular basis, and my degrees are in art education. Can I pull it off? I do my best, organizing slides of interiors I've done and reviewing notes from the design classes I've taken and community college classes I taught in Bend.

The night before the interview, Jim is on a business trip when I have a panic attack. I awaken the next morning in my day clothes, not remembering that I'd gone to bed. *I'm such a mess. How can I even consider finding a job?*

I don't know how much my nerves are apparent during my afternoon presentation. I show slides of the mansion I decorated for the Patels. I project photos of the log home I worked on in Bend with a much different vibe.

Despite my fears, the presentation seems to go well, and I feel I haven't made a fool of myself. Maybe I will survive despite my fears. I go home and have two glasses of wine, not my normal MO.

I'm disappointed I don't get a call back. I'd love to teach design, and the program had an ideal schedule. Later, a new friend who works as a counselor for another community college tells me how impressed he is that I'd gotten as far as an interview. He explains that, by law, open positions have to be advertised, but in typical practice, the college already has someone to fill them. I feel a little better. I suppose the interview gave me good experience.

An acquaintance connects me with an admissions coordinator at a local community college. He's a compassionate man, and encourages me to consider college teaching, suggesting I envision the life I would like to have. I want to continue to write, but I also know I can't make much money as an author.

If I am going to enter some kind of professional field, I need to adjust my identity. I'm no longer the western woman from Bend. I'm in a sophisticated metropolitan area now. No more prairie skirts for me. I find a brown tweed pencil skirt and silk blouse at Goodwill for starters.

I rework my résumé and send it out in response to a few ads in the paper. I'm excited to get an interview with Easter Seals in Portland. One of the two women interviewers asks if I'm good at multitasking. Without hesitation I say, "Of course! I'm a woman!" The women nod and chuckle. I go through more hoops with success, including generating a list of suggested events to raise money. However, I realize their biggest event of the year is on Easter Sunday. I tell them I can meet all their requirements except helping on that day—that I'll be celebrating Easter in church.

The woman who calls to let me know someone else has been selected is apologetic. "We really liked you," she says. I get the distinct impression that my unwillingness to work on Easter Sunday torpedoed my chances. Although I'm a little disappointed, I also feel relief I won't have to spend an hour each day commuting to Portland or venture into this unfamiliar work environment. Perhaps rejection is God's protection.

My exchanges with Jim become stranger than ever. As I'm dressing to go to the store, he glances at me and says with surprise in his voice, "You're really a nice-looking woman." I shake my head. *He's just now realizing it? It's too late, baby. It's all too late.*

As we're going through some stuff in our garage, Jim catches me by the shoulders and looks at me with a sorrowful expression in his eyes I've not seen before. "Are you sure you want to do this?" he asks.

"I ask myself that question daily, and each day you give me a reason to leave. You can be good at the hero stuff—I'll never forget the time you drove all those miles to get that Keiko radio for me—but the ordinary stuff is much different. You don't even pick up the dog poop, which you agreed to do, and you barely take care of the yard. And when I try to answer a question you've asked, you walk away while I'm talking. You're arrogant and demeaning to me every day."

He frowns and asks, "But who will adjust your back and help you with your computer?"

"I have no idea, but you're fooling yourself," I say, raising my voice as he walks away, "if you think I'd stay just for that."

At breakfast the next morning, he prays, "Dear, Lord, please put Linda on a righteous path." He doesn't say "we," he doesn't say "me." He says, "Linda." *He's trashing me to the Lord. And right in front of me! No wonder I grind my teeth at night.*

I read every self-help book and article I can get my hands on. While waiting in my doctor's office, I read an article on the science of a good marriage. It suggests that the most destructive emotions in a marriage are criticism, contempt, defensiveness, and stonewalling. I sigh. That's my experience with Jim to a T.

I write down a quote from Ann Lamott's *Traveling Mercies*:

> "I have read that this is how you induce psychosis in rats. You behave inconsistently with them; you keep changing the rules. One day when they press down the right lever, expecting a serving of grain like they've always gotten before, they instead get a shock. And eventually the switching back and forth drives them mad. The rats who get shocked every time they press the lever figure out right away and work around it." [4]

I think if I hadn't kept a journal, I might have gone a little mad like those rats. *Does Jim know what he's doing when he keeps changing his story? Oh, that's right, its crazymaking.*

Twenty-three

Beyond Belief

The future is beyond knowing, but the present is beyond belief.
—William Irwin Thompson

Since I don't know who to use as an attorney, I call the Oregon State Bar Association, which recommends Ludwig. I meet with him and like his low-key sense of humor. I take it as a good sign his name is the same as my favorite grandfather's middle name, and I'm pleased with myself for talking Ludwig down a bit on his fees. Together, we plan the rest of my life finance-wise. I'm scared. I haven't been on my own for twenty-five years. I have no idea of how much money I'll need. He says if I get a decent job, as well as receiving the support payments he's calculated I should get based on Jim's salary history, I will be "comfortable." I'm not sure what exactly that will look like, but I have to trust this man.

Ludwig and I have a conference call with Jim. I'm extremely nervous, wondering what his reaction will be to my proposal. I have no desire to punish him financially. I just want what seems fair. I'm pleasantly surprised when Jim quickly agrees to the monthly spousal support payments we've penciled out—much better than his attorney had suggested—but if I'd known what was about to transpire, I might have wanted to stick it to him big time.

Jim and I continue to live together to save money. When the divorce goes through, we'll go our separate ways. He's being super nice. Every night he helps me clean up after supper. He points out that he's stopped belching out loud and farting because it isn't "respectful" toward me. I'm not impressed with his new behavior. I figure it's so that I can't say he hasn't been a good husband. It's definitely too little, too late for him to make that claim. I realize he's heard my pleas all along to help out in the kitchen and made the conscious decision to ignore me. *Why change now?*

I'm discouraged about my struggles with balancing my checkbook when Jim and I sit down to go over our financials. He especially wants to review my "unusual expenses."

"I bought a few new business clothes for my job interviews. Is that what you're talking about?" I ask.

"No! You've been withdrawing funds from my account!"

"I have not! Look at my ATM receipts. Your bank account number isn't on any of them. Who's making those withdrawals, anyway? And by the way, what's happened to my couch money?" I'd made some money selling an article to a children's magazine about Keiko; there was the check from the moving company for damages incurred; and I'd saved money from last Christmas. I put it all together in one of our accounts and told Jim it was money for a new couch. I still have the dream of that cozy red velour couch. It's a symbol of taking care of myself.

"You pissed that money away!" he says.

I'm livid. "No! *You* must have pissed it away, and I'd better get it back!"

I had hoped we could extend some grace to one another. I love Jim, but not enough to live with him for the rest of my days. I still consider myself a married woman and assume Jim still considers himself a married man, both honoring our vows. I'd hoped we could treat each other with respect even after the divorce goes through. Nevertheless, I'm not going to let him get away with his accusations.

Journal Entry – May 22, 1999
4:00 p.m.

Jim called late this afternoon to say he wouldn't be coming home for dinner, that he'd made other arrangements. No explanation, no apology, nothing. As if he didn't care a whit that I'd already started preparing it.

11:00 p.m.

It's getting late and Jim's still not home. What's going on?

Next Day Journal Entry

Another shift in our relationship. Jim got home at 1:00 in the morning. I let him know he'd "dishonored" me by calling off dinner at the last minute and giving me no indication that he might be out late. He told me he and a female real estate agent went to Skamania Lodge for a "light meal." I couldn't believe my ears. That place is known as one of the most romantic spots on the Columbia River. If that wasn't a date, I don't know what is.

The next day we talk, and I say, "We need some ground rules. Are you planning to date? Because I'm not—not as long as we're married and living together."

"No, I'm not planning on dating."

"What about this dinner thing?"

He dodges the question. "I've been thinking that I ought to learn how to do my own cooking rather than depend on you."

"Okay," I say.

"And laundry," he says. "I should do my own."

"If that's what you want," I say. "I don't mind doing it, as it's cheaper that way."

"Okay," he says.

"And doing things together. I don't think we should, except for your Mom's birthday and your niece's graduation."

"Okay," I say. "What about my computer? Will you help me if I need it?"

"Yes."

So now I'm suddenly more independent. A bit of a shock, although, since we did so few evening activities together, it probably shouldn't feel so strange. I need to build up my friendship with some single gals, so I don't feel so alone. My, my, what a difference a day makes!

The Next Day Journal Entry

Jim didn't get home until one this morning after going to a church service and potluck with the same woman. And then "We talked and talked and talked."

Sounds like a date to me, and I'm feeling extremely upset that he won't admit it—that he's lying to me.

Maybe it's a kind of blessing, as I don't feel so guilty for leaving him alone. Maybe this is one reason he's rethinking his desire to get that job in San Diego. Maybe he wants to stay for this new woman.

Later

I'm so very angry. Took Mom and Dad on a little two-and-a-half-hour trip. Got home to a note saying Jim was out looking at condos with "a real estate agent" and he wouldn't be home until after dinner. I'm sure it's the same woman he's been out with the past two nights. This is totally contrary to what we agreed to yesterday. Not only that, he just assumed I'm taking care of the animals. My blood is boiling. If this isn't dating, I'm a fool!

11:15 p.m.

Jim isn't home yet. This is so very weird. I hope he hasn't flipped out! Oh, I guess it's me who's doing that! I feel I'm going out of my mind. I don't know what to do with myself. I yearn to somehow escape my body and this living nightmare. While I wait, I'm ironing and watching the history of golf. I hate watching golf!

3:15 a.m.

Jim finally came home. I'd gone to bed, but I hadn't slept, my mind in a never-ending loop. I got up and asked him what he thought he was doing. "What do you mean?" he says.

"Jim, this is not right."

"But you're divorcing me!"

"But we're still married and living under the same roof. This is a slippery slope you're on."

"We're just talking."

"Yeah, sure! You ask God if this is right!"

I'm in shock. Only a few months ago, Jim had been telling me he was going to fight for our marriage. I took that to mean he still loved me. Despite our problems, I've clung to that belief. But I've been delusional, protecting my ego, I suppose. How could he love me and yet hurt me like this while we are still married and living together? Jim has done many hurtful things over the years but lying to my face now makes it so much worse. The one thing I've always wanted from him is honesty, and yet now he won't even give me that.

I ask Jim if we can talk. "This is a very delicate time we're in. The decisions and actions we make now will affect us the rest of our lives. We have to be very careful to respect one another and not do anything to create animosity between us. This new relationship of yours is a big problem. When you see your Promise Keeper friends in Bend, I want you to ask their opinion about you seeing this woman. And be honest. Don't tell them half-truths like you do sometimes. Do they believe you're doing the right thing?"

Jim nods. "Okay."

I think I've done well by staying calm and firm, when I really, really want to kick him you-know-where.

Jim's going out with his lady friend feels similar to the watershed moment when Rex had a vasectomy without my consent, then divorced me. I hurt like hell, but I clearly saw there was no reason whatsoever to hang on to the relationship. Jim's behavior is the visible sign of the poison that has been happening underground all those years.

I'm in such turmoil I don't know what to do with myself. I call Ros. (Rosalind's Twenty-Four-Hour Broad Shoulders for Distraught Women), and she urges me to come over. She and her partner, Tom, embrace me, feed me, and listen to my heartbreak. Ros and I take a walk and then she tells me to lie down and take a nap. I'll never forget their love and care when I needed it the most. I feel a little saner when I finally leave.

When Jim gets back from Bend, he doesn't volunteer any mention of his Promise Keeper friends. I finally ask.

"They couldn't agree. But three of them told me it wasn't right, so I asked to be forgiven."

"From whom?"

"Jesus."

"That's good," I say, "but what about me? Do you want my forgiveness?"

"I haven't had the chance to ask."

Give me a break! "Interesting that you didn't answer my question."

"What question?"

"Do you want my forgiveness?"

"Yes, I'm sorry. I didn't mean to cause you pain. I hope you'll forgive me."

I don't feel as if he's said it with much sincerity, but then I remember that is his problem. So I say yes, I forgive him. "I can be forgiving if I'm asked," I tell him. "It's just that I'm rarely asked." Then I add, "You need to move out."

Twenty-four

Drama Queen

To wish that certain things didn't happen is to wish that I am not myself.

—**Mary Pipher,** *The Shelter of Each Other*

It's four in the morning. I'm awake and having a crying fit. I'm wishing I'm not myself. I keep envisioning Jim and Lady Friend going to Skamania Lodge for a romantic dinner. When did he have time to take me anywhere special? But he has time for her. The thought of them together eats at my gut. I beg God to let me see the truth in my decision to leave him. Has my leaving caused him to turn his back on his Christian principles? Am I to blame? All I want in this moment is clarity. *Lord, show me what I did over the years to push Jim away.* Clarity does not come.

Since I hear Jim get up, I get up too. I have to ask, "Who is this Realtor, and how did you meet her?"

"Oh, a Christian singles site on the Internet," he answers casually.

That gets my blood boiling all over again, but I stuff it so I could learn more. "So how does that work?"

"I connected with her in a divorce chat room. She's been divorced for ten years and has a seventeen-year-old daughter with severe mental disabilities and a twenty-seven-year-old daughter with a child."

Jim has a history of helping and making friends with people who aren't as accomplished as he is. In the last several years, he's been the nicest to me when I'm at my weakest. I suspect he enjoys feeling superior, so I ask, "How educated is she?"

"High school."

Aha! That fits.

"So, does she think you're divorced?" I probe.

"I said my wife is divorcing me."

"It didn't bother her that you are still married?"

"No. She just liked talking to me and sending me little jokes."

I try keeping my voice steady. "So, is she the Realtor you've been seeing?"

"Yes."

"Excuse me," I say, trying not to explode, "I have to go upstairs."

Jim turns his attention to fixing something on my computer as he had promised.

Entering the master bedroom, I grab his pillow and give it some hearty whacks against the wall accompanied by my screams. I'm sure Jim can hear me. Maybe the neighbors too. Perhaps it's helpful to blow off steam like this, but it gives me a headache.

Later, Jim tells me it looks as if he'll be moving to San Diego at the end of the month. This news leaves my stomach feeling queasy. I'm thinking his move must mean he's leaving Lady Friend behind. Okay, that's good. Go to San Diego! Git! Be gone!

A friend tells me when your horse dies, get off. My marriage has died, but I'm finding that letting go is not so easy. Twenty-five years is a long time with someone.

Someone else tells me that divorce is like removing ivy from a brick wall. Even though it's cut off at the root, the tendrils still need to be pulled away, leaving the brick face raw. I have some painful pulling away to do, and I'm already feeling raw.

In the midst of all this drama, I get word that my publisher might pull the plug on my Keiko book. *Swell!!*

Journal Entry - June 5, 1999

Jim began the process of moving out today. I'm sad. We talked over the details of the divorce this morning. We agreed that I would take the two oldest animals, Tillie-dog and Rachel-cat, and Jim would take, JazzPurr. He said he would pay any vet bills for the animals.

I asked him how he discovered the new church he's going to. Last time I asked, he avoided the question. This time he said, "Oh, from my lady friend."

I'm feeling angry and shaky. I wish this connection he has with Lady Friend didn't affect me so.

I find a tape on Jim's desk, probably lent by Lady Friend. On the cover it says, "How some of America's most well-known pastors have corrupted our president and endangered the security of our nation and safety of the entire world." I feel rattled all over again at the change in my husband in the last few years. Our religious and political views had once been similar, but I'm astounded by the broad gap that has developed between us.

I go to the attorney's office to pick up the divorce papers. I ask Ludwig if I might say something. He says, of course.

"Twenty-six years ago, I fell in love with Jim, in part because he helped kill the tomato horn worms in my garden. In the last several years, if I'd asked him to do something similar, he'd have said, 'I'm busy. Besides, it's raining.' On the other hand, if anyone else had asked, he'd have been there in a flash."

Afterwards, I go to Carl's Jr. I pick at my charbroiled chicken salad and do some more reading in my library book, *I Could Do Anything If I only Knew What It Was*, by Barbara Sher. I'm feeling tragic and lost, and then Barbara's words jump off the page. "If you can make yourself go after a goal when you're feeling stuck, you will activate … and expose … all the resistance that is causing you to be stuck."

Somehow that message lifts my cloud of gloom. *Linda, Linda*, I say to myself, feeling full of compassion and a little sheepish. *You silly woman! You have so much. Jim has given you much. Your parents have given you much. And God has given you much. There is little holding you back.*

I wipe my nose and stride out of the restaurant and over to the Hallmark store to buy Jim a nice Father's Day card.

I keep looking for work, doing informational interviews and crafting my résumé for various jobs. My career class advisor makes me promise to make fifty contacts. I have no answers from my previous calls and feel discouraged. Instead of making the new calls, I develop chills and go to bed.

On the few interviews I have, I wear my new professional clothes, which help me feel more confident. I've shopped with care, and most of my clothes are bargains. However, I splurge on a hundred-dollar blouse. I've never bought a garment that expensive before or since, but I like the feel of the silk against my skin. How nice it is to pamper myself just this once.

Even though I've been working out with David on a regular basis, I continue to experience pain. One of the books I'm reading suggests there are psychological reasons for our pain. I ponder that. My neck pain hurts me most: Jim has been a pain in the neck. My back is hurting too; this burden of divorce and all the uncertainty is too heavy to bear. My leg has started bothering me; steps to extricate myself from my marriage are painful. My spine is out of adjustment; I feel disjointed.

Since I'm on my own now, that means, after twenty-five years, I'm in charge of all aspects of my life, including my van. Since I've noticed an intermittent noise for a while, I take it to a mechanic, and he discovers one of the engine mounts is broken. I give myself a pat on the back for paying attention and seeing to the problem. Despite Jim's advice, I'm not selling it.

Jim calls. "I'm coming home to get the preliminary divorce papers. Can I bring you lunch?"

My heart breaks a little. *Not "home" anymore.*

I come down with strep throat, the smoke alarm batteries go bad in the middle of the night, I can't get the TV remote to work (dead batteries, but how am I to know?), I'm scheduled for a root canal, and a growth has to be removed from the bottom of my foot. Still, I'm working on being grateful. I have insurance and see the doctor who gives me medicine for my throat. I have fresh batteries and a stepladder so I can replace the bad ones in the smoke alarm. I have good dental insurance and a dentist who seems friendly and competent. That he's handsome and appears to like me doesn't hurt either. He admires my healthy gums.

I talk with Jim's mom on the phone. She understands and is sorry for both of us. She gives me credit for keeping our marriage together as long as we have. I feel a little better, but I'm a little sorry for Jim that his mother isn't in his corner.

Journal Entry - June 12, 1999

It's a beautiful day, but I wish it was raining. There's nothing lonelier than coming home after church and having no plans for the afternoon. I took Tillie for a long walk. It helped.

I have an illogical feeling in my gut that Jim is abandoning me by moving to San Diego.

Did he ever tell me, "I don't want you to leave because I love you?"

A friend calls me to ask how I'm doing. I tell her my mind wants to play tricks on me. It keeps telling me that life with Jim had some positives, and that, in losing him, I'm losing too much. I have to remind myself over and over why and how I've gotten to this point.

"I know just what you're saying," she says. "The old way seems the safest, and the new way sometimes seems too scary. Now go get yourself a blanket and hug yourself."

A friend from California calls and is shocked when I tell her we're divorcing. "You know what I think?" she asks. "I think you wanted too much from Jim. He must have had to work too hard to give you that beautiful house in Bend."

"You're right about working hard," I say, trying not to betray my astonishment. "We both did. Did you know that I took snacks to the workers daily and, when our general contractor didn't show, we discussed the work plan and any questions they had? I even did some of the tile work myself. Did you know that before we built, I told Jim it would be okay with me if we decided not to spend all that money on a house? If he wanted to go back to school and get his degree so he'd be more employable, I would support us by going back to teaching? And, did you know he said 'No'?"

"Oh, I didn't know," she said quietly.

"Exactly."

Journal Entry - June 15, 1999

Jim is having JazzPurr's claws removed. "I might be getting some new furniture for my new house," he says. He never cared that our cats ruined the new leather couch in Bend. Why now?

Journal Entry - June 21, 1999

Jim sent me an email, and one sentence is driving me crazy: "... I was trying to keep my eyes on the Lord and not on getting too involved too soon. ..."

I've forwarded his email to a few friends. I also send him an email urging him to get counseling as I intend to do. I remind him that each of us has to guard our hearts and souls over the next few months.

One friend replies the same day: "Linda, it sounds as if he's fallen in love with someone!"

This can't be happening!

Another friend emails me: "Received an email from Jim about your divorce. What did he mean by it "coming through just in time?"

It's happening soon!

I meet with the pastor of our Beaverton church to discuss forgiveness with him. How do I forgive Jim for deceiving me and then lying about his new relationship?

"Forgiveness is absolutely necessary, and you should do it as soon as possible," he says. "Remember, God has forgiven both you and Jim." He points to some of the passages in the Bible that deal with forgiveness.

"For if you forgive men when they sin against you, Your heavenly Father will also forgive you." (Matthew 6:14).

"Get rid of all bitterness, rage and anger, brawling and slander, along with every malice. Be kind and compassionate to one another, forgiving each other, just as in Christ God forgave you." (Ephesians 4:31-32).

I know these passages. He might as well as said, "Just do it." *Right. I would if I could.*

Jim comes by again to clear out more of his stuff. I don't ask him about his email; I'm working on forgiveness. I give him some pocket duct tape (he loves duct tape) to tape his life back together, some sun block for his new life in the sun, and a housewarming card. He hugs me.

That same day he gives a friend a nice set of drawer caddies I could have used. I ask him why he hasn't offered them to me. "Oh, those came from my business."

I'm furious and walk away before I say something ugly. He has no consideration for the sacrifices I made while he pursued that business. It took up all of his time and put us in financial jeopardy when we had to mortgage our home.

After he leaves, I drive to the convenience store and buy a pack of cigarettes. I don't smoke but I'm feeling crazy, and this is the one crazy thing I can think do at the moment. I go out in the back yard, sit on a lounge chair, and light up. I feel calmer and somewhat rebellious. Afterwards, I hide the butt in the trashcan.

Twenty-five

Pants on Fire

She was so blinded by divorce craziness that she couldn't see the oxygen
mask dangling in front of her.
—Virginia Gilbert, *5 Ways to Stay Sane When*
Your Ex Is Driving You Crazy

Now that Jim is out of the house, my curiosity gets the better of me. I wonder what I can find in his email messages. I go into his office, open the email program on his desktop computer, and discover he's been exchanging messages with some woman and signing off as "Lover Boy." My stomach lurches. Is this another woman or Lady Friend? I pace the floor, trying to wrap my mind around this new revelation, but I don't have the resources to absorb the blow.

Les happens to be in town, staying with our parents, and comes over to calm me down.

"He can't be doing this! He can't have someone else already." I pound my fist on the kitchen counter. "We're still married!"

"Look, I know this is hard, but you're freeing him, and he *is* doing this," Les says.

"It's not right!" I insist.

Les shakes his head. "It's not right, but you can't stop him, you can't control him. He'll do whatever he wants with whomever he wants whether you like it or not. The sooner you realize it, the better off you'll be."

"I know, I know," I sob, collapsing in my brother's arms. "I'm worried about what he's doing to himself and his Christian witness. This rush into another relationship is not likely to end well for him. I know that some Christians will condemn me for choosing divorce and claim I'm a poor witness to the world. However, if Jim acts on these emails and marries right away, he's going to look like a man who had an affair while married. That makes him an even worse witness. And what is this news going to do to Travis?"

"The important thing right now is to take care of yourself, Sis. I know you're hurting, but you're tough. Trust me, you're going to get through this. You don't have to do anything but hang in there right now. Promise me you'll hang in there, okay?"

"Okay," I say weakly. "Okay."

Les has been able to talk me down, but after he leaves, my rage builds. I want to tear Jim limb from limb. I tear apart a picture of the two of us and take off my wedding ring, one of the matching bands we'd had made by a Santa Fe jeweler, designed with circles (my preference), and squares (Jim's preference). I leave the photo and the ring on his office chair. What symbolism!

Jim is staying at a residential hotel, and I call him several times. When he doesn't answer, I leave little messages as I envision Lady Friend entangled next to him. "Hey, Lover Boy, what are you up to?" I leave one last message. "You better come get your computer before I do something ugly to it."

I smoke two cigarettes, take two sleeping pills, and drink a glass of wine, before I pass out.

The next morning, I put Jim's computer on the front porch and tell him where to find it. *That computer always meant more to him than I did.* He doesn't take long to come get it. At last I've gotten his attention. His jaw is set and his eyes are hard, but he doesn't say a word. A thrill runs through me as I see the anger in his face. *Why didn't I do this long ago?*

I send an email to a friend, "This divorce stuff has left me a little crazy. I let the drama queen in me strut her stuff. My attorney says not to worry, that temporary insanity is part of the picture."

Jim continues to send me emails, dropping hints of his romance—to hurt me? I ask him to spare me the details. I'm hoping the relationship will fail, that he will have to look in the mirror and come to grips with what he's done. I send a response.

> *Dear Jim,*
>
> *I'm puzzled by your message. What do you mean by 'too involved too soon'? Are you trying to say you're in love with someone? And please, don't plead, 'I didn't mean for it to happen.' Be honest for a change!*

I call my cousin Carolyn and ask her if she'd like to go to dinner. I'm relieved when she says yes. We talk and eat, and I learn she had similar marriage and divorce experiences. I tell her some of the things Jim has done. "He sent me to Iceland. He arranged for yard service after he left the house we're renting. He owed me that much, since he'd promised to take care of the yard after we moved in but had done almost nothing."

Carolyn laughs. "How much personal effort did he put into your relationship?" she asks. "Jim's generosity is like sending aid to Nicaragua, but not being willing to serve in the local soup kitchen on Thursday nights."

It's my turn to laugh. "I feel like such a fool, trusting him to be kind during this time," I tell her.

"You've tried to think the best of him for all these years," she tells me. "That's to your credit."

Journal Entry - June 29, 1999

Jim came over in the evening to get more of his stuff. I gave him some of our dishes and the tortilla press. When he saw the press, a half-smile passed across his face. He and I had attended a session at the Santa Fe School of Cooking, implying we might try making some of the dishes together when we returned home. We'd purchased a can of Chimayo chili and the tortillas press, but he had too much work to do to follow through. When I gave in and made them myself, he claimed he didn't like tortillas.

I also gave him the toaster in which he often burned his toast, even though he knew I didn't like the smell. He'd claimed the toaster didn't work right, but I knew otherwise. Pushing these things off on him felt good.

I make sure I get my share of the tools. Jim says, "This sander is mine."

"Oh, no it isn't," I counter. "You used it once or twice. I used it when I refinished our front door in Bend. I earned it!"

I make him take a sack of packing peanuts he's been collecting in the garage.

"What am I going to do with these?" he asks.

"I don't care what you do with them. They're yours. Take them. I recycled the peanuts and cardboard from your business for four years."

I ask him, "What are you going to do with the boxes of records, tapes, and CDs sitting in the family room?"

"Leave them here."

"Oh, no, you're not."

"Is that an attitude?"

"You bet!"

He asks, "Well, what do you want me to do with them?"

"That's your problem. Just get them out of my sight."

Journal Entry - June 30, 1999

We seem to have come to a kind of peace, thanks be to God. Jim comes over tonight to do a little more packing, then again for a short time tomorrow night to say goodbye. Ros will be waiting with open arms after he leaves. I'm not looking forward to the moment, but know having a definitive goodbye will be best in the long run.

Our divorce will be finalized on July 24. Jim paid extra to speed it through, apparently so I can be eligible for COBRA benefits through the company before he leaves his job. Divorcing is like cutting off a diseased limb you once loved and had been an integral part of your body. It will never grow back, but you can heal and live a healthy life without it.

This may be the last I see of Jim. We hug. He tells me he loves me.

"I love you too," I say.

He says, "You know me better than anyone else."

And that's why you want to get away from me.

As he's driving away, I see him wiping tears. I confess I feel a mixture of sadness and satisfaction to see him a bit sorrowful.

Twenty-six

Truth Will Out

If you shut up truth and bury it under the ground, it will but grow, and gather to itself such explosive power that the day it bursts through it will blow up everything in its way.
—**Emile Zola, attributed,** *Dreyfus: His Life and Letters*

My life is rapidly changing as I struggle to find firm footing. I have to deal with mail coming for Jim. I have a problem with my new health insurance. I have to open a new bank account and close our old joint one. I cancel department store credit cards I haven't used for years. After the unsatisfactory talk with the pastor about forgiveness, I'm looking for a new church. I have to find a cheaper place to live. I need a job. I need to make new single friends. I need to find my mind.

My family is taking good care of me. Carolyn invites me for a little get-together with her mother's family. I'm glad to have someone to cook for and something pleasant on which to focus. I bring my homemade strawberry pie and corn salad with yogurt-dill dressing.

Uncle Gordon, a retired prosecuting attorney, asks in his gruff voice, "Did you make this pie?"

"Sure did."

He grins. "It's delicious. Does Jim know you can cook like this?"

"Yup."

"Well, he's got to be crazy not to treat you right."

I snort. "That's what I told him." I'm touched that my curt and crusty old uncle has obvious sympathy for me.

Carolyn's Aunt Hazel says, "You're vivacious, charming, educated, capable, and talented. You're going to be fine after you get over this little hump."

This "little hump" seems like an unscalable mountain. I've jumped a wide chasm and I'm still airborne, scared of either falling, or if I do make it to the other side, of what will greet me there.

Journal Entry - July 7, 1999

I'll be honest. When I look back on my life, I'd classify both my marriages as big mistakes. People have told me, "You got what you needed then, and now it's time to move on."

Oh, yes, I can see it that way, but deep down, I don't believe it. I made errors in judgment. I should never have married Rex. Jim and I didn't give ourselves time to get to know each other before becoming intimate. Consequently, when he disparaged my cooking and didn't want to discuss the problem, my judgment was clouded and I overlooked those warning signs. What is ultimately concerning is that I neglected to consider what kind of relationship God wanted for me. I declare I will not make that mistake again.

Journal Entry - July 11, 1999

Didn't sleep well last night ... thinking, thinking, crying out to God in loneliness. "Oh, God, save me! Oh, God, help me!"

Journal Entry - July 16, 1999

I feel as if I'm falling to pieces. Just opened an envelope from AT&T, expecting to see a phone bill. I saw a credit card bill instead. Jim spent $117.23 faxing to a woman in Washington State, plus $50.00 for women's clothing, and another $50.00 for men's clothes. All but the men's clothes must be for his Lady Friend. There's also a charge from a porn site. Makes me wonder what he did all those late nights "working" in his office. Why didn't I make it a practice to study our credit card statement each month?

Our divorce becomes final. I scribble a note to Jim in my journal.

Journal Entry - July 24, 1999

Congratulations. You are now divorced and free to spend your time any way you like. Do you like being alone without having a wife begging you to spend more time with her? Am I angry? Am I bitter? Yes! I'm angry because you ignored me. I'm angry with your parents for not nurturing you better. I'm angry with your grandparents who damaged your parents. We've all become victims.

I'm bitter because I tried so hard to make our marriage work, and you didn't. You've spent much of our marriage in rebellion, fashioning me into your parents' and grandmother's surrogates. Do you have a right for self-pity? Maybe a right, but what good does it do you to exercise it? Only you are responsible for your decisions and how you've chosen to live your life. Our divorce is one of many consequences that will haunt you. I swear it.

Unforgiveness has raised its ugly head.

Journal Entry - July 26, 1999
I'm walking around with a huge wound. It's scabbing over,
but then something rubs against it and I'm raw all over again.

Trying to regain my footing, I write a list of *"Positive Changes I Expect from My Divorce."*

1. *Self-reliance – I don't have to be dependent on another person for advice, taking care of the house, making sure the bills are paid, etc.*
2. *I don't have to try to please Jim anymore. (This is already a relief, as what pleased him changed in unpredictable ways.)*
3. *My home can be a complete reflection of who I am, not a compromise.*
4. *I am free to explore activities, such as outdoor ones, in which Jim had no interest.*
5. *I am forced to find meaningful employment. I can feel worth in being a capable person.*
6. *I don't have to worry over Jim scarring my walls or his cat destroying my furniture.*
7. *I will have more opportunities to meet interesting people of like minds, instead of spending time with Jim's friends with whom I had little in common.*
8. *I don't have to deal with temper tantrums and rude behavior in my home.*

In looking for a new church, I find a Four Square congregation and attend a few Sundays. I tell my situation to the pastor, and he seems welcoming. When I mention I'd been the one who filed for divorce, he says "Oh, in that case, you would never be able to serve in any position of leadership here. In fact, why don't you try Rolling Hills Community Church down the road? They have a good singles group. I think you'll be happier there."

His words hurt, but I'm not surprised. He must be one of those conservative Christians who believe I'm wrong to have divorced my husband who may or may not have committed sexual adultery no matter the other circumstances. On the contrary, I know my God is a God of love, not legalism. I wonder how the Lord will deal with this man and his church over the lack of understanding and compassion, but I decline to dwell on it. Instead, I make a mental note to check out Rolling Hills.

I'm having problems with a deviated septum and see a doctor. In checking in, I notice the receptionist's eyelashes look strange. As I'm speaking with the doctor in his office, I see photos of patients who've had eye lifts. I'm no spring chicken, and one eyelid droops a bit from the Bell's palsy I've had. Looking a little younger appeals to me. I ask him about the eye lifts, and he declares, "It's like getting two for one. Your insurance covers the anesthesia for the septum, and while you're under, I can do your eyes. You pay only one anesthesia cost."

I'm guessing Jim is feeling guilty for what he's been up to, because he agrees to pay the extra cost of the eyelift without an argument.

Because my eyes have to be bandaged for a couple of days, I stay at Mom and Dad's. They've been worried for me, and I think their taking care of me is good for all three of us. After the bandages come off, I look in the mirror and discover the eyelashes on my left eyelid are gone!

"What happened to my eyelashes?" I ask the doctor on my follow-up visit.

"I hoped you wouldn't notice," he says. "Your eyelid bled more than expected and I had to cauterize it, which burned off the lashes." He points to his receptionist. "If they don't come back, you can apply false ones like Carol's."

Perfect!

I'm fortunate they do come back. I also have my teeth whitened. I continue to dye my mostly gray hair a natural-looking auburn. My mother and grandmother both had all white hair by the time they were my age. Okay, I admit it; I want to appear attractive, looking my best, no matter what comes my way. It's one thing I have some control over.

Old habits die hard, and I'm still trying to save Jim from himself. As his birthday approaches, I worry over the state of his spiritual condition. I fear he is going down a dangerous path and needs to step aside and analyze his situation. In an earlier email to him, I'd urged him to get counseling, and he reassured me he would. However, when I call his mom, she tells me he's thinking of remarrying and will be bringing Lady Friend to Santa Fe to meet the family. I hang up, shaking and feeling like a bloody fool. The counseling he's been getting is marriage counseling!

I'm obsessed with the fear that, by marrying Lady Friend, Jim will be making the biggest mistake of his life. I tell myself that maybe our marriage hadn't been so bad. After all, we solved our big issue over food.

I've been in communication with Jim's Promise Keeper friend, John. When I tell him Jim is planning on remarrying, he urges me to write him, standing on the Bible, and ask for reconciliation. He directs me to confess my error in divorcing Jim, for being controlling, and not accepting my husband for the man he'd become.

I drive myself crazy, wanting to stop this train Jim is on. I wake up the next morning with John's words in my head. The first thing I do is sit at my computer in my pajamas and slippers and compose an email following John's advice, hoping I'll reach Jim before it's too late.

> *Dear Jim,*
> *I miss you and still love you. I see now that I was wrong in divorcing you. I've been talking with John, and he's convinced me that the best path for spiritual and emotional healing is for us to reconcile. Is there any possibility of working on our getting back together?*

I'm late. Even though I have little respect for Norma's advice, I have one last prepaid counseling session and I want her to know what Jim's been up to. As I'm about to go out the door, I glance one more time to see if Jim has answered perhaps the most important email I may ever write in my life. Yes! There it is. I give it a quick glance. Not registering what it says, I print it and bring it with me. I immediately hand it to Norma and begin explaining what it's all about.

"Stop!" she says, holding up her hand, cutting me off in midsentence. "Linda, he's married!"

"What?! No!"

"Look. It says right here!"

> *I'm sorry this has worked out the way it has for you, but it is too late. I understand the pain you must be enduring. I gave up all hope by last February after asking you several times if you still wanted separation, and resolved I was going to make a new life for myself. If I have sinned against God and you in my decisions and actions, I can only pray for forgiveness and release.*
>
> *As for reconciliation, our marriage is ended, and I am starting a new one. Margot and I are now married. I delayed telling you, as I had hoped to tell Travis first, but that's not possible since he's not been home. If I am under anyone's condemnation, then so be it. I have to move on with my life.*

He felt free to move on six months ago without giving me a clue? A gale-force wind slams into my body nearly knocking me over, and a primal scream bursts from my gut—a cry full of pain and despair. My heart is being ripped apart.

"Shh, shh, shh," Norma soothes.

I'm dimly aware my howls can be heard far beyond the walls of the room, but I'm beyond caring.

"It's over. It's over," Norma murmurs, holding me and stroking my hair. "I should have seen it; you've had truth written on your forehead from day one. Now you must let God be your husband."

Part Two

Trusting God and Doing the Next Thing

Twenty-seven

God in the Dark

Why are you doing this to me?
Because knowledge is torture, and there must be awareness before
there is change.
                                    —**Jim Starlin,** *Captain Marvel #29*

My motto has become, "Trust God and do the next thing." It worked for the publication of my two books when both seemed to be lost causes, and I'm still doing my best to trust the Lord. However, "doing the next thing" often feels impossible these days. I'm tortured by the end of my marriage, my shattered illusion that at least some degree of love and respect remained between us, Jim's slamming the door in my face by his quickie marriage, and all his lies. Yes, I had wanted to leave, but not like this. Yes, I would have been hurt if he'd been truthful about his wanting me to leave and his new relationship. However, discovering he played out a lie day after day for several months has pushed me to the edge.

Trying to put together pieces of the puzzle that would have forewarned me of Jim's activities, I swing between total rage and hurt. In February, he told me that, as long as I couldn't forgive him, he had no hope for our marriage. He must have figured this conversation gave him permission to move on. When I returned from my trip to Bend in April, he informed me, "I'm thinking of buying a house." I can now see his plan involved Lady Friend, a Realtor. And his magnanimous gesture of speeding up our divorce so I would be eligible for COBRA benefits? He was in a rush to get married!

Who is this man I once loved? How could I have been so stupid to trust his good will? Oh, the betrayal! Daggers stab at my heart. I've plummeted over the waterfall and plunged to the bottom of dark water.

I drive down the freeway, pounding the steering wheel and calling him every bad name I can think of at the top of my lungs. I work like a madwoman in the yard, attacking the thick rhododendrons with my pruning shears even though I will soon have to leave this house. Whack! Whack! Whack! I'm sure I'm the talk of the cul-de-sac.

And what of Travis? I doubt Jim has told our son that he's married. Travis has to know, and I will have to be the one to break the news. I call him, my heart hurting for us both.

"What's new?" I ask when he answers, a death grip on the phone.

"Not much."

"Have you talked with your dad lately?"

"No."

I try to keep my voice steady. "Well, then, there's something you need to know. Remember, I told you he's considering getting remarried?"

"Yeah …" Suspicion is in his voice.

I choke out the words, "He's already married."

"Oh, my God! What an idiot!" he yells.

I begin to cry. "I'm still trying to wrap my mind around it."

"I'm so sorry, Mom. Dad's an idiot. I'm going to tell him loud and clear!"

I try to soften the blow. "It's bad and stupid that he didn't let you know, but remember he's still your dad and he's been a pretty good one. You know he loves you," I say through my tears.

I hear him sigh. "Yeah, I guess."

There's not much more to say, and I reluctantly say goodbye.

A part of me feels good that Travis and I have solidarity in our pain. I'm also immeasurably sad how our family has been torn apart and the impact on our son. I hug Tillie, crying into her warm, furry body. She licks my tears. I imagine my grief is affecting her too.

My days are painful, but my nights are worse. I reclaim the queen-sized bed, but still keep to my side. Night after night I dream of Jim. Sometimes he's returned, and I'm so glad. Other times, I beg him to leave Lady Friend and come back to me. I wake from these nightmares to the void on his side of the bed and howl with rage and loneliness. I have no defenses in those dark hours. Once my energy is spent, I curl into a fetal position, begging God to put His arms around me. *Oh, God, oh, God, help me, help me. This hurt is beyond hurt. Jesus, you understand betrayal. You understand what it's like to be abandoned. Thank you for sharing my pain. You are the God of all comfort. You carry me when I cannot walk. Carry me now Lord. Hold me tight. Hold me. Hold me.*

I wonder what truly separated us. Besides food, work, and religion, had there been something else I didn't know? Jim has been hiding behind his religion, but what does it matter now? I chastise myself for wasting so much emotional energy on him. I need to let God, who knows the whole truth, deal with him. A passage from Hebrews 4:12 keeps coming to mind. "The word of God is living and active, sharper than any two-edged sword … it is able to judge the thoughts and intentions of the heart." *Watch out, Jim!* When I consider this scenario, I burn with anticipation of that glorious day, envisioning myself dancing on his broken body. In my saner moments, I want him to understand his sin and be reconciled with God.

I have to face both the end of my marriage and deal with Jim's new one at the same time. I remind myself over and over he's done me a favor. I have no more illusions. Once I recover, I'll be free to move forward.

Recovering is the challenge.

Jim's remarriage opens my dad's eyes. "I see it now," Dad says. "Jim set you up. He wanted the blame for your divorce to fall on you, when all the while he made it impossible for you to stay. That way his hasty marriage doesn't look so bad."

"Thanks, Dad," I say, and hug him, relieved he understands. Once again, he is my champion. "It's true I opened the door to divorce, but Jim gave me a boot to the rear."

I begin hearing stories from other women who'd left their husbands because they felt emotionally abandoned. Later, they discovered these men were having affairs, addicted to pornography or gambling, or engaged in some other secret dysfunction. Although these women hadn't known the exact problem, they sensed it deeply. My feeling that things in our marriage weren't right had not been a fantasy. My God-given intuition and my dreams had been trying to get my attention for a long time. I vow to put more trust in my discernment from now on.

When some people go through a trauma like divorce, they want to hide out, nurse their hurt in the dark, and not talk to anybody. Not me! It seems as if I talk with everyone I've ever known. I send emails to several friends, pouring out my pain. I cling to their responses. Bill and Alice, my dear friends in Albuquerque, say, "We're so sorry. We always thought Jim had been too wrapped up in his work." Knowing I'm in shock, they call me once a week, wanting to make sure I'm okay. They point out my patience and trust is being stretched.

"Maybe that will make me taller," I joke.

A divorced friend replies, "In hindsight, it's easy for me to say let go of anger and bitterness, but I admit I had them after my divorce. Even now, one of them creeps back in. I have to remind myself it does me no good whatsoever and can cause me great harm if I let it fester."

A friend in Bend writes, "It's amazing to me that, with all the counseling through the years, Jim didn't change. Kinda makes you think he didn't want to." *I can see that now.*

Another friend offers me hope. "Mine is a magic story, perhaps because I believe in magic. Two years after my divorce, I met and married the 'love of my life.' I am in a good place: happy, intellectually stimulated, loved and appreciated. I wish the same for you. Trust it will happen—perhaps not in the same way, but just as rewarding."

The majority of my male friends have an opposite take. "Well, it didn't work out. You're damaging yourself by holding on to your hurt and sorrow. Get over it. Move on." My mother tells me Les has this attitude. "Linda sounds like a broken record," he'd observed.

I swat this sting away. I don't need this from my own kin. I tell myself this attitude is a good reason to give up on men for a long while.

A couple of months later, David, my trainer, voices the same male philosophy. He can read my physical and mental state the minute I walk in the door. "Isn't it about time you got over this emotional stuff?" he asks one day.

I shake my head and go to fill my water bottle. Lucille, another client, rushes to my defense. "Hey, give Linda a break."

I glare at David and move to the first station, hanging my heels off the step, stretching the ligaments in my legs.

He follows, intent on getting his point across. "Well, how long have you been coming here?"

Since I know David's tendency to provoke, I answer without emotion or elaboration. "Since November."

"Well, gee!"

Lucille remains my defender. "It'll take a year at least!"

I'm touched and amused at her stance. "I've been doing a little research," I say, not letting David get to me. "Men approach this recovery stuff in different ways than women."

"That's right," Lucille says, her face flushed with indignation. "Men just go out and screw the first skirt they can get under!"

I laugh as David stomps off, waving his hand in the air as if to brush us both away. Lucille and I give each other a high-five. I've grown emotionally as well as physically tougher since joining David's studio, and I'm not taking his attitude personally.

The one male exception to the "just get over it" mentality is my first husband, Rex. Since our divorce, he's called me every year on my birthday. Now he calls more often. "It's okay to stay in bed for a few days and to take care of yourself," he consoles. "Jim has been giving you signals for years that he wasn't committed to your marriage. He was too much of a coward to admit it."

Who could have predicted my first husband would be defending me against my second? I appreciate the sympathy while pondering my strange new reality.

Perhaps Lorraine has told Phil about my divorce, because I receive a letter from him. In it is a religious tract claiming the Bible is clear that only if Jim had committed adultery would God have condoned my divorcing him. My heart sinks. I knew Phil's wife had initiated their divorce, but I didn't realize his entrenchment over this issue. He and I are not as compatible as I once imagined.

I see a new counselor but spend most of the time filling her in on my marital history. She makes the observation that Jim's taking up with Lady Friend the way he did seems like an angry act against me. I'm certain of the anger, but I believe he feared the possibility of being alone and unloved. Contrary to forgiveness advice from my pastor, this counselor says working through my feelings is going to take some time. Good advice, but it doesn't take me long to realize she's avoiding any discussion of my faith. No need to waste any more time with her. I have no desire to try separating my emotional life from my relationship with the Lord.

I find a new counselor who identifies himself as a Christian. Although most of the time I believe I had every right—maybe even an imperative—

to leave Jim, part of me is still processing this issue. My counselor is fine letting me talk it out. Because I'm such an emotional mess, he puts me on Paxil, an antidepressant, and suggests I write a list of what I know about myself.

I am brave.
I have loved deeply.
I have developed patience.
I have spread my wings and tried many things. (A cliché, but true)
I have proven myself to be a good mother, homemaker, friend, writer, interior designer, singer and song leader, church leader, and innovator.

Sometimes these affirmations work. Other times, not so much. I'm struggling to understand who I am—a weak sob sister, or a capable, confident woman. My counselor assures me I'm in transition.

At times, I feel I can't rest until Jim admits the error of his ways. I send an email telling him how much he's hurt me and to ask him if he thinks God approves of his deception.

He writes back, "If I am under anyone's condemnation, so be it."

I email a friend. "It's six a.m. and I'm beside myself with anger and bitterness. I wish I could be swallowed by a big black hole so I couldn't feel the pain. I desperately need to talk with someone."

She replies, "What a way for him to start a new marriage—on the heels of his lies and deceit."

Her message sends chills up my spine. God will not be mocked. I write back, "I'm barely hanging in there. Good people are looking after me. God is sustaining me. Someday, I will be okay. Thank you for your prayers."

I've been in touch with Susan, my counselor in Bend. "I'm so sorry you are going through all this. Divorce is more difficult than death because the rejection lives on. It's a tough, step-by-step process. Believe me, God knows what Jim has done and will deal with him."

I highlight my Bible with reassurances of God's protection for me ...

"A righteous man may have many troubles, but the Lord delivers him from them all." (Psalm 34:19).

"... I have made you and I will carry you; I will sustain you and I will rescue you." (Isaiah 46:4).

"... Be strong and courageous. Do not be afraid; do not be discouraged for the Lord your God is with you wherever you go." (Joshua 1:9).

"Don't worry about anything, instead, pray about everything. Tell God what you need, and thank Him for all He has done." (Philippians 4:6 NLT).

"Trust in the Lord with all your heart and lean not onto your own understanding. In all your ways acknowledge Him and He will make your path straight." (Proverbs 3:5-6).

... and possible punishment for Jim:

"It is mine to avenge; I will repay. In due time their foot will slip; their day of disaster is near and their doom rushes upon them." (Deuteronomy 32:35).

"Do not take revenge, my friends, but leave room for God's wrath, for it is written, 'It is mine to avenge; I will repay,' says the Lord." (Romans 12:19).

"Let no one deceive you with empty words, for because of these things the wrath of God comes upon the sons of disobedience." (Ephesians 5:6).

"Do not be deceived: God cannot be mocked. A man reaps what he sows. The one who sows to please his sinful nature, from that nature will reap destruction" (Galatians 6:7-8).

Okay, I get it. I'll concentrate on obeying the Lord, and let Him, who is all wise, deal with Jim in whatever way He sees fit.

Several people tell me, "You're an attractive woman. You'll make it." I wonder what being attractive has to do with making it. Their comments seem to imply that I'll soon find another man to take care of me. Yes, I'd love to have a good man in my life someday, but I'm not clear how being attractive is going to heal my pain now and sustain me in the days ahead.

I receive another email from Jim, "I do care about you, but it seems that I screw things up without even trying. I hope you can forgive me for the things I've done that have hit you so hard. I'm just trying to make it through these heartbreak times and put my life back together. I didn't plan any of this, and I've been praying and asking the Lord, why now? I was trying to keep my eyes on Him and not getting too involved too soon. Maybe this is God's way of keeping me sane and my mind off the self-pity and depression I'm so good at."

No mention of what "these things" are. No naming what "any of this" is. If his eyes had been fixed on God, he wouldn't have served me his lies and deception that are so much more hurtful than truth. Yet, self-pity is all Jim chooses to give me. Coward! For weeks I feel as if I'm going to vomit. I have no appetite but choke down Arby's Junior Roast Beef sandwiches to sustain myself.

I come home one day to a message for Jim on the answering machine. It's a car-servicing place, thanking him for his business and inviting him to come back again. Hearing Jim's name in my kitchen is an affront to my senses. At this point I'd erase him and his name forever if I could. I call back, telling them to never again call him at this number. I envision myself as a dog just after a bath. I want to shake myself free of the man I once loved.

Twenty-eight

A Moving Experience

You keep track of all my sorrows. You have collected all my tears in your bottle. You have recorded each one in your book.
—Psalm 56:8 NLT

I must find another place to live, but how can I, when I have to drag myself out of bed on most days? I'm not even sure what I'm looking for. I have a fair amount of furniture, including the old oak table and chairs. These familiar things give me a sense of security and normalcy. What will I be able to keep?

And then there are my pets, Rachel and Tillie. They're used to being outside for extended periods of time. So am I. I can't imagine the three of us cooped up in an apartment. I think of the small house in Bend I fantasized about. The thought of something similar remains appealing.

I have three weeks to find a place and get moved. Finally, Sunday afternoon I buy a newspaper and study the homes-to-rent section. I find two in the Beaverton area that seem interesting. I boost Tillie into the van and set out. The first house is in an iffy neighborhood, and I drive on. That next one looks run-down and I nix it too. I drive a block down the street and notice a "For Rent" sign on the brick wall of a townhouse development. I stop, back up to the sign, and write down the phone number. I tool through the little community, noting the neat landscaping and tall evergreens. My heart beats a little faster. Could I dare hope this will be the site of my new home? As soon as I get back to Tualatin, I call the number and leave a message.

A few days later, I receive a return call from the landlady. She questions me concerning my situation, my pets, my finances, etc., and tells me she will be showing the place at such and such a time. Can I meet her there and see the place? Since I want this woman to know I'll be a respectable renter, I bring along my interior design portfolio that includes photos from What-A-View. When I get there, she's been showing the place to a young couple. I hadn't considered I'd have competition! The landlady shows me around, and I picture myself living in this two-story, two-bedroom townhouse. I'm glad to see that there's a greenspace a couple of doors down where I can take Tillie for a ramble and she can do her business.

It turns out this woman has a drapery workroom and sells her products to interior designers. I hope my portfolio has given me an edge, and I'm on pins and needles awaiting her call. Two days later she does. With a hefty pet deposit, the place can be mine. In a few weeks I can move in. Hallelujah!

Since the lease on my current house is set to expire soon, I ask my landlady if I can stay one more month with reduced rent. She agrees, seeing how much I've improved the yard and kept the interior in good shape.

I make a furniture plan of my new place and begin the process of downsizing once again. I put an ad in the paper for my upright grand piano but get no takers. I give it to a music company in Portland in exchange for a substantial store credit. *Will I ever have a piano again?* I donate an uncomfortable antique rocker to the Tigard Historical society. I take a few more items to an antique store and make $150.00. I'm certain they are worth more, but I don't have the patience or time to try to get a better deal. I'll be able to keep the big entertainment center I worked so hard designing and painting; it's going to fit in the townhouse just fine. The oak table and chairs will be a snug fit. I won't be able to use the table's four leaves, but right now, I'm just happy to know where I'll be living for a while.

Mom has been experiencing crying jags that neither she nor her doctor can explain. I'm frustrated with her refusal to take antidepressants. She's also concerned about her memory, discouraged that gingko biloba isn't helping. However, she seems fine as she helps me get boxes—mostly containing my Elfery furnishings—out of the attic. All that's left is a paper grocery bag. "Look," she says, pointing to the big bold letters on the side that read, "CHANGE FOR THE BETTER." "That's a message for you."

My heart warms at Mom's observation. After she leaves, I cut out the words and tape the piece to a wall in the kitchen. I'm moving forward, even though I'm hurting and can't fully envision where I'm going.

Ros comes over to help with my garage sale. I sell the tent that we seldom used along with silver, china, and the crystal Jim's mother had given me. We do a happy dance when she totals the proceeds; I've made almost $1,000. What a blessing.

After the sale, I take a big box of Jim's things to the post office, remembering the character in the movie *Saint Maybe*, who spent her last dime getting rid of her ex-husband's stuff. The postage comes to $16.00—a cheap price for "shaking off" more of Jim from my life.

Journal Entry - July 27, 1999

I went to a concert on the commons but seeing all the couples enjoying the music hurt too much. How casually they seemed to take their coupledom. I miss living with someone, sharing my life on a daily basis. I got used to being alone when Rex left; I suppose I will adjust. But right now, it sucks.

I become friends with some of the women who work out at David's fitness studio. One of them asks me if I'm keeping my husband's name.

"Since I've had that name for twenty-five years, I didn't change it in the divorce decree," I explain, "but now, knowing Jim is married, I'm sorry I didn't."

Eva, a woman in her late seventies pipes up. "He's married?"

"Yep."

"The jerk!"

I can't help but smile at her response. "Time wounds all heels," I reply. "I'm counting on it." This gets a laugh.

I have a burning desire to get my name changed as soon as possible, but I don't want to go back to my maiden name. "Linda Moore," seems generic. I want to go forward with something unique but not strange. In the end, I choose my maternal grandmother's maiden name of "Kurth." I like it because it's not common and because it reflects my Swiss heritage.

After posting my intention in the local paper, I'm to appear before a judge in the county seat of Hillsborough. As I try to figure out the MAXX light-rail schedule and how to pay, anxiety gets my stomach churning. It's as if I have a mini-Jim on one shoulder and a mini-Ros on the other.

Jim: "You'll never be able to do this on your own. You're going to need help. Where are you going to get it now?"

Ros: "You're fully capable. Just take a breath and do it one step at a time."

Ros wins. Soon, I'm at the courthouse, and, with the stroke of a pen, I'm a different person—Linda Moore Kurth.

I change my name on everything, even my car registration. I'm told it's not necessary, but it's necessary to me. I don't want *his* name on anything of mine. The photo on my new driver's license is one of my best ever. I have a theory of why that is. I believe in times of great loss, we are at our most vulnerable. I've heard it called, "sacred time." Although I hurt to my core, I feel as if I have an aura protecting me. It shows in my countenance, and many people respond to me in a kinder, gentler manner than before.

Moving day is almost here. A friend comes over a week early to help me pack, but I'm emotionally and physically exhausted. We spend the afternoon just talking. I'm grateful she understands this is what I need.

By the time moving day is almost upon me, I've made some progress. There is more to be done though, and I'm not sure I'll be ready. My family comes to my rescue. Carolyn carefully wraps my most fragile and valuable belongings. On the day before my big move, Les and Sandy drive up from Eugene. The two of them plus Mom and Dad, Ros and Tom, and my Amazon cousins (because they are both so big and strong) all converge on my house. They pack much of the remaining items and move most of the boxes to the garage of my new place. By the end of the day, my body hurts but my heart is brimming with gratitude.

When the professional movers arrive at the Tualatin house, the neighbors rally around, wishing me well. By now, they all know Jim has a new wife. One man, whom Jim had been proselytizing, tells me he'd thought Jim a better man than he turned out to be. *There goes Jim's Christian witness. No wonder he had to leave town.*

After the last box is removed from the truck, the mover hands me a bill for $859.15. I'd budgeted a thousand dollars. If my family hadn't helped me, I would have gone way over.

After everything is unloaded, I have nothing to sit on for TV viewing. Mom and Dad bring over an old navy mohair upholstered rocking chair and footstool that's been in their attic for years. Dad reminisces how he rocked me in it when I was a colicky baby. It's shabby chic with its worn arms and seat, its familiarity comforting. Miraculously, it matches the entertainment center.

It's dark by the time I take Tillie out for her nighttime poop at our new place. Carrying a scooper, I follow her around with my flashlight, not wanting the neighbors to be upset with me and my dog.

Despite the hectic day, it takes me a while to get to sleep. My new place backs onto a busy street and I'm not accustomed to the noise. My head whirls with all the activity of the last few days. At last I drop off, counting my blessings.

I begin making the place my own. The one big question is how to get my desk, an old kitchen table I've rescued from my parent's basement, upstairs and into the second bedroom, which will be my office. The movers hadn't been able to get it through the office door, but Dad is sure he can find a way. He and I struggle and struggle, turning it this way and that on the stairs, my mother cheering us on. We're close to admitting defeat, but I'm determined to make it work.

"Hang on, Dad," I tell him. I squeeze past the table balancing at the top of the stairs and run to my toolbox. I return with my hammer, my jaw set.

A smile blossoms on Dad's face as he deduces my intention.

Bam! Bam! Bam! I hit at the legs, trying to loosen the old glue and nails. Bam! I'm shouting, "Take that, Jim, you SOB!" "How does that feel, Jim?" "You're a stinking turd, Jim!" Bam! Bam!

"Not so loud, you'll disturb the neighbors!" Mom pleads.

My parents have never heard me use this kind of language, but I don't much care. I don't care what the neighbors hear, either. I keep at it until I dislodge all four legs. In triumph, Dad and I carry the top of the desk into the room. "Boy, when you make up your mind to do something, you get it done!" he says. "We can put the legs back on with brackets and screws. You'll never have to worry about getting this thing into any room ever again."

Mom tells me later that on the way back home, Dad laughed about my little performance. "That did her good," he assured her.

At long last, I take a load off, resting in the rocking chair while rubbing my hands over the raised pattern of the fabric. Rachel jumps in my lap and almost tips me backwards. After regaining our balance, we settle in for a little snooze. I dream Jim has a choice between eating three pieces of bacon and saving our marriage. He chooses the bacon. Pretty accurate, I think, when I awake.

Since the garage is detached, I can't put Rachel's litter box there. Instead, it goes in the little half bath/laundry off the kitchen. I buy a fuzzy toilet seat cover so she, who is not so limber anymore, can cling to it as she jumps up and onto the sink vanity where I will keep her food away from Tillie. Carolyn is impressed when I hang an entire utility closet worth of cleaning tools on a rack on the back of the door.

I call Jack, Jim's friend who had done some work for his business. Since I had visited Jack in the hospital and gone to his wedding, I feel comfortable asking him for a favor. I need help getting my computer equipment set up. Being afraid of a "newly divorced woman," he arrives with his wife. As he works, I mention Jim's marriage.

"What are you saying?" Jack asks me, stopping his work midair.

"Didn't you know?"

"I've talked with Jim several times on the phone, and he's never told me."

"You both sinned," Jack and his wife tell me, once they recover from the shock of my news. "You should pray that Jim comes to his senses and returns to you."

The part of me that still misses him wants to believe them. Another part knows they are delusional.

Since I'm not a regular TV viewer, I sign up for basic cable. One night in my new digs I settle into the old rocker and slide a movie into the VCR, hoping for a distraction from my sorrow. When the movie is halfway through, Jim's ghost is in the room.

"Let's pause it here, and I'll make some popcorn," he says in his habitual way.

I run around the house, sobbing. I curl into a fetal position and rock on the floor. I pray that what I'd just seen is reality, and the divorce I've gone through is fiction. I know this is crazy, and I'm desperate to talk with someone. I call Ros, but she doesn't answer. I call Les. When I try to explain what has just happened, he quietly says, "I know."

I realize he does know, that he must have had similar experiences when Matthew died. We cry together over the phone for our own losses and for each other's.

Twenty-nine

Forgiveness

We must develop and maintain the capacity to forgive. He who is
devoid of the power to forgive is devoid of the power to love.
—Martin Luther King, Jr.

By nature, I'm an energetic person who is able to accomplish a great deal, but I'm adjusting to the shock of my circumstances. I need rest after even the simplest of tasks. It's been nearly two months since the divorce, and I'm grateful I don't need a job right away, allowing myself time to fully process the pain of Jim's abandonment.

One Sunday, I pull myself together and go to Rolling Hills Church for the first time. After the service, I ask for the location of the Single Adult Ministries (SAM) class. I'm jelly inside as I'm greeted at the door of a large room with over fifty people. I feel their eyes on me but do my best to look confident. A few people say hello, and I'm directed to a round table where four women are seated. We chat briefly, and I detect their acceptance. I'm hopeful I've found my peer group. I like the presentation and feel encouraged to return.

After class, I'm invited to join the group for fast food on the commons. One guy, with Irish good looks, tall and dark haired, who's been checking me out during class, slides onto the bench next to me. We make small talk and he asks, "So, have you been single long?"

"Not long," I answer, "not long enough to be over the anger I feel toward my ex. I understand how people can become full of rage against their cheating spouses. There are times I still I feel that, if I had the chance, I'd take a baseball bat to him."

"That's a great topic for a first date," he says, instinctively grabbing his crotch. He quickly drops his hand, realizing what he's done.

I'm amused. "Well," says I, quick as you please, "That's why I'm not into dating right now."

Our conversation dies a natural death, and the guy finds an excuse to talk with someone else. I almost laugh out loud. *Maneater. She's a maneater* plays in my head.

I've read about spiritual cleansing ceremonies, and I ask my friends in Bend if they will help me with one. Patty, the co-pastor of my former church, agrees to preside over a divorce ceremony, and Trudy, my friend since California, says I can stay with her and her husband. I'd planned the ceremony to be held on Saturday in a park by the Deschutes River, but a terrific thunder and lightning storm builds, with sheets of rain pouring down from the sky. A few of my friends, including Lorraine, gather under the shelter, shivering in the cold and damp. Trudy, who seemed ambivalent about the ceremony, doesn't show. Although she hasn't said so, I suspect that since she's a Catholic, she doesn't approve of my divorce.

While the rain continues to pour, Patty suggests we adjourn to the church, saying it will be better there anyway, adding spiritual weight to the cleansing. During the ceremony, I burn our marriage vows, and the papers from Jim's desk that fateful night I discovered his betrayal —a receipt from Skamania Lodge and programs from church services he attended with Lady Friend. I resolve to no longer let those bitter memories have a hold on me. Instead, I'll rely on the Lord's help in creating a better future.

One of the older women who has not been in my circle of close friends, joins us and gives me a sparkler—a reminder to let myself sparkle. My heart fills with gratitude for this woman's gesture. I feel surrounded by love, acceptance, and hope.

When I return to Trudy's, she gives me a weak excuse for not coming. Somehow, I feel inoculated against this slight, as I've never felt welcomed to discuss my problems with her. I tell myself it's all right; Jim can have this couple. All our other mutual friends are now *my* friends.

At church coffee the next morning, several people cluster around me. "How's Jim?" one asks.

"Remarried," I answer. *Wait for it.*

There's a collective gasp. "I'm so sorry!" someone says. I try to look tragic, but smile to myself, getting some mileage out of this moment by imagining what's going in their heads. *Vindication!*

On my return, I join a divorce support group. The stories I hear are heartbreaking—much worse than my own. Nevertheless, I tend to overshare my experiences concerning Jim. After a while, the leader tactfully suggests I change my focus to myself—what am I feeling and how am I coping? Angry, sad, lonely, hopeful, scared, blessed, loved. I'm a mess of emotions.

We learn the Five Stages of Loss and Grief first identified by Elisabeth Kubler-Ross. I'm relieved to learn people often proceed along the different stages but find themselves doubling back to those they thought they'd left behind. That's my pattern for sure.

Our group leader speaks of taking responsibility for our part in our divorce. I admit to not having an understanding of what I did wrong; Jim didn't often share what I did to bug him. If I had to do it again, I would tell him how much I loved him and how much I missed his love rather than give him a long list of things I hoped he'd change. It wouldn't have solved our problems, but it would have been a better attempt. I know that toward the end, I found myself on the alert for the next hurtful thing he'd say or do. My natural response was to snap back.

The support group discusses forgiveness and how we need to strive to achieve it for our own sakes. Holding on to anger will eat us from the inside. If we wait for our exes to ask for forgiveness, we'll waste our time, the likelihood of getting an apology being miniscule. We've allowed the very people we want to leave behind us to hold us as psychological hostages. Our leader explains that forgiveness is seldom achieved in an instant. The process is more akin to peeling an onion, one layer at a time. Time, caring for ourselves, and prayer, are prescribed.

I still waver between wanting to forgive Jim and inviting God to roast him and toast him. I read *Forgive and Forget: Healing the Hurts We Don't Deserve* by Lewis B. Smedes.

"[Forgiveness] cannot heal our narcissistic resentments toward people for not being all that we expect them to be—Nobody can forgive people for being what they are." [5]

I'm beginning to shed the illusion that I could have somehow changed Jim to be the person I thought he would be happier being. My resentment toward him for being difficult is a waste of my good time. If I have anyone to forgive, it's myself for being wrong in believing I could fix him. I need to forgive myself for staying so long and letting him get away with his behavior.

Forgiving, yes, but forgetting? First of all, it isn't my nature to let things go to the point that I forget. Second, if I forget, I might not retain the lessons I've learned. Perhaps there should be a partial forgetting— the part that eats away at me and poisons my soul. In the end, I must release and forget the part I carry in my body—the part that clings to the hurt and the desire for retribution. However, I see no good purpose for complete amnesia. Hopefully, in time I will achieve my goal of forgiving and remembering without emotions attached.

I find the *Definition of Forgiveness* by the International Forgiveness Institute to be helpful: "The concept of forgiveness is not a matter of forgetting the terrible things that have happened. Forgiveness is a gift, not a deal. It is the abandonment of resentment and the offering of goodness toward the other. It is a choice and a process. It means trying to understand the other, to experience compassion for the offender, and to focus on forgiveness as a moral gift. It does not mean condoning or pardoning or forgetting about justice. Forgiveness and justice often exist side-by-side."

Mark, the Associate Pastor in charge of SAM, gives a talk on the importance of forgiving and continuing to have compassion for one's former spouse. I'm impressed with his wisdom and decide to discuss my struggles with him. I'm shocked when he declares, "Not only do you need to pray for Jim, you need to pray for his wife. Wishing their marriage will break up is wishing for another broken marriage. It's clear that Jim and his wife need God's presence in their lives. I know it's a difficult thing I'm suggesting, and I don't expect you will get to that place for a while, but I want you to consider it."

I understand what this man is saying but doubt I can ever get to the point of wanting to pray for Jim's marriage. I hope someday I can release the bitterness and hurt I'm carrying, but I also need to distance myself from Jim as much as possible. Let someone else pray for his marriage!

My forgiving spirit is stretched in another, unexpected direction. One day I receive a hate letter from John, Jim's Promise Keepers friend in Bend. It's full of accusations, claiming I'm a controlling, bitter, and angry woman, and deserve the heartache of losing my husband to another woman, missing out on God's blessings.

I'm stunned, then furious. I take another screaming drive down the freeway before I can consider how to respond. Jim and I email occasionally to straighten out minor matters. I email him a copy of his friend's letter, asking if he knows if John has a problem with women. I'm surprised when Jim says he thinks John is way out of line, and, yes, the man did have difficulty with some women in his former church. I wonder if Jim sees some of his own words in that letter and maybe feels a little ashamed at how he's portrayed me to his Promise Keepers brothers.

I know if I trade angry words with John, I will be confirming how he's characterized me. I pray and decide on a different approach. I write back, telling John I feel as if he's thrown rocks at me instead of extending compassion. Is he a man without sin, anointed by God to judge me? I ask him how much he influenced Jim against me and the Bend Presbyterian church. I know the men in that church who'd been following him have all left. I tell him he has only heard Jim's side, and has little idea of the whole truth.

I write, "If you mean to bring me to repentance, I suggest your message would have been better received had it been written through the mind and heart of Christ." I tell him I don't expect to change his mind and don't care to correspond with him any further. I think that's the end of it.

Despite my wishes, I receive another letter from John. I open it with trembling hands, expecting the worst. I catch my breath as I read the opening sentence.

"Dear Linda, I violated you. God has shown me that my letter to you, while the content was from scripture, my motive was not pure. I know I hurt you. Please forgive me and let me know if there is anything I can do for you. I'm sorry."

A better apology than Jim ever gave. My heart feels lighter. I cannot be defined as an angry, bitter woman.

The SAM class has become one of my anchors for sanity. The speakers address issues with which we single Christians are grappling. I become acquainted with several people there and begin making women friends. I also escape being asked for a date for the first time.

One evening I receive a phone call from one of the SAM men. He's been sending vibes that he's interested in me, and I'm prepared when he calls. When he seems ready to ask me out, I break in: "Sergei, there's something you need to know. I appreciate your interest, but it also makes me uncomfortable because I still have feelings for my ex-husband. In fact, I'm in a spiritual battle for his soul right now. I can't be distracted with dating."

It's true I've been praying for Jim's spiritual health and have promised myself I will not date for a year. It's also true I'm not attracted to this man. I hope my little "confession" will deter him just as I did with that first male encounter at SAM. I guess it's good to know that a few men are finding me attractive, but they feel rather like mosquitoes—an annoyance.

The subject of permissible divorce becomes a topic of conversation one Sunday in SAM. A woman asks Pastor Mark how he understands the Bible's view of remarriage after a divorce. He says he believes the Bible says it's okay if your spouse has "released" you. I look at my situation. Whether or not Jim committed adultery, he did much to get me to leave. According to Mark's understanding, if Jim hadn't remarried, he could prevent my remarrying by not releasing me. I've never before heard this line of thinking. Why would God keep me from finding love again because of the actions of my ex? Again, I might not be a Bible scholar, but I believe I know God's heart. I like Mark, but I believe he is incorrect in his understanding of this issue. My conviction is strong.

Journal Entry - September 28, 1999

Dreamt of Jim again. There is a problem with Lady Friend. She won't let him keep his cat and decides they can't go to church on Sundays. He realizes he's made a mistake in marrying her and comes back to me.

After each Jim dream, I awake with a hurting heart. My ego must be trying to protect me from being rejected. I can't believe there are still a couple of friends who insist he will come back. I've got to tell them to stop.

I continue to dwell on Jim way too much. One day, though, I think to ask myself how I'd respond if a friend said to me, "I want to introduce you to someone I think you're going to like. He's a Christian and a nice guy. His wife of twenty-five years dumped him, and he's quite sad. He's a bit overweight, I hear he snores like crazy, spends all of his time at the computer, wants to be waited on, and is a picky eater, but he really is a nice guy. Maybe a little passive-aggressive too, but nice."

"You've got to be kidding!" I'd say. "I deserve so much better!"

Thirty

Substitute

Like a small boat adrift in the fog, she caught glimpses during patches when the mist cleared of a world far away, in which everything was changing.

–Ruth Ozeki, *A Tale for the Time Being*

Journal Entry – October 8, 1999

A dream: I am in a house. There's something wrong with me. My perception is way off. It's as if I'm standing on the floor, but the place has been turned upside down … the floor is on the ceiling and the ceiling is on the floor. I can't move for fear I'll fall. Mom comes along and sees I'm in trouble. She encourages me to walk, helping me move my feet one step at a time. They move, but my body remains behind at a crazy angle. Mom has to push my torso forward to catch up to my feet.

I'm still feeling my world has turned upside down. I'm thankful for my parents, cousins Ros and Carolyn, and others to help me regain perception and balance. I'm trusting God I will eventually get through this. My animals are a source of joy and comfort, just as Yum Yum had been when Rex left. Each night, Rachel settles at the foot of my bed, and Tillie lies nearby on her pillow.

After our SAM class, many of us go to either a restaurant or someone's house for a potluck. At one such gathering, I mention to a woman that I need to find a part-time job at the least. She asks for my background and finds out I have teaching credentials. "Why don't you substitute teach?" she asks. "That's what I do."

Having sworn off that line of work, I answer, "Been there, done that. I don't think I could take all that stress anymore."

"If student discipline is your concern, you might be surprised how things have changed. We substitute teachers are considered professionals these days, and we have the backing and respect of the administration now. You should look into it."

Because I don't have any better options, I apply to substitute for the Beaverton School District.

Tillie has always been a nervous Nellie, with food allergies causing bladder and bowel problems which have persisted as she's grown older. Since she can't be left alone the entire time I'm teaching, I search for a pet sitter. I find Julie's little ad in the paper, and chat with her on the phone. I'm impressed with her references and invite her to come meet us. Tillie and Rachel are shy with her, but she is calm and understanding. Julie and I work out an arrangement. As soon as I'm called to substitute teach, I call her, and she comes by around noon to let Tillie out for a bit. Julie turns out to be a wonderful young woman who leaves me little notes telling me how her visits go. I'm relieved to have figured out this piece of my new life.

My first teaching assignment is for a high school art teacher in my SAM class who has requested me. That morning I wake in the dark with a sick, lonely feeling in my stomach. There's no one to share breakfast with or to wish me good luck as I go out the door. No one will be wondering how my day is going. I feel small, insignificant, and alone.

The teacher has warned the students that, since I'm a personal friend, they'd better be nice. I'm relieved when they comply. I'm not feeling myself. It's as if I'm a substitute for my real self, playing a role in an alternate reality.

The subbing soon averages out to three days a week. Each morning I read scriptures describing the armor of God. I envision putting on each piece of armor: the belt of truth, the breastplate of righteousness, the shoes of peace, the shield of faith, and the helmet of salvation. This practice gives me a sense of the spiritual protection and strength I need to get through challenging situations with students and my own frailties. When I get home from work, I let Tillie out again, and collapse with a glass of wine—a new habit—exhausted and my back hurting. After recovering, Tillie and I walk a few blocks to a nice wooded park with trails.

The days when I receive calls in the early morning rather than the night before are most difficult as I scramble to get ready and find the school. One morning I'm called to sub for a music teacher in an elementary school. Beaverton is a sprawling city, and I get lost as the minutes tick away. I arrive fifteen minutes late, hot and sweaty, my pulse racing. I'm directed to the music room where I find instructions for the day. I must play the piano, run the tape recorder, show a film, and use an overhead projector. I've barely kept up my piano practice, and I'm not a good sight reader; I only used the piano I gave away to practice my singing. I stumble through the piece while trying to get the wiggly students to sing along. I have no idea of how to run the projector. As I fumble with it, the students grow more and more antsy. I switch to directing them in a song. The day continues with technical challenges.

To make matters worse, one little girl complains that another child is bothering her with unwanted hugs and other touching. I reprimand the child causing the problem, but in a few minutes, she's doing it again. Since her actions are beyond the norm, I send her to the office. At the end of the day, I talk with the school secretary and learn the child is a new student. Concerned over what might be happening at the child's home, I suggest a school counselor evaluate her. When I'm asked to return the next day, I decline, crossing elementary school off my availability list. I'm glad this job gives me the option to opt out when I'm not feeling well or when I know it's not something I feel equipped to handle.

Knowing I don't want to substitute teach forever, I snag an interview with a start-up computer educational company. I wear my Goodwill tweed pencil skirt, silk blouse and a new jacket I scored at the Rack and carry my briefcase. I make it clear my recent divorce has left me wide open for new opportunities. I sense I've made a good impression on the woman interviewer, who is close to my age. She calls me back a month later for a second interview. Wanting to know more, I question her concerning the job's specifics which seem a little fuzzy. She offers to bring in the three people who have the same position as the one I'll have so I can get a better idea of what it entails.

When I arrive at the company, I am ushered into a room with three young women sitting at a conference table. Each briefly outlines her work. They nod to each other when describing having to take work home. All three appear exhausted, overwhelmed with how much there is to do.

When the session is over, I hasten out of the building. This is not the job for me. Like Jim, I'd be too busy to have a life. Besides, while substitute teaching, I've discovered a position that might suit me better.

Between these job interviews, I substitute for a library media specialist in a new elementary school. The position requires me to complete a mix of activities, including teaching lessons to visiting classrooms, helping students with their research, and monitoring computer use. I enjoy the work and feel inspired. At lunchtime, I seize the opportunity to question the co-librarian, asking what it would take to get a position like hers. She tells me of a program at Portland State University where she's received her credentials and gives me the name of the department head.

Turning my attention away from the computer-related job, I meet with a human resources person at the Beaverton School District office. I ask what opportunities there are for teachers with library media credentials. He says the specialty is in demand, and he encourages me to pursue it. I scurry to get my transcripts sent to the Portland State department head as well as a letter telling them why I'd make a good school librarian. My Masters in Art Education degree and my published books give me credibility, and a few months later, I'm back in college. Going back to school for this credential is another leap of faith, as I don't know how working in this position will affect my health.

As I ride the MAXX into Portland for class, I step out of myself in a déjà vu moment. I'm right back where I began after my first divorce, attending university classes and substitute teaching. Have I made any progress in my life, or am I on one long, endless loop? I can only keep trying to move forward and pray for the best.

My first class is cataloging, and I struggle. My brain isn't used to studying, and the technical detail required is difficult. I squeak by on the exams but compensate for my poor exam grades with a paper. Thank goodness I'm good at researching and writing. I earn a B.

A birthday card from my friend Lorraine fills me with warmth. "God is leading you and there is a future. It's bound to be blessed, because you know God more profoundly and personally, having been through tough times. My prayer for you is healing, hope, and wonderful surprises." Her friendship is a true blessing.

That same month I join the Rolling Hills praise choir. *You've turned my mourning into dancing again. You've lifted my sorrows.* [lyrics by Ron Kenoly] It's great to be singing again, and there is no room for Jim in those moments. Only God. My friends in SAM say I'm glowing. I believe it must be so; joy fills me.

When I put my author hat back on, I'm assured I'm moving forward. *Keiko's Story: A Killer Whale Goes Home* is nearing release, and I'm working on my next children's book, *How Do You Mail a Whale?* Since my editor is enthusiastic over this new book, I proceed, even though I haven't yet received a contract. The concept centers on unusual things that have been flown long distances in a "How did they do that?" style. I include descriptions of the various aircraft that have been used for these transports.

In order to obtain firsthand information for these stories, I sit in my new office (the second bedroom) in the townhouse and phone people who have been involved. *I have my own office now!* Sometimes it takes many calls to speak with someone on my list, but I'm persistent and persuasive. My first subject involves a concert that John Tesh played on top of a mesa in Arizona. After watching a video of it, I begin to wonder how his crew got all the equipment up there, particularly the grand piano. From a phone conversation with Tesh, I learn the name of the helicopter company he hired. I call a local piano store and the helicopter pilot and find out that the grand piano weighed too much for the helicopter. The pilot confesses the guts of the piano had to be flown separately. I'm a detective!

My greatest thrill is speaking with Johan Reinhard, the explorer and archaeologist who discovered the Inca Ice Maiden, a frozen mummy buried for centuries on top of a snowy peak in the Andes. Since I'd read that Reinhard had been looking for a find like this for some time, I say to him, "You must have been thrilled to have found this treasure at last."

He says, "All I could think of at the moment was, how in the heck are we going to get her down the mountain?" I don't put that part in my story, but I love that I'm privy to this little anecdote.

The contract for *Mail a Whale* is offered but withdrawn, and the story is not published. After spending the time and energy in research, I'm disappointed, but I know emotional pain, and this is nowhere close to that. Carolyn, a far more accomplished writer than I, says one should not become a writer unless one must, because there are so many disappointments waiting for writers in this business. I will keep on writing.

Meanwhile, I revel in the freedom of making the interior of the townhouse my own. I indulge myself, buying yards of paisley-and-rose-patterned Ralph Lauren fabric and make a duvet cover of my own design. *I'm crazy for paisley.* I spend hours sewing, and it turns out well, with a big, contrasting welt around the sides and bottom. I also buy new sheets, untouched by Jim's skin, and silk pajamas, giving me comfort these dark nights.

The final piece is my couch. I order it to fit my small living room. It's a bit longer than a love seat and designed with seat cushions that allow the feet of a short-legged person like me to touch the floor. The cozy chenille is even more beautiful than I envisioned, its deep red fabric glowing with golden tones in certain light. I sink into it with a satisfied sigh.

Journal Entry - November 20, 1999

Family and friends filled my little place at a party this afternoon. It gave me an opportunity to thank everybody who helped during my divorce and move, and to celebrate my new digs with my new red couch. I made a little speech, mentioning each person's unique contribution. I concluded by reversing Dickens' saying, "It was the worst of times, it was the best of times." I read, "And we know that in all things God works for the good of those who love Him, who have been called according to His purpose." (Romans 8:28). I explained that all of them had helped things work for the good for me, and I am most grateful.

Thirty-one

Dance Lessons

Opportunity dances with those who are already on the dance floor.
—H. Jackson Brown, Jr.

I learned several lessons from my divorce from Rex. This time around, I vow to trust God with my relationships, sure that hooking up with someone as a means to avoid the pain of lost love is not part of His plan. A platonic companion is what I need. The divorce support group I've joined is another lifesaver. I don't feel so alone, as I get acquainted with other folks who are also struggling to make sense of this new single reality in which we find ourselves. I begin to make friends there and invite four of them to a homemade New Mexican dinner. Of the four, just Ed and another man arrive. I discover that Ed, a college counselor, and I, have quite a bit in common. We're the same age, have the same level of education, like talking and philosophizing, love our dogs and our homes, and enjoy the out-of-doors. Our friendship grows to occasional Saturday brunches as we share each other's tales of divorce woe.

We both tire of talking out our divorce issues in class these last four months. Ed mentions he wants to learn ballroom dancing and wonders if I'm interested in going with him. We leave the group and begin taking lessons at a recreation center. I have no background in dance and don't view myself as graceful, but I'm musical and have long wanted to give dance a try. What I don't realize is that my education will go far beyond learning dance steps.

The sessions are managed with the men learning their part, the women learning theirs, and then all practicing together, rotating partners. My muscles tense the first time Ed takes me in a dance hold. I've not been in the arms of any man, other than my husband, in twenty-five years. Ed's pressure on my back is tentative, indicating he's as nervous as I am. I try to relax, adjusting to the sensation. I smile, easing the tension between us.

"One, two, three. One, two, three," our teacher claps and chants as we move in a waltz step. Time to change partners. Ed and I nod at each other and move on. My new partner has sweaty palms. *Brave man. I'll bet he's here for his wife.* I have an epiphany. *I have the power of encouragement.* I smile at him and relax into his hold. "You're doing great," I tell him. And so it goes. By the end of the night, I'm still getting used to being in a stranger's arms. I need work on relinquishing control and trusting my partner's lead. I drive home, smelling men's cologne on my clothes. As strange and unsettling as this experience is, I'm pleased with myself for giving it a try. *I might even learn to be good at this.*

Ed and I continue on to the next class. I'm doing well, but Ed is having difficulty catching on. He tells me he doesn't want to hold me back, that I should go on ahead without him. I bid him a fond farewell as my dance partner and move to the next leg of this journey.

The idea of spending my first post-divorce Christmas with my family fills me with dread. I imagine being an object of pity and a third wheel at Les and Sandy's, with Sandy's family all discussing sports. "Make good new memories" has been one of my goals since the divorce. I accept Ros' invitation to join her, her three brothers, and their families. I bring eggnog pudding and *biscochitos*, a New Mexican sugar cookie, glad to have the opportunity to cook for someone other than myself. We share memories of our childhood mischief, and I laugh myself silly over a tale of the boys buying a monkey from a catalog and trying to keep their mother from discovering it in their closet.

Members of SAM make New Year's plans to attend a Christian Singles dance and then ring in 2000 at one of their homes. I'm excited and nervous; it's been years since I've been to a real dance. I buy myself a long, sparkly dress that covers most of me, some strappy, glittery heels that are totally wrong for dancing, and sexy black underwear that no man will ever see.

I enjoy hanging out with my new girlfriends but since I've promised myself I'm not going to be a wallflower, I ask several men in our group to dance. Some turn me down, but I don't let it bother me; I put them in a "not interesting" category.

I'm surprised when a younger man I've never met beckons me onto the dance floor. We do the swing, and we are terrific together. He's fun and easy to dance with, and I'm laughing by the time we're finished. He tells me I have a beautiful smile, and I realize I've been holding back that smile for a long time. What a boost to my confidence!

Journal Entry – February 14, 2000

Some people tell me I've done well, landing on my feet, but in truth, I've landed on my knees. I suppose it's where God wants me right now. I remember the words I taped to my computer when working on the Keiko book—"Trust God and do the next thing." This is akin to the trust exercise I participated in several years before, when I allowed myself to fall backwards, trusting my partner to catch me. Even though I've often felt frightened these days, I vow to continue to put those fears aside, and trust my Provider—Jehovah Jireh.

Valentine's Day for the newly single can be painful. No gifts, no lover's promises. No hugs or phone calls. As I walk into Fred Meyer, where I do most of my shopping, dozens of shiny Mylar Valentine balloons float before my eyes. The weight that had been dissipating instantly sinks back onto my shoulders and into my bones. Part of me wants to leave. Another part doesn't want to be defeated by a bunch of balloons. I remind myself of other Valentine's Days when I stood before a card rack, holding back the tears, reading sweet messages to loved ones, and wishing I felt that way about my husband. I grab a cart and, after finding what I've come for, add a box of good chocolates, a pot of cheery red tulips, and a bottle of champagne. I leave the store in triumph.

Later that week, I receive a carton of my newly released Keiko books. They are beautiful, with interesting charts and stunning photos, some of them taken by me. Oh, happy day! I send a copy to Jim, since he supported me in many ways with this project. He sends me a disturbing letter. In it, he whines about his expenses, saying he's trying to encourage my financial independence by promoting my book and hopes I have plans to get a good job soon, so he won't have to continue paying alimony.

That man can still yank my chain. I know my ex has no legal grounds to discontinue my spousal support. I write back, telling him I'm not responsible for any bad financial decisions that put him in this difficult spot. I don't tell him this is a school and library book, not something generally distributed in bookstores and not something that will bring me much money. Neither do I tell him of my disappointment in the sparse attendance to my book signing at my local Barnes & Noble, or that I haven't yet developed a group of friends to celebrate with me. None of that is any of his business.

Journal Entry – February 20, 2000

Went over to Mom and Dad's this afternoon and found their back door wide open and them gone on a three-day trip. Nothing seemed disturbed so I locked up the place.

Journal Entry - April 5, 2000

Dad is in the hospital. He will be undergoing angioplasty tomorrow. Went over to their house tonight to give Mom some comfort.

Journal Entry - April 8, 2000

Dad came through the surgery just fine.

Journal Entry - April 9, 2000

Last night I dreamt Jim and I argued over something to do with our divorce and his betrayal. I longed to be cleansed of all the ugliness between us and to be free of bitterness and reconciled in love. The cold light of day tells me I need to let that dream go.

Rex calls with startling news. He's just signed divorce papers from his fourth wife who has a terrible problem with alcohol. "I hope this will be a wake-up call for her, but it's not likely."

"I'm so sorry," I say, listening to him describe her bizarre behavior.

"To make matters worse," he says, "we had plans to go to Tahiti next month. I've already spent five thousand on the trip." He pauses. "Say, would you like to go with me?"

I can't help but laugh, "Don't tempt me! I'm committed to celibacy now, but that doesn't mean I don't have sexual feelings. Being with you would be hard. You well know this would not turn out good for either of us, but thanks for making me smile."

The Tahiti invitation is a small, bright flower blooming in my brain. I reflect on it from time to time and allow it to amuse me. I don't regret my decision, but I'm touched that one ex-husband thinks well of me.

Thirty-two

A Home of My Own

God know what is best for me and He's working on it right now!
—**Linda M. Kurth** *Journal Entry* **February 14, 2001**

The hope of owning my own home has stayed with me since my house fantasy in Bend. It would give me a sense of security and allow my design creativity to flourish. I like the townhouse's little community, and have been thinking of the possibility of settling there permanently if I find the right floor plan at the right price.

One Sunday afternoon as I'm picking up Tillie's poop, a young woman who looks familiar walks by. "Didn't I just see you at the SAM lunch today?" I ask her.

"Yes, I remember you," she replies.

"Do you live around here?"

"No, I'm visiting my dad, Bruce. He lives over there." She points to a unit four doors down the street.

I recognize the name, and the next time I see Bruce, mention we are neighbors. "Would you be willing to show me your place?" I ask.

"Sure," he says, inviting me to drop by.

As I walk through his place, I'm impressed. Each room is somewhat larger than my rental, and there is a small bonus den adjacent to the living room. The master bedroom upstairs has a balcony, and I swoon over the master bath, which has a large jetted tub and a separate shower. That tub might help my back pain. The separate shower would make it easier to bathe Tillie, as currently I have to haul her in and out of a tub. The second bedroom looks out onto a large evergreen tree and would be perfect for my office. My oak table and chairs might feel a bit tight in the dining area, but not impossible.

The double attached garage has room for a workbench, storage, and my van. There's also a nice deck out back with a few pretty azalea bushes and a gate opening to a semi-private greenspace.

"This plan would work well for me," I say.

"Are you thinking of buying something here?" he asks.

I nod.

"Interesting, because I'm thinking of selling."

I try to restrain my excitement at the possibility of owning this place.

We discuss a price that seems to be average for the area. Since I'm not sure if I can afford it, I meet with a mortgage broker I know from SAM. She looks over my finances, assures me it's doable, and tells me she can handle all of the paperwork. I make an offer, but Bruce is disappointed with the amount. I'm disappointed, too, but I believe my offer is fair. I tell him to think it over, content to leave the results in God's hands.

A few days later he approaches me at SAM. "I've been thinking about your offer," he says, "and I accept." I blink, letting his words sink in. *I'm going to have my own place!* I'm feeling excited and scared all at the same time. I pray I'm making the right decision.

Now to get the paperwork signed. On the day of the signing I go to my bank in a panic; I've had difficulty getting funds transferred from my investment account. The clerk tells me she can't help me and that I have to wait a few more days. She shoos me away. I don't have a few more days!

In a moment of sheer desperation, I stand in the middle of the lobby and shout, "I want my money, and I want it now!"

The bank manager appears and hustles me into her office. "Let's not get excited," she pleads.

"I *am* excited! I'm signing the papers for my house today and I need my money. It should have transferred by now."

The woman makes a few phone calls. "It seems your funds have been held up because of possible fraud."

"Fraud?!"

"Your name is listed in a different way on the investment account than on your bank account."

"I notified the bank four months ago of my name change. I supplied all the proper paperwork. Hasn't it been processed yet?"

The manager turns apologetic and says she'll get me a cashier's check while I wait.

I breathe a sigh of relief. I'm disappointed, though, when I go to the signing and discover my married name is on the deed. Regardless, I'm a single homeowner for the first time in my life! My heart fills with joy.

The next hurdle is moving. It has been less than a year since my last move, and I don't want to rely on my family this time around. Once again, God provides. SAM has a volunteer group that helps move class members—singles seem to move a lot. They agree to move me even though I warn them of my heavy furniture. Moving day arrives, and it's a sight, as the women carry clothes down the street to my new place. The men manage to bring the three pieces of my big entertainment center around back and through the sliding door. Since I've taken apart the old table desk, it goes up the stairs and into my new office without a hitch. After the helpers leave, I collapse on the couch, thanking the Lord for these friends who have blessed my socks off.

After I get settled, I host a potluck to thank them, and I help move others. I'm so glad that pastor who didn't want me in his congregation suggested I check out this group.

At last I have my own place. I become something of a madwoman, making my townhouse all I imagined it could be between substitute teaching and on my limited budget. First, though, I acquaint myself with all parts of my house. I summon the nerve to inspect the attic, as I balance on the rafters. Next, I lower myself into the crawlspace, getting covered in dust and insulation. I'm proud of myself for doing this on my own.

I don't have much time to think of Jim as I steam and scrape off dated wallpaper and learn to skim-coat the resulting rough walls. I've become friends with my neighbor Sharon, and she helps me some days.

Off come the floor-to-ceiling mirrors surrounding the fireplace. My Amazon cousins volunteer to remove a small wet bar, carrying it into the garage for a workbench. I have fun experimenting with various painting techniques for all but the tall living room walls. The kitchen backsplash fools people with its trompe-l'œil tile in a blue and ivory checkerboard design.

Travis takes the train down from Seattle to help me sand the kitchen's old dark parquet flooring, which has lost its finish. I suspect he's wanted to give me some emotional support since the divorce and feels guilty he hasn't been able to do so. This gives him something concrete to contribute, and helps us connect. I'm so happy to be able to give him mom hugs and find ways we can laugh together again.

I stain the newly sanded floor in a blue and white checkerboard to match the backsplash. My office walls are a mix of sunny yellows and corals. I paint wavy vertical stripes of blue and red against a soft yellow background in the hall bath and a sky-blue ceiling with clouds. I hang photos of my Mom, Grandmother, and other relatives in their old-fashioned bathing suits. I call it my Coney Island bath. The downstairs powder/laundry room walls resemble saddle leather when I rub bronze glaze over the base coat.

I imagine my bedroom as a turn-of-the-century dressmaker's atelier. I sponge on gold glaze over a green background, which sparkles through more sponged-on pistachio green paint. I pull together pieces from other rooms in my past. Since the Ralph Lauren coverlet has roses on it and there's a lace bed skirt I made and tea-stained, I tuck vintage silk roses in bows that tie back the lace valances on the windows. I fill a large silver vase with more silk flowers. My Grandmother's sewing machine sits under a window with an old wicker upholstered chair and a woman's dress form nearby. With framed paper doll vintage fashions, the room is complete.

Out back, I rip out a few overgrown shrubs and transplant others. I teach myself to fix the existing drip system and install a picket fence around the heat pump. Pots of herbs provide seasoning for my cooking. In rare moments of leisure, I sit in my deck chair and reach for a mint or basil leaf and crush it between my fingers, releasing the pungent aroma.

Ros and Tom have been traveling since she retired from nursing, but they come over to help. Tom power washes the deck while Ros and I attempt to install a couple of new light fixtures. We discover we have to modify parts, but we work so well together, it's fun. Most nights I go to bed exhausted and hurting but happier than I've been in a long time. I feel showered with blessings.

I go to the Salvation Army Thrift shop to look for a T-shirt to wear during my workout sessions. I find one depicting the Oregon Trail for two dollars. It's perfect, since my ancestors were Oregon pioneers.

On my way out the door, I'm brought to a screeching halt. It's a craftsman-style oak china cabinet. There's something about craftsman furniture that touches the core of me. Maybe it's the straightforward lines and genuine materials. Whatever it is, I'm a true fan, as I told Lady Mander some years ago. I look at the price tag and try to walk away, but my feet are rooted to the floor. It's calling to me. Can I afford it? I don't know! Just like purchasing the townhouse, this decision is all mine.

I ask a clerk, "How long has this cabinet been on the floor?"

"It came in this morning. Because it has a small flaw, the store gave the people who purchased it a new one and told them to donate this one."

"How long do you suppose it will take for it to sell?"

"I expect it will go pretty fast. It's half the retail price."

"I have to check my bank account. Can I put it on hold?"

"No holds."

Lord, I hope I'm doing the right thing! I feel it's meant to be mine. Here goes ...." I want to buy it, but I have to figure out how to get it home," I tell the clerk.

She tells me I'll have to pick it up before the store closes that day.

I think of my dad and his pickup, but they're on a trailer trip. My Amazon cousins aren't home either. Noting her impatience, I say "I believe I can get it in the back of my van, if somebody can help me remove the back seat." The clerk agrees, and two strong men from the store take out the seat and place it in front of the store with a "Not for Sale" sign. I will return for it later. With some effort they slide the cabinet into the van.

As I drive home, I pray. *Please, God, help me find someone to unload this.* Upon arrival, I begin knocking on the doors of people I know, but no one is home. I'm desperate. Then, I remember having passed a couple of men working on a utility box a few blocks away. I drive back to them and ask, "Would you gentleman be able and willing to help a damsel in distress?"

"Sure, ma'am," they answer without hesitation. They follow me back to my place and soon the china cabinet is sitting in my living room where the wet bar had been. *Thank you, men! Thank you, Lord!*

I figure out later I can afford it, and it completes my living-dining area beautifully.

My SAM friend Ed helps me install new ceiling fans in the bedrooms. He assures me he doesn't mind helping, saying it's better than staying home feeling sorry for himself. We often share home-cooked meals, with each of us making a dish, and enjoy going on little walks, discussing how best to live our lives from here on out.

I begin to suspect Ed is something of a whiner, though–similar to Jim. For example, he hates cheese and is a picky eater. I could never consider someone like him a possible mate.

"Women are of two minds when it comes to what you want in men," he complains. "On one hand, you desire men to be sensitive and caring, but that makes us appear weak. On the other hand, men are supposed to be strong and stalwart, impervious to pain and sadness, but that makes us appear insensitive. We men are in a no-win situation in this day and age, and there are no role models to follow."

"Sounds like an opportunity," I respond. "You can become your own role model, forge a new path. Consider looking at Jesus. He had both strength and compassion."

Ed shakes his head. "I never feel I can be open. With all three wives, I felt I couldn't be honest about a problem with them. I thought they'd say, 'Fine, I'm packing my bags and I'm out of here.'"

"That's interesting. I think if you'd asked Jim if he felt he could have been honest with me, he'd say the exact same thing. I can tell you that keeping his mouth shut didn't work well for either of us. So how has it worked for you?"

"Terrible," he concedes.

With Ed, I begin to articulate what has been percolating in my mind and my soul. In one of our conversations I tell him, "I'm trusting God to find me the right mate at the right time."

"Not me," he says. "I have a window of opportunity, health and age-wise. What if God wants me to be single and celibate the rest of my life? I couldn't take that."

"How much success have you had doing things your way?" I ask him.

He laughs sardonically. "None!"

"If it's sex you want," I say," you can find that without God's help for sure. But if it's a good marriage you want, I'd recommend the matchmaking services of the Almighty God. He can work in supernatural ways, whereas you work on a human level."

"I'm stubborn and hardheaded. I just don't think I can trust God. I'm afraid he'll find me an old bag—someone with whom I'll be miserable."

"Maybe God is preventing you from meeting that attractive woman with the right traits until you give it over to Him," I suggest. "All those negatives you've mentioned—height, hair, income, status, age—will be irrelevant in God's hands. He's not bound by statistics and percentages either."

Journal Entry - July 11, 2000

I dreamt last night that Jim and I are still married. He informs me he's fallen in love with someone else. I'm devastated, and I press him for details. He tells me it's Pat, our friend.

"Pat? What a mismatch!" I say, sick at heart. "You have nothing in common."

"Well," he says, "She doesn't fart. I can't stand your farts."

"You fart!" I say. "How could you have another lover and leave me?" But in mid-thought, I stop. "All right, go to her. She can have you! I want a husband who will love me and stick by me!"

I wake in my lovely bedroom with a big smile on my face. I'm cured! (Well, mostly.)

Thirty-three

Revelations

When you stop chasing the wrong things, you give the right things a chance to find you.

—Unknown

Journal Entry - November 25, 2000

Went to a Christian Singles dance with Trish, Sarah, and Gloria. What an impressive group of women we are! Attractive, intelligent, gracious, fun-loving, God-fearing. One of the men in SAM said we were downright intimidating. I'm okay with that.

Trish grabs my arm. "There he is!" she whispers. We're attending a gallery opening packed with people when she points to an ordinary-looking man across the room. Trish is my best friend in a group of several women at SAM with whom I've become close.

She grabs my arm and begins to shake. "Let's go!" she says, pulling me outside.

"What's that all about?" I ask, my curiosity on high.

"I'm ashamed to tell you. We had a thing. I slept with him—quite a bit."

"What?!"

"I know, right? But you have to understand—my marriage was in shambles. My husband had become controlling and had a terrible temper. Once, he almost killed our cat. But, as a Christian, I didn't think I should leave. Then, I met that guy. He said all the right things—how beautiful I was, and how smart, and how he'd love the chance to treat me right. His words were like water in a desert. I couldn't get enough of them—or him. You must think I'm terrible."

I recall my own temptation. "It's not for me to judge," I tell her. "I had a crush on someone during the latter part of my marriage. If he'd been less principled and made advances, I might not have been able to resist. I thank God I didn't have to make that choice and be burdened with more heartache and self-incriminations for failing to resist."

"Yes, be thankful. Our affair couldn't last, but I hurt like hell when it ended. At the same time, I knew I deserved the hurt. I guess I'm still not quite over it."

"Stay right here," I say, running back into the gallery. I come back with two glasses of wine. "Let's drink to better men in the near future!"

I begin to hear other stories of how bad marriages affected these beautiful, intelligent women of God: mental breakdowns, affairs, poverty, children turned against them—the list goes on. Like me, they struggled with the question of staying or going. Now they face the challenge of recovering their true selves. I count myself fortunate to be among these brave souls.

I'm grateful to Rolling Hills for supporting us through SAM. Encouraging divorced people is not an easy choice for many churches, especially concerning women. In fact, I've heard rumors that this church is conflicted about the issue and has removed a woman in music leadership because of her recent divorce—a divorce that seemed warranted. Although

I attend service, tithe regularly, and sing in the choir, I've declined to formally join the church because it doesn't believe women should be preachers, an issue I consider related.

Jim is still playing games. Now that I own a home, Travis asks if I will keep his boxes of keepsakes, currently stored at his dad's place. He's not seen Jim since his marriage, nor met his wife, and he feels more comfortable with my keeping his stuff. Jim mails them to me and I notice one of the boxes has a scanner logo on it. Inside, I find a sample piece of hardwood flooring. Since, throughout our marriage, Jim kept every single box his electronics came in, I'm quite sure he's letting me know he has a new scanner. The floor sample must be a hint he's remodeling his house. What a guy! I'm thankful I'm no longer triggered by Jim's crazymaking.

I gather the few gifts Jim has given me over the course of our marriage, with the intention of mailing them to him. I plan to say they remind me of all the years of neglect. But the next morning I awake with these words in my head: *Accept the love that had been there.* I realize I've been so intent on separating myself emotionally from Jim, all I've been seeing is evidence he didn't love me; it's been too painful to remember the good times. But, now that I have some distance, I can allow myself a few good memories. In the big picture, I'm grateful for our son. In the early years Jim had been a good father, much better than his own father. On a small scale, I will always cherish the little pewter whale pin Jim bought me while vacationing in Friday Harbor. It has a permanent home on the lapel of my favorite jacket.

As Christmas approaches, Jim emails me, saying he's received a card sharing Les and Sandy's plans to host my parents and me for Christmas. It's his way of telling me he knows what's going on in my life because he's still close to my brother. And I thought Jim's behavior could no longer trigger me! I'm angry with Jim, but even madder at Les for staying in contact with someone who hurt me so badly. I call, telling him I don't want Jim to know anything about me. Les doesn't understand why I'm upset, which upsets me even more.

Journal Entry - January 22, 2001

Celebrated Dad's eighty-third birthday with family today. He seems to be doing well.

Ed has become busy with dating. Sometimes he cries on my shoulder when things aren't going well, but when they're good, he doesn't pay much attention to me. Men! However, I'm busy learning web design and HTML at school, substitute teaching, working on my house, seeing my family and friends, and dancing.

In fact, dancing has become a passion for me. One of the women I meet at my regular dance venue in Portland suggests I look into taking lessons at Heather's Dance Studio in Tigard. Soon I'm enrolled in a weekly ballroom dance class there, beginning with the cha-cha and quickly moving from beginner to intermediate. Baby, I can dance!

Journal Entry - March 25, 2001

Now that the semester is over, my school projects are finished, and it's spring break, I'm feeling a vacuum. You'd think I'd have become more okay living alone, but I'm not. I feel lonely, wanting someone special to love.

Since I'm feeling low, I sit on the stairs and call Rex. His divorce had been put on hold when his wife went into rehab. However, the damage to her liver was too severe, and she passed away. He and I have been talking more since then. He assures me I couldn't have done anything more to make Jim happy. "You did nothing wrong in showing your anger to him. You showed your honest feelings. You are an upfront person and don't play games. You know it doesn't work to try to change yourself for someone else."

His assessment helps relieve the self-recriminations I'm still carrying. However, a question pops into my head—one that has never occurred to me before. "Did you ever cheat on me?" I ask. My breath is shallow and my hand trembles.

There's a pause, and I *know*. "What's her name? Did you love her?"

He tells me, and I remember his mentioning her. "I was stupid," he tries to reassure me.

"Thanks for telling me the truth. Well, gotta go!"

A few hot tears run down my cheeks. "Of course he did," I say to Tillie who's sitting beside me. I take her muzzle in my hands, staring into her soulful eyes. "I guess I should have known. I hope God agrees I'm due for a good husband one of these days."

"Lord," I say heavenward, "please give me one more chance to get it right. I don't want any substitutes this time. I'm willing to wait as long as it takes for the real thing."

Journal Entry - May 22, 2001

I've been substitute teaching almost every day, even though I often have low-grade to medium pain levels. I'm getting used to the pace and often have some energy at the end of the day. Tillie and I always walk when I get home.

Summer is approaching, and I won't be substitute teaching. A writer friend, who is about to quit her hospitality job at an exclusive Portland athletic club, suggests I look for employment there. I apply, not telling them I'm only looking for summer work. I'm hired after I'm told not to mix with the members and to always wear nylons. I find myself stationed at the check-in desk. "Good morning, Mrs. X. Your meeting is down the hall and on the left." *Smile. Crinkle your eyes.* "Down the hall and up the stairs." *Tilt your head in acquiescence.* "Over there to your left and go in the first door on your right." *Gee, I wish I didn't have to wear panty hose on such a hot day. This is not the real me.*

I find common ground with my boss. She's a Christian and tells me about her divorce a few years earlier. "My husband had been a successful building contractor," she says, "but when he turned forty, he quit his work and tried to become a professional skateboarder. Got tats, wore the baggy shorts, the whole thing. He became a stranger, and I no longer mattered to him. We lost our beautiful home, and I had to go back to work. However, God has blessed me with a nice place to live and this job."

The lovely woman I work beside at the hospitality desk has a divorce story too. Before my own divorce, I hadn't tuned into the reality that half of all marriages end this way, and I'm disturbed.

At the end of summer, I'm sorry to leave my new friends, but relieved to leave the job. The high society atmosphere is not for me. I want to be where I feel at home, a part of a community where my best abilities can be put to use. Time to finish my library media credentials.

Thirty-four

Dating

Okay, so you look like John Wayne. That don't impress me much.
—[based on] Lange, Twain, "That Don't Impress Me Much"

It's time to put the divorce books away and move on. The book that speaks to me these days is introduced to us by SAM's pastor. *Finding the Love of Your Life* by Neil Clark Warren, founder of eHarmony—a Christian singles matchmaking service—claims physical attraction is an important part of a good marriage, but that "sexual expression can take control of the relationship and blind the couple to reality." Warren states, "When sexual expression is not kept in check, the emotional, cognitive and spiritual aspects of the relationship become slaves to the physical desires." He advocates celibacy "until the moment that permanent commitment is pledged." [6]

Having gone through two marriages that began with sex beforehand, I understand the wisdom of Warren's thinking, knowing it comes from a biblical as well as a psychological perspective. I vow to be celibate for as long as I'm single, and to take plenty of time to know the person who might become the love of my life. If God doesn't want me to marry again, I will remain celibate the rest of my days. I memorize "Commit your way to the Lord; trust in Him and He will do this: He will make your righteousness shine like the dawn, the justice of your cause like the noonday sun." (Psalm 37:5, 6).

Since I like lists, I make an extensive one detailing the kind of husband I long for. Some might say I set the bar too high, but I know what I want and need, and I'm not going to settle for less.

What I Want in a Husband

1. *He is spiritually grounded. He is an integral part of his church. He has an active prayer life. He studies the Bible and trusts God as a wise and loving Father.*
2. *He is willing to stay celibate until marriage.*
3. *He believes in mutual submission of marriage partners; we honor each other.*
4. *He listens and hears me. He is interested in what I say.*
5. *He enjoys play. We take turns initiating fun activities to do together.*
6. *He is self-confident. He knows his strengths and weaknesses and continues to grow in wisdom.*
7. *He accepts other people for who they are but is not afraid to express his wants and needs when appropriate.*
8. *He is financially stable. He is wise in spending his resources.*
9. *He is engaged in his professional work, but it does not rule him.*
10. *He is a good communicator. He lets me know in non-blaming ways how my actions affect him. He shares his dreams and fears with me.*
11. *He enjoys outdoor and indoor activities without being obsessed by them.*
12. *His mind is open to new learning, new possibilities, new insights of himself and others.*
13. *He takes pride in his home, keeping things repaired and in reasonable order.*
14. *He has a plan for his life, while being open to unexpected opportunities.*

15. *He has dealt with emotional issues of the past, and they do not rule his present-day thinking and actions.*
16. *He enjoys being with family. He has a good relationship with his kids, and he gets along well with my son and my parents.*
17. *He takes good care of his body, has vitality and energy, and keeps active.*
18. *He has a zest for life. He is a joyful person with a good sense of humor.*
19. *He is willing to encourage and support me in following my dreams.*
20. *He is trustworthy and honest. His words and actions reflect one another.*
21. *He is brave, steadfast, and loyal. He does the right thing, even if it is difficult. He doesn't run away when things get tough.*
22. *He is intelligent and has common sense. Our levels of education are similar.*
23. *He is gentle but not weak, strong but not harsh. He has a well-developed instinct for nurturing and protecting.*
24. *He is courteous and has good manners. He is aware of others and is able to put them at ease.*
25. *His friends are much like him in integrity and social conscience.*
26. *He is physically and verbally affectionate.*
27. *He enjoys cooking with me and is willing to help with the dishes and other duties around the house.*
28. *He is able to be vulnerable with me. He allows me to nurture him.*
29. *His birthday is within five years of mine.*
30. *He won't want me to move far away from my family.*

I put a brief description of who I am and what kind of man I'm looking for on the Friend Finder site. A guy named Steve connects with me. We exchange a few emails and decide to meet. The first things I notice are his crooked teeth and a polyp on his lip, both turnoffs. We chat and I suggest we go for a little walk. He declines, saying he's a runner and never walks. Besides, he's allotted an hour and a half for our meeting. Time's up.

I assess him as rigid and a strong introvert, and beyond that, he hasn't done any personal work or counseling since his wife left him for another woman. Nice guy, but not for me. Perhaps all is not lost, though. In our conversation, I find out he's worked with Jonathan, a high school classmate of mine, and mentions Jonathan has recently divorced. I'd always liked this classmate and made a mental note to find out his situation.

I contact Terry, our high school class president, and ask him if he knows anything of Jonathan. He says he doesn't but he'll call and chat with him. A couple of days later, Terry calls back.

"Jonathan says yes, he's divorced, although he's still in love with his wife. The thing is, Jonathan is gay."

I have to laugh at myself. At our next class reunion, Jonathan and I give each other knowing smiles and a good hug.

Next, I meet Don for coffee in Portland, Dutch treat. He's intelligent, urbane, tall, slim, and balding, with a good smile and laugh. We enjoy talking with one another and agree to meet again. He asks what the kind of relationship I'm seeking. I tell him I'd like to marry again someday. He mentions the different levels of relationship, one of which includes intimacy. I tell him I intend to remain celibate as long as I'm single.

"Whoa, that's not in my plan," he says.

"I understand," I reply, not at all surprised.

"Hmm, you're quite a challenge, but I'd like to see you again."

I'm happy to be finally dating. I ride the MAXX into Portland to meet him on our next date. The sun is shining with a little breeze, and Don and I walk side-by-side on the new Eastbank Esplanade along the Willamette River. Even though I know he's not husband material, I enjoy his company and invite him for barbeque salmon at my place. We eat on my deck. He worms it out of me that he's my first date. "Wow, the pressure," he jokes but says he will take me kayaking soon.

He calls a couple of days later, saying he's decided we aren't a good match. He sounds surprised when I agree with him. He says, "I don't think you know what you want in a man."

Oh yes, I do, and it's not you, bud!

"You'll have trouble finding someone who's on the same page as you in terms of being celibate."

"That will make it easier to know who's the right one for me, won't it." I feel I have the upper hand, and I'm enjoying our little repartee. Still, I'm mad at myself for going out of my way to make him dinner. There goes my kayaking trip, and he hasn't spent a dime on me–didn't even buy me coffee. I've extended myself too much. Lesson learned. No more letting a man take advantage of me.

I contact one guy who's portrayed himself in the paper as a "Tux to Jeans" kind of guy. He calls me back, but all he can discuss is his truck. I'm finally able to cut in and tell him he seems nice, but we aren't a good match.

"Oh!" he says, and hangs up.

I'm sorry I probably hurt his feelings, but glad I didn't waste much time on him.

I briefly date a couple of other men I meet dancing. Early on, we get to a question similar to the one Don had, "Where do we go from here?" This is code for, "When are we going to have sex?" I give them the same answer I gave Don, and their reactions are similar. By then, I'm somewhat amused. I'm enjoying taking my time, not being desperate to find someone.

Fred finds me through a Christian Singles ad. We have several phone chats, and I can tell he's a genuine Christian. We agree it's time to meet, and he invites me to dinner at a nearby restaurant. I'm excited and carefully plan my wardrobe. I've lost quite a bit of weight, working out with David and dancing an average of three nights a week. I wear my straight, calf-length leather skirt, leather boots, and a white sweater that flatters my bust. I'm looking good!

Fred says his friends tell him he resembles John Wayne, and that I can recognize him by his maroon shirt and big smile. As I step into the restaurant lobby, my heart pounding, a man moves toward me. He's wearing a cheap-looking maroon shirt, a big smile, has a huge pockmarked nose, and a comb-over. I literally feel my heart drop to my stomach. Lord, save me! During our meal, he reaches out to touch me—my hands, my arms. I sit on my hands to get away from him. It's all I can do to get through the evening. I'm disappointed in the outcome but I can also see the comedy. *Oh, well.*

I try once again, signing up with eHarmony, a Christian matchmaking service in its infancy. After several weeks with no matches, I query them. They respond by saying I'm "so unique" they're having difficulty finding anyone.

I laugh out loud. "I quit, God," I say. "Now it's your turn."

Thirty-five

Tough Calls

Praise be to the God and Father of our Lord Jesus Christ, the Father of compassion and the God of all comfort, Who comforts us in all our troubles, so that we can comfort those in trouble with the comfort we ourselves receive from God.
—2 Corinthians 1:3, 4

I t's evening. I get a rare call from Travis. "Mom," he begins. By the tone of his voice, I know something's wrong.

"Honey, what's the matter?"

"My world is falling apart!" he moans. "I think I may be going crazy. I don't know what to do!"

My son hasn't been open with me about his life for years. This openness is new, but the circumstances are troubling. "Tell me what's going on."

"Not over the phone."

Having had a dark-in-the-night crisis myself, I intuit his pain. I need to be there for him. My mind whirs with plans. "I'll be there as soon as I can. Promise me you won't hurt yourself, okay?"

221

He promises. I warn him it will take me a while to get there since I have to find someone to take care of Tillie.

I call my neighbor Sharon, who says she'll check on Tillie early in the morning. I jump into the van and put the pedal to the metal. I hate that I have to stop on the way for gas. I try calling Travis but realize I don't have his new number. Four hours seem like a lifetime. "Please, God, take care of my boy. Please, God," I chant. At long last I reach the crumbling old house where he lives on the second floor. I ring his doorbell and wait with bated breath. I'm relieved to hear his footsteps on the stairs. He opens the door, and we fall into each other's arms.

Sitting on the threadbare rug of his living room, he lights a cigarette. I sit next to him and reach for the pack, lighting up too. His eyes widen, and he barks a laugh. We smoke while he gathers himself and begins to tell me his troubles. He pours out his pain from the time in the Army and his sadness and confusion over the changes he sees in his dad. And now his primary relationship has just blown up.

I feel honored as he shares his deepest raw feelings with me. "I know, I know," I murmur. "I'm so sorry." I mean this from the bottom of my heart.

He winds down in exhaustion. I tell him through my own tears, "I've been close to where you are, and I feel your pain. I also know that when you reach out and allow others to help you, you'll find your way out of this darkness and into the light again." In the past I've tried quoting "God is our refuge and strength, an ever-present help in trouble," (Psalm 46:1) but he doesn't want to hear scripture. Instead, I say, "You know I will always be here for you, right?"

He nods and we embrace.

I sleep on his couch that night, and the next day we go for a walk and talk some more, wondering what caused his dad to become a stranger to us. Travis feels guilty he hasn't been able to take care of me during the divorce aftermath. "Oh, honey," I say, "you're so sweet, but I've got an amazing support system. Just knowing you love me and are thinking of me is enough." Before I leave, he promises he'll go to the VA for mental health care.

As I head for home, I think how having my own breakdown has allowed me to understand and bear Travis' pain. *Thank you, Lord, for using my sorrow for good.*

Journal Entry - June 20, 2001

Dad is back in the hospital again, this time with pneumonia. I think Mom is scared. I spent a lot of time with her. Hope he comes home tomorrow.

I call Les to discuss our parents' situation. As our conversation winds down, I ask my brother if he still thinks I made a mistake in divorcing Jim.

"No," he says. "I can see you're in a much better emotional place. With Jim, you often seemed on edge."

I'm relieved we're on the same page again, an important development considering the challenges ahead of us.

Shortly thereafter, I call Mom's doctor because we've been concerned over her deteriorating memory. In the middle of the conversation, he mentions Mom's Alzheimer's.

I clutch my chest. "She has Alzheimer's?"

"Didn't you know?"

Since Dad has been in and out of the hospital, this news convinces Les and me that our parents need to sell their home and move to some sort of assisted living. We've been trying to keep up the family home and make sure Mom is doing okay. Les has been coming up from Eugene weekly to take care of their large yard when Dad can't. I've been staying some nights with Mom while Dad is in the hospital. I worry what she's up to during the day. These tasks have grown to be too much for all of us.

Dad has been stubborn and in denial over the seriousness of Mom's problems. I confront him in his hospital bed, feeling awful for talking tough while he's so vulnerable. I hold his hand. "Dad, I need to tell you something—something very difficult."

"What is it?" he croaks.

I gather my courage. "Mom's memory has concerned Les and me. I talked with her doctor. Dad, Mom has Alzheimer's."

His face falls. "She does? I don't think her memory is that bad."

"Her doctor diagnosed it two years ago, Dad. I can't believe you didn't know. Didn't Mom or her doctor tell you? Sometimes she calls me three times a day and doesn't remember the previous calls. The other night, after she left here, it took her two hours to drive home. I'm sure she got herself lost for a while. You know it should have taken only about fifteen minutes."

He begins to cry.

"It's awful news, and it means you and Mom are going to have to make some pretty big changes. With you in the hospital so much, and Mom getting so confused, let's find someplace where you can both have some help."

Dad is in shock, but, by the end of my visit, he agrees it's time to sell the old home place. Our roles have been reversed, and my parents will be the ones needing me now. I thank God I'm in a good place and can be there for them.

It's July third. Tillie has vomited. I clean it up, but I'm busy and don't think much of it until early evening when I notice her behavior is lethargic. I rush her to the emergency vet, and eventually an assistant comes to get her. I'm not allowed to go into the exam room and am told to go home; they'll call me when they have news. My beautiful companion looks back at me as she's led away.

I drive home, feeling sad and scared. Since Jim loved her, too, I decide to call him. We haven't had a phone conversation since his marriage, but maybe enough time has passed that we can offer each other a little sympathy. I nervously dial his number.

"Hello," a girlish voice answers.

"I'd like to speak with Jim, please," I say.

"Who?"

"Jim. May I please speak to him?"

"Dad!" I hear her call.

A tremor goes through me. Travis has told me Jim's mentally disabled stepdaughter is living with them, but the reality of him having an entirely different life and family is now in my face. I'm just a stranger on the phone.

"Hello." *So weird to hear his familiar voice. Maybe I should hang up.*

"Jim"?

"Yes?" *As if he doesn't want to acknowledge me.*

"This is Linda."

"Yes?" *Awkward!*

"I just thought you'd want to know that I had to leave Tillie at the vet tonight."

"Oh."

"I just thought you'd want to know."

"Okay."

"I'll let you know more when I know more." *No, I won't. This is too painful. Your voice sounds the same, but you speak like a stranger.*

"Okay, honey," he says in a flat tone.

What? Jim has never called me *honey* in all our years together. So weird. I'm twice as upset.

I call a friend and her husband answers. He asks me if I'm okay and I break down, telling him what happened. "I just don't understand how he could have been married to me, and then so soon afterwards, has a different family and life," I say through my tears.

That dear man says, "I don't understand either."

Oh, how good to know I'm not alone in my confusion. "I suppose someday I'll get used to it," I say, "but I'm not there yet."

"No, of course not."

It's two thirty the next morning—July Fourth—when I receive the call. Tillie stopped breathing while they worked on her. They are keeping her alive until they can speak to me. Do I want to give permission to open her chest?"

No.

Since Tillie was a foundling, and since, contrary to most dogs, she loved fireworks, we'd arbitrarily chosen July Fourth as her birthday. It's somehow fitting that she died on her birthday.

I'm alone in my grief. She's been my goofy, loving companion for fourteen years. I hug my pillow, crying my heart out.

After I send Jim the final vet bill, he emails me with a complaint over the cost and states he can't afford any more charges like this one. I email back, "Look at the bill again. This is the last one. Tillie has died."

He doesn't respond.

I don't bother to tell him when it's Rachel's turn to go. I've been giving her subcutaneous injections, but, after a few months, she's dragging again. I make arrangements with the vet to come to my home so she can die in relative comfort. Travis comes down on the train again to support me. I hold my sweet kitty-girl in my lap until she's gone, and after the vet leaves, Travis and I cry together. I believe God has kept my animals alive until I'd be okay on my own. Still, my home feels empty without them even as they remain forever close to my heart.

Thirty-six

Dance Code

At first sight, his address is certainly not striking; and his person can hardly be called handsome, till the expression of his eyes, which are uncommonly good, and the general sweetness of his countenance, is perceived.

–Jane Austen, *Sense and Sensibility*

Now that my pets are gone, I'm feeling a bit unmoored. The responsibility for their care has been lifted, and I'm experiencing some guilt for enjoying more freedom.

Journal Entry - July 14, 2001
Last night I danced with the man in the moon at a Midsummer's Eve party. It was heavenly.

Since I want to dress in costume for the midsummer's eve party at the dance studio where I've been taking lessons, I shop at the Tigard Value Village. A seafoam-green lace dress with a beaded bodice and flared skirt catches my eye. Accessorizing it with a crown of artificial flowers will work nicely. Returning home, I spot Sharon and stop to chat. "Look what I found," I tell her, joking. "It's my wedding dress!" That night, I'm transported by a dreamy nightclub two-step with a mysterious man wearing a moon mask. It's like being in a movie with just the two of us surrounded by drifting clouds. Afterwards, I'm slowly deposited back down to earth.

My experience on the dance floor is instructive in a personal way. I'm learning what I want from a partner, and I've developed the confidence to deal with the various behaviors I encounter.

My Dance Code
General Principles:
1. *If I've turned down an invitation to dance, I do not accept another invitation from someone else for that dance.*
2. *I must not confuse a wonderful dance experience with romance. Just because I've danced well with someone, doesn't certify him as life-partner material.*
3. *I make sure I don't have bad breath or body odor.*

How I Deal with Difficult Dancers:
1. *Men who try holding me too close: I stiff-arm them. And if that doesn't work, I step on their feet and refuse to dance with them again.*
2. *Men who have bad breath: I carry breath strips with me and offer them one.*
3. *Men who smell of alcohol: No second chances.*
4. *Men who have body odor: No second chances.*
5. *Men who try to tell me in a know-it-all-way what I'm doing wrong in my dancing: I leave them alone on the dance floor.*
6. *Men who are good dancers, but don't show any interest in me as a person: I match their disinterest and concentrate on the dance.*

7. *Men whose only topic of conversation is themselves: I concentrate on the dance.*

How I Treat Other Dance Partners:
1. *Men who seem nervous: I compliment them for having the courage to give dancing a try and encourage them in their efforts.*
2. *Men who want to give me a simple tip to fix a misstep: I try to learn and be grateful.*
3. *Men who are bad dancers: I don't let on that I notice. I do my best to follow them, and I never turn them down because their dancing is poor.*
4. *Husbands who are dancing because it pleases their wives: I tell them what heroes they are.*

New Year's Eve 2001 has come and gone. I've been chosen as chair of my homeowners association. I love living in this little community, and I'm happy, as well as challenged, to be involved. I have to exercise tough love with the committee at times, keeping our discussions factual rather than emotional, similar to what I do in the classroom. I'm pleased with how well that works.

I continue to work on my townhouse. It takes me several coats to get the color of the hall bathroom just right, and my friend Sharon jokes that with all that paint, the bathroom will turn out to be much smaller.

My dancing continues to improve along with my number of regular dance partners. Although there's no romantic feelings involved, I seem to have some sort of telepathic connection with one of the men. I send out a message to come dance with me, he turns around, looks at me, and off we go. We both comment on the phenomenon.

Mike, one of the men in my mambo class at Heather's Studio, asks if I'd like to be his dance partner. He seems like a nice guy and we are well-matched ability-wise, so I agree. Having a dance partner is pretty common in my dance circles. It's kind of a guarantee there will be someone to practice with at the dances we choose to attend. These days I'm all about being upfront and honest about who I am and what I want. As Mike and I get better acquainted, we agree that although we are good dance partners, we are not a good romantic match. That's fine with the both of us.

On the last Friday of July, I've arranged to meet up with Mike at a singles dance at the Beaverton Elks Club, which is one of the regular venues in the area. We dance a few dances, but then he becomes interested in a woman across the room and disappears. I'm not happy he's abandoned me. I've had enough abandonment during my marriage. I silently rehearse the little talk I'm going to have with him. We need to discuss what each of us thinks it means to be a dance partner, since our ideas don't seem to be the same. If we can't agree, there's no point in continuing our partnership.

While I sit at a table steaming over Mike, a man I've not met before asks me to dance. His version of the foxtrot, to put it kindly, is not the current one. But, true to my Dance Code, I follow him as best I can. He's short, balding, a little overweight, and is wearing a small gold cross necklace. He introduces himself and asks me my name, wanting to know a little something about me. I tell him I've just received my library media credentials and am looking for a teaching job. It's in God's hands, I add. The man tells me he is a mathematics teacher and has just become a mathematics specialist in an elementary school, believing his placement is part of God's plan.

Nice. And then I go home and forget him. He hadn't impressed me much.

Later the next week, I call Mike and we have our little talk. We agree that before each dance, we'll discuss our expectations of one another. Our talk must have gone well, because when I see Mike at dance class, he tells me he appreciated the nice things I've said about him. Who knew I could be such a diplomat?

A couple of weeks later, I go to Rose City Dance Club in Portland. I come here most Sunday nights without Mike. At Rose City we have a lesson followed by dancing to a live band.

Tonight, the man I'd met at the Elks Club asks for a dance.

"You're Linda, right?" he asks as he takes me in his arms.

"That's right. I'm sorry; I don't remember your name."

"It's Bill. It's good to see you again. Say, how's your job hunting going?"

He remembered. "Nothing yet."

"Would you like me to pray with you over it?" he asks, giving me a warm smile."

"Ah, okay."

He takes me by the hand, leads me out to the lobby, praying for God to bless me in my search. Now, I'm impressed.

In August, I buy a ticket for a Saturday Christian Singles Midnight Dance Cruise on the *Portland Spirit* sailing on the Willamette River. By the night of the cruise, all my friends have bailed. If I hadn't already paid, I'd have backed out too. On top of that, parking my car by myself in downtown Portland so late at night concerns me. I say a little prayer and slip a book into my dance bag in case I get bored. I board the ship, not knowing what to expect.

I'm asked to dance a couple of times, and then I see Bill. He looks nice in his suit, in contrast to most of the other guys who are casually dressed. *Oh, I like a snappy dresser.* He greets me with a happy smile, and we dance and talk. *His swing dance is pretty good, much better than his foxtrot. This is fun!*

#18. He has a zest for life. He is a joyful person.

Even while dancing, we're busy discovering more about each other. I tell him I don't want to get involved with anyone more than five years older or younger than I am. He's a year and a half younger. My attractions have been to tall men, but Bill has charisma. I can tell he's intelligent, and when we share what schools we've attended, I'm not surprised to learn his Master of Arts in Teaching Mathematics degree is from Harvard. Nice! He tells me he lives across the river in Vancouver.

#22. He is intelligent and has good sense. Our levels of education are similar.

#29. His birthday is within five years of mine.

We're having difficulty not dancing all the dances together. Somehow, it doesn't matter that his dancing skills are not as developed as mine. After a time, we tear away from each other. *I don't want him to think I'm crowding him.*

At one point I climb to the upper deck to watch the river, half-hoping he'll find me. He does! We talk and dance some more. When it comes time for the last dance, we go looking for each other, and we dance close. Except for the tango, it's the first time I've allowed someone to hold me tight. *So nice. Watch out, Linda.* He holds my hand up the boat ramp. On the way to my car, I ask if I can take his arm, and he seems pleased.

#24. He is courteous and has good manners. He is aware of others and is able to put them at ease.

I'm liking this guy. I hope he'll ask me out.

He asks me if he'll see me at Rose City the next evening. *Okay, promising.*

He's there the next night, and as we dance, he asks, "What would you say if I asked you to dinner?"

I feel confident and sassy, "You'll have to ask me to find out."

He laughs and asks me, and I say "Yes." *Of course!* We can't stop grinning at each other throughout the rest of the evening, as if we are sharing a wonderful secret.

I mention I'm going to a country western bar on Tuesday for a West Coast swing lesson. "I'll see if I can make it," he says.

When I arrive, he's there to greet me. *Impressive that he's come all this way to connect with me.* We spend the night talking and dancing. I learn he's been married and divorced twice. I guess that makes us even.

"I know I'm going to see you Friday night, but the ads say the stores are getting in fresh salmon. Would you like to come to my place Thursday night for some salmon barbeque?"

Interesting reversal to my experience with the first guy I dated. I've never had a man pursue me like this. Is this good or bad? I hope he's not some kind of weirdo.

"I hope you don't think I'm rushing you," he adds. *Is he reading my mind?*

Bill lives twenty-five miles north of me in Washington. On my way I begin second-guessing myself. *This is a long way to drive. What am I doing? I don't really know this guy. Can I trust him? He could be faking this Christian stuff.* I'm prepared to tell him my boundaries.

Bill's condo is older than my townhouse, but nice, with tasteful furnishings.

#13. He takes pride in his home, keeping things repaired and in reasonable order.

We go for a walk and then put the salmon on the barbeque. While it's cooking, I venture, "Since you mentioned 'rushing' on Tuesday, I think it's time to discuss boundaries. You see, I've decided to conduct my relationships God's way. I hope, someday, He'll give me another chance at marriage. Until then, I've pledged to remain celibate."

Bill raises his eyebrows. "Interesting. This summer I decided to do the same. I've been single for ten years, and all that time I pursued relationships my way. It's taken me that long to finally realize my way didn't work. Two Sundays ago, I went up to the altar and told God that, from now on, I wanted to follow His guidelines. I feel at peace with my decision."

Hallelujah! My friends have been telling me maybe I haven't found the right man yet because he's not ready for me. Maybe Bill is Mr. Right, and now he's ready. Whoa, Nellie! It's early yet. Don't get too excited.

#1. He is spiritually grounded; he trusts God as a wise and loving Father.

We're so engrossed in our talking, we burn dinner. We laugh at ourselves as we eat charred salmon

#27. He enjoys cooking with me.

He wants to kiss me, and I sure want him to kiss him. *Oh, man, this is hard.* Instead, I open my purse and hand him the book *Finding the Love of Your Life.*

"What's this?"

"Our relationship has grown so quickly, I wanted to be prepared," I explain. "This book has some solid reasons for staying celibate until marriage. Dr. Clark maintains that having sex beforehand clouds our judgment of the other person. From my experience, I would agree. I want to get to know you better before we get too romantic."

"Does this mean I don't get to kiss you now?"

"Not until you read the book."

"Well, I'm not a fast reader, but that sure gives me an incentive to get through it as soon as possible!"

#18. He has a good sense of humor.

We confirm plans for him to pick me up the next night and take me out to dinner. Our date is to be at a restaurant near where I live.

That afternoon, while substitute teaching, I experience bouts of dizziness. Although disconcerting, it's the only symptom I have, and I really want to see Bill. It isn't until I get home and try to get ready, that I realize I must be ill. I try calling him, but he's already left home. I greet him at the door in my sweats.

Thirty-seven

Falling

Wise men say only fools rush in, but I can't help falling in love with you.
—Haley Reinhart, "Can't Help Falling in Love"

ill's mouth flies open at my appearance. I explain my plight, apologizing profusely. *He's going to turn and run.*

Instead, his face morphs into concern. "Let me take care of you," he says, walking in and steering me to the couch.

#23. He has a well-developed instinct for nurturing and protecting. I'm liking this.

"What sounds good?" he asks, heading toward my kitchen. It isn't long before he presents me with a bowl of tomato soup and a grilled cheese sandwich. We chat for quite a while and he seems to listen to me.

#4. He listens and hears me. He's interested in what I say.

The next morning, he drives from his home to see me, to make sure I'm okay. He takes me to breakfast, as I'm feeling better. *Is he too good to be true?*

#21. He is brave, steadfast, and loyal. He does the right thing, even if it is difficult. He doesn't run away when things get tough.

On Sunday afternoon, I go to his place again. He's read the book. We discuss what it means to be celibate and agree on what level of intimacy we should allow ourselves. We kiss. A lot. It's been so long and it feels so good. My heart and my body are singing.

#26. He's physically affectionate.

Bill and I see a lot of each other after that. I observe he irons his clothes and makes his own lunches. He even cans, using his mom's pressure cooker. *He's a real grownup.*

I'm pleased to learn Bill loves his new job, but he doesn't let his work stop him from biking and dancing and seeing me. I invite him to a hike sponsored by the Tualatin River Keepers. He comes along, obviously enjoying himself.

#5. He enjoys play. We take turns initiating fun activities to do together.

#11. He enjoys outdoor and indoor activities without being obsessed by them.

I attend a mathematics workshop he gives at the Northwest Mathematics Conference in Portland and observe him in action. Like many people, I'm math phobic, but he makes it fun and understandable.

#9. He is engaged in his professional work, but it does not rule him.

We've only been dating for three weeks, when he begins calling me every evening. On one hand, I'm enjoying his attention, but on the other, I'm concerned I'm getting in too fast, too deep. Still, it's wonderful to have Bill unafraid to show he's smitten with me. I'm touched when he tells me that, for the first time in a long time, he has someone with whom he enjoys sharing his life. "I admit I've been kind of lonely," he says.

#28. He is able to be vulnerable with me.

September 11, 2002

I love Bill's sense of humor. I suggested he take an Enneagram test to understand better how our personalities might mesh.

"Of course, this test might prove we aren't compatible," I tease.

Bill laughs. "In that case, we'll just have to keep it physical."

I laugh too. "In your dreams!"

"Would you like to go to the Vancouver Symphony Concert on the Columbia?" Bill asks. "It's my birthday and I'd love to spend it with you. We could take a picnic dinner."

"Sure," I say. "What can I bring?'

"Just yourself," he says. "We'll pick up some fried chicken and salad on the way."

I surprise him with my homemade Black Bottom Banana Muffins, which he pronounces "amazing." During intermission, we notice a flock of swallows swirling above us. We stand to watch, but I become aware that Bill is watching me instead, and rather intently at that. I look at him quizzically.

"Your eyes are golden," he says with awe in his voice.

I blink and smile. It must be the angle of the setting sun, but I like that this guy is seeing me in a special way. *Has an angel given me a little boost?*

I'm pleased Bill shows an interest in my writing. When he asks to read *Home of the Heart,* I explain romance novels have different levels of sensuality. Mine is considered a "subtly sensual" romance, just beyond the "Kisses" stage. After Bill reads it, he tells me it made him cry in places. "You are such a good writer. I hope you write more stories."

#19. He is willing to encourage and support me in following my dreams.

Then he says, "After finishing your book, I realized I'm falling in love with you."

Oh, wow! The L word! I think I love him too! I'm excited and scared at the same time.

I'm scheduled to practice the mambo for an exhibition. Bill says he'll meet me at the dance studio and we can go out afterwards. I agree and tell him when I should be finished. He arrives a little early and our practice goes overtime. I'm getting more nervous by the minute, worrying he has to wait so long. When we finish, I run to him and apologize.

He shrugs his shoulders and smiles, "No problem. I loved watching you."

I relax, realizing that, after all those years with Jim, I've become habituated to expecting my man to be displeased if a situation turns out differently than planned. It's an unhealthy habit I need to overcome.

Bill expresses an interest in joining my intermediate level foxtrot class. Although I appreciate his desire to improve his dance skills and participate with me, he has a lot of catching up to do. Heather suggests he show her what he knows, and I can see she's trying to hide her concern. After an awkward ten minutes or so, she begins giving him directions. "That's right," she encourages. "That's right." Twenty minutes pass and her face has brightened. He's a fast learner and can join the class. I give him a big hug, pleased and proud for him.

#12. His mind is open to new learning, new possibilities, new insights of himself and others.

When I share this with Sharon, she frowns. "He's trying to monopolize you." I've discovered she has a bitter streak toward men in general and her ex in particular. Fifteen years earlier, her husband had an affair and divorced her. Even though they have children and grandchildren together, she can't stand to be in his presence. She seems as angry toward him now as when he left. I'm sorry for her and have promised myself I won't follow her example.

"I've got to say I'm not used to this kind of attention," I tell her. "And with some guys, I might find it creepy. With Bill, though, it just feels nice."

Bill has begun attending church service with me at Rolling Hills. One Sunday we drop in afterwards to see Ros. *I want to see what Ros thinks of Bill.* We sit and chat for a little while, and, as we leave, Ros whispers in my ear, "I like him. He has kind eyes."

Bill's parents are deceased, but he takes me on a couple of road trips to introduce me to his four kids. It's clear that his six grandchildren are crazy about him and vice versa.

#16. He enjoys being with family. He has a good relationship with his kids.

The trips give us plenty of time to learn more about each other. We talk about what went wrong with our marriages. Bill first married when he was twenty-two and in graduate school. They were married for five years and had two sons. Unhappy with the life of a teacher's wife, she chose to pursue a more exciting lifestyle.

His second marriage lasted fourteen years and produced a daughter and a son. "After the birth of my third son," he said, "my wife lost interest in me physically. She told me that my intimate touch caused her to think of pregnancy, and she never wanted to be pregnant again. Although she sometimes carried out her 'wifely duty,' the emotional connection we'd enjoyed wasn't there anymore. I stayed in the marriage for ten more years, hoping we could regain the love and closeness we once had. However, being rejected for so long was soul-crushing. I had to leave to restore my sense of self, my joy. I prayed God had something better for me."

"Copy that," I said, telling him my similar story.

As we drive, I read *The Love Languages: How to Express Heartfelt Commitment to Your Mate* by Gary Chapman. We learn that each of us has a natural way to communicate love to our partner. That method may not match our partner's "love language." When each of us knows what is pleasing to the other, we have an important key to a satisfying relationship. I tell Bill my love languages are "Acts of Service" and "Quality Time."

"'Words of Affirmation' and 'Physical Touch' define mine the best," he says. "Love, appreciation, and respect have always been important to me, and I think those fit into these two love languages. I know that when I stopped receiving those from my wives, our marriages deteriorated."

#15. He has dealt with emotional issues of the past, and they do not rule his present day thinking and actions.

I tell Bill there are a couple of other things he should know about me. "I love being a redhead, but my hair is actually white. And, another thing, I'm never changing my name again."

"No problem!"

#7. He accepts other people for who they are but is not afraid to express his wants and needs when appropriate.

We discover we have much in common. Being close to the same age is nice. He often breaks into song, choosing lyrics from our childhood and teen years. I love that he feels so comfortable being fun and goofy with me.

I call Travis. "I've been dating someone and I'd like you to meet him. Can we take you out to lunch?"

"Why? Are you thinking of marrying this guy? Aren't you taking things pretty fast?"

"I like Bill a lot, and it's important to me that you give me your opinion of him."

Travis and Bill obvious enjoy each other's sense of humor. After lunch, Travis gives a thumbs up. This confirmation is huge.

I introduce Bill to my parents. Dad can appear pretty gruff sometimes, but Bill sees right through him, and they hit it off, laughing and joking. Because of her Alzheimer's, Mom's reaction is varied. What impresses me is the respect Bill shows both of them. He's lost his own parents and understands how important mine are to me. His attitude is essential to our relationship, because, just as we are getting serious, I become involved in my parent's move.

#16. He gets along well with my son and my parents. This is vital.

It's time to move my parents from the home that has been in our family for three generations. It's no simple task. Mom wants to take everything with her and harangues Dad because she can't. This is the Alzheimer's taking over but knowing that doesn't make dealing with her any easier.

Before the house sells, I take Bill through it, showing him my childhood bedroom and the attic. We go down to the cool basement, with its musty, basement smell, where some of Mom's canning goods are still standing in neat rows. I pat the big smooth concrete basin where we soaked our swimming suits and rinsed off our muddy clothes. It gives a resounding thunk.

We go out to the barn to see the chicken house we kids scrubbed clean and made into a playhouse, and the hayloft which provided a view of our neighborhood. Then out past Dad's big garden to the tree-shaded area we called "The Park," where we often held summer picnics. For the last time I caress the smooth piece of obsidian that's part of the outdoor fireplace my grandparents fashioned. I close my eyes for a moment, remembering the carpet of wildflowers that bloomed around our feet each spring, planted long ago by Grandma Moore, and the heavenly scent of wild violets I picked for my elementary school teachers.

I'm so glad Bill can see where I spent my childhood and can get a sense of what the place means to me. Not only does he respect my need to care for my family, he tells me he admires me for how I treat them. His support during this hard time endears him even more to me, as I help my family deal with all these changes.

On October sixth, while Bill and I are attending Rolling Hills, he leans over and whispers, "I love you."

I surprise myself by whispering back, "We're meant to be together." It's as if I'm uttering some deep, immutable truth that has come from above.

That afternoon while we snuggle on my red couch, Bill says, "I agree that we're meant to be together. The thing is, I'd already planned I'd ask you to marry me today."

Thirty-eight

God Bless My Broken Road

2002–2003

I'm sorry," Matt said softly, drawing Meg into his arms. His sympathy released more tears, and he petted and rocked her as she grieved the loss of her childhood home. When she had quieted, he spoke. "We'll make our own home, Meggie," he said, brushing away her tears. "A home where we and our loved ones will always be welcome. A home of our hearts."

—**Linda M. Kurth**, *Home of the Heart*

"I love you too, and I want to marry you," I tell Bill. "I do believe God has meant us to be together. But I've made two mistakes already, and I promised myself that if I was to marry again, I'd have to know my prospective husband really well. We've only known each other for three months!"

"Can't we somehow speed up the time it'll take to get to know each other better and to see if we're as good match as we think we are?" he asks.

"Well, my church offers premarital counseling," I tell him. "If the counselors decide we're a good match, I'll agree to marry you sooner rather than possibly later."

Bill kisses my forehead. "They're gonna love us being together," he says with a big grin.

I go to bed that night, wrapped in warm thoughts of Bill's love, but the cold light of morning gives me pause. When I see Bill the next evening, I'm ready with a $64,000 question. "What is your understanding of the roles of husband and wife in a marriage?"

"What do you mean?"

"Do you think the wife should be submissive to the husband, or do you believe it should be a mutual submission?"

"I think couples can draw upon the strengths of each other in building the strongest marriage possible. There will be things in which the wife is more adept. In those areas, the husband would be wise to submit to his wife. I believe the reverse is true."

"What if it is an area in which both are strong?"

"I think the two can discuss the situation and decide on a way that satisfies both."

I bore in. "What if the two cannot come to an agreement on how to proceed?"

Bill thinks for a moment. "Unless it's critical, I think no decision should be made. The two should pray about it and wait for God's clear direction. What do you think?"

"I agree. However, if it is a decision that needs to be made immediately, I would trust you to make the best possible decision."

"I'm glad we talked this through," he says.

"Me too." I'm feeling optimistic, and I'm curious what more we'll find out about each other in our counseling sessions."

#3. He believes in mutual submission of marriage partners; we honor each other.

My head is spinning. I've spent time, energy, and money getting my townhouse just the way I want it. I figured out I have room to host a dozen people at my oak table with its four leaves if I swap out some of the living and dining room furniture for occasions such as board meetings. I've recently been elected to my second year as president of the homeowners association. Now that I'm feeling settled, I could be looking at another big change in my life.

Besides leaving behind my beloved home once again, a bigger factor looms. My spousal support means I'm able to make independent financial decisions. If I marry Bill, I will be financially dependent on him. The "world" might tell me I'd be smart to simply live with him and not marry. We talk it over and decide the moral and ethical decision is to make the financial sacrifice and get married.

Journal Entry - October 8, 2002

Bill is "walking on clouds." I guess I'm in shock. I believe he's the man for me, but my life seems to be changing so quickly, I feel as if I'm being swept along and have no footing. The thought of leaving my townhouse just when I've almost finished it is hard.

In the beginning of our sessions with our marriage mentors, we take two detailed personality tests that are sent away to a professional testing service. When the results come back, our mentors say they are amazed we know each other so well. One of these tests identifies Bill as a high optimist. I'm not surprised that I'm regarded as a realist.

We are scheduled to have eight sessions, but, after the third, they ask us to come back for a final time. "You're ready," they say. "You know each other better than many couples who've been together for months or years." We're not surprised, considering all the things we've read and done to get to know one another.

Having gone through the counseling, we feel confident that God approves of our marrying. We set our wedding date for February 15,

2003, and begin the process of notifying family members. Les and Sandy meet Bill and take to him right away. The leader of SAM pulls me aside to tell me she has "a good feeling" about Bill. Some of my friends, Sharon in particular, are concerned our courtship has been short, but most are hopeful when I tell them of our counselors' assessment. There are no red flags anywhere.

Emotionally, I feel ready—Bill is the man for me. But much has to be done before the big day. Because of Bill's job and the tax situation, we decide to live in Washington. That means we need to finish little details on my townhouse before we put it on the market, prepare Bill's condo for rent, find a new home for us, and transfer my teaching credentials across the Columbia River. We also have to plan the wedding. *It seems just a bit crazy!*

Transferring my credentials requires passing tests on reading, writing, and mathematics. I have no worries about the reading and writing parts, but I am terrified by the prospect of the mathematics test. Bill understands and offers to help. I'm wary. My poor Dad tried to help me with my math as a public school student, and our sessions usually ended with me crying. But Bill explains, "I'm happy to tutor you, but only under one condition: I will show you the reasons behind the processes, not just how to get the answer."

I do my best to lay aside my fears and to trust Bill. As we go through the various topics, I'm surprised by how much I learn. I wasn't taught this way in school, and I have suffered from the belief I wasn't capable for all these years. I take the three tests in January, breezing through the reading and writing portions, and just missing the qualifying score in mathematics. I'm sure, though, I can pass that test on a second try. Bill's work with me has given me a confidence in mathematics that I didn't have before.

#10. He is a good communicator. I add *patient*, too.

The night before our big day, we snuggle together in my bed, dreaming of our wedding and honeymoon. It's not been easy for us to stick to our vows of celibacy. We yearn to express our love without restraint, but we also believe the Lord will bless us in our obedience to Him. Bill's commitment to our vows of celibacy gives me peace concerning our future. He didn't just give lip service in the beginning and press for things to be different as time went on.

#20. He is trustworthy and honest. His words and actions reflect one another.

Since I have many friends and family in the area, we decide to hold our wedding ceremony in the chapel of my home church in Tigard. Coincidentally, the pastor is someone I knew in Bend. Dad has given me some money and asked me to help Mom find a new outfit, and she's managed to get herself together for our big day. Trish directs people to the chapel. Travis does a superb job of playing our favorite music from the boom box. All of Bill's children are in attendance plus a couple of the grandchildren. Some of the wedding guests are my parents' friends and attended my first wedding in the same church all those years ago. A friend takes photos. My trainer, David, is here, and I'm touched by the tears he tries to hide.

I wear my seafoam-green lace dress and flowers in my hair. Bill looks handsome in his new tuxedo. We smile at each other while listening to *Annie's Song* by John Denver. Ros steps up to take my bouquet. Bill takes me in his arms in front of the altar and we waltz to Anne Murray's *Could I Have This Dance (For the Rest of My Life)*. We recite our vows with Bill promising to keep his spirits up and the toilet seat down. I promise to let him teach me more mathematics.

As Bill and I walk back down the aisle to the tune of Natalie Cole's rendition of *At Last (My Love Has Come Along)*, Mom dances along behind us. We're eager to begin our life together as long as we both shall live.

Epilogue

Have I forgiven Jim? Though I will never condone his hurtful behavior during the last years of our marriage, I've forgiven him. Along with that forgiveness, the sorrow and pain I experienced have faded away. We are civil to one another, exchanging occasional emails and good wishes on birthdays. He is still married to "Lady Friend," and I pray for his well-being, but not, I confess, for his marriage.

What about that "What I want in a Husband list"? Bill fits all of my criteria except for a portion of one or two. (It wouldn't be fair if I told you what they are, but they're minor.) There's one piece I didn't think to put on the list—shopping. Bill enjoys taking care of the majority of our household shopping. What a nice surprise. This gives me more time to write. I'm fortunate Bill didn't make a "What I Want in a Woman" list. I can't imagine measuring up in as many ways as he has.

I admit I didn't realize he enjoyed so many sports. I can't believe I watch televised golf with him and enjoy it. *In the hole, Rory!* I even go fishing with him sometimes.

A month after our marriage, I retook the mathematics part of the teaching accreditation test. Since we had spent so much time learning how processes worked, our review was much shorter. I left the exam knowing I passed.

My life with Bill has been blessed. He cheerfully adjusts my back, helps me with my computer, and enjoys my cooking. I enjoy his too; we take good care of one another.

Since Bill wanted me to have an Elfery again, we bought a house with a space under the stairs, and, with some modification, it became another Elfery and a magnet for the neighborhood children. We also redeemed my certificate for a piano.

A few years later, we made hopefully our last move to be closer to our children and grandchildren. The yard reminds me very much of the one I enjoyed as a child in Tigard, and the surrounding area is much like the Willamette Valley where I grew up. I was able to use my interior design experience for a remodel to the "Home of Our Hearts" that will accommodate us in our old age. And there's room in the dining area for the oak table with all four of its leaves, where kids and grandkids, our Bible study group, critique writers, and Christmas drops-ins comfortably gather.

My son, Travis, received a PTSD diagnosis from his time in the Army. Since then, he's had good help and become an emotionally strong and loving man. I'm proud of him for the work he's done to get to this place. Recently I asked Travis if he thought I should have left his father while Travis was still living at home. Would it have been better to spare him from our struggles? "I don't know, Mom," he answered. "I was painfully aware you and Dad were in conflict, but I can't imagine what my life would have been like if you had left him when I was a teenager. That would have been pretty rough, too."

My parents are gone now. For several years they leaned on one another, Mom seeing to the physical responsibilities and Dad, the mental ones. I carried out the difficult task of having their driver licenses taken away. Les and I took care of what needs they couldn't, but Dad's heart gave out and we had to place Mom in a home for women with dementia. Bill and I lived nearby, and I was able to visit her on a regular basis until she passed at the age of ninety.

Ros, my dear cousin and "sister," developed a brain tumor. For two years I visited her, keeping her company and bringing her and Tom meals to tide them over. My heart broke when she passed away. I'm so grateful I've had Bill to comfort me in these sorrows.

I believe the manner in which my life has unfolded has been a kind of miracle. The Lord knew I would make mistakes and bad choices, He knew I would reject Him in my young adult years, and yet, He never let me out of His sight. He had a plan bigger than mine. When I think of my journey, an Oregon girl marrying a man who brought me to Albuquerque and later left me there, meeting and marrying an Albuquerque man who was born and raised in upstate New York, moving to California and then to my home state of Oregon, and eventually settling near my hometown of Tigard, I'm confident that God had His hand on me throughout. I landed where I could be supported by friends and family when I needed them most. After I recovered, my proximity meant I could support them in return. The cherry on the top was meeting Bill, the love of my life.

At this writing, Bill and I have recently celebrated our seventeenth wedding anniversary. People tell us how lucky we were to find each other. We gently correct them, saying we believe it came from a blessed, heavenly plan, not luck. God used our broken roads to bring us together. Our love has grown sweeter through the years, and we still love to dance. We've both experienced hurts in our pasts, and sometimes we're challenged not to carry old bad habits into our relationship. As painful as it can be sometimes, we don't hide from our problems and let them fester; we talk them out. Remembering the Lord brought us together makes it easier for us to work through the few difficult times and celebrate our many good ones.

I don't pretend to understand how God worked all this out, but I'm certain He had (and still has) plans for me, to prosper me and not to harm me, plans to give me a hope and a future. God has blessed me in ways I'd never allowed Him before I walked through the Refiner's fire. When I was cut to the core, I discovered what is important in life and what are mere trappings. In the dark depths of the night, He cradled me in His arms. Now I feel His hand on my shoulder. I am secure in Him and nothing much shakes me these days. I know without a doubt that God is good all the time, and I look forward to my final home in heaven with Him.

Journal Entry - Not long ago

In my dream I'm walking behind Bill in an airport terminal, trying to catch up. He turns and holds out his hand, waiting for me to walk beside him.

Reflections

As a Christian woman, I experienced the tug-of-war between "conservative" and "liberal" Christians and their churches over the biblical understanding of marriage. This dichotomy of beliefs had a strong influence on my struggle during my marriage and the ultimate decision to divorce my Christian husband. This conflict chose me, not the other way around. I'm no biblical scholar, but I endeavor to understand how God wants me to live. I feel called to:

- Give glory to God who has sustained me throughout my life, even when, at times, I turned my back on Him. The Lord has not forsaken me.
- Bear witness to the good people—Christian and non-Christian—who embraced me in my darkest hours.
- Encourage Christians who are going through divorce to trust our merciful God to help them through the heartbroken times in their lives. For those Christians who struggle to discern God's view of leaving a marriage, I hope my experience and understanding will help them.
- Shine a light on spiritual abuse—Christians using their understanding of biblical law to shame other Christians. Legalists of today are progeny of the Pharisees of Jesus' day. We need Christ's mercy, because even the most religious and spiritual among us sin and fall short of perfect holy life.

- Encourage Christians to open their minds to what the Holy Spirit wants to reveal concerning marriage and divorce. We understand the Bible best when we are aided by scholars who take into consideration the times of the books of the Bible. I am amazed how the Holy Spirit continues to reveal insights into the meaning of Scripture.

- Shine a light on the subtle abuse of crazymaking, and to let those who have experienced such abuse know they are not alone and not crazy. Our worth resides in the Lord, and we can find strength in His word and in the words of His people who speak love and wholeness into our lives.

- Use the example of my unhappy marriage to help others avoid the mistakes my former husband and I made. We live in times that challenge our marriages. I urge everyone to follow the Golden Rule and love your spouse as you love yourself.

- Use the example of my courtship with Bill to help those considering marriage to maximize their chance for success.

(See my blog articles on these issues: https://www.lindamkurth.com/divorce-and-faith-articles.html

What I believe about divorce

First, I don't believe that, if a marriage gets tough, the only answer is to leave. I've heard Christian people declare "God just wants us to be happy," using that as permission to divorce. This idea cannot be found in the Bible. The following passage, written by the apostle Paul, is the bedrock of my understanding that we have a choice and how we are to make it.

> "You, my brothers and sisters, were called to be free. But do not use your freedom to indulge the flesh; rather, serve one another humbly in love. For the entire

law is fulfilled in keeping this one command: 'Love your neighbor as yourself.'" (Galatians 5:13-14).

I believe God calls us to do our best to make our marriages work. I also believe this passage means we are free to make the choice to leave if done out of *agape* love—love that is merciful, full of grace, and unselfish, seeking the best for the other. In other words, doing to others what you would have them do to you. Carrying out this command can be difficult and against our human nature. Discerning the most loving path can be a challenge.

Did I divorce Jim out of this kind of love? I tried my best, doing all I knew to make my marriage work, although my efforts proved to be far from perfect. And when it didn't work, I tried to leave in love, although that didn't work out as well as I'd hoped either.

God planned marriage to be a lifelong union. He hates divorce, but He Himself chose to divorce the Israelites because of their unfaithfulness (Jeremiah 3:8). Because of Jim's unfaithfulness, shown by his "fruit" (his treatment of me) time and time again, I lost the capacity to be a loving wife to him. I discerned neither repentance from him nor a sustained desire to change. Staying married to Jim meant living a lie.

There is evidence that, as our marriage neared its end, Jim had an affair. According to many Christians, that would have given me permission to divorce him. However, I refuse to claim my right on those grounds. Even if Jim hadn't had an affair, his abandoning me emotionally was an act of unfaithfulness. His behavior told me he did not want to remain married to me. As in many areas of our life together, he left it up to me to make the difficult decision to leave.

I'd hoped my leaving would cause Jim to examine his behavior. I have little insight into whether or not that happened. It did cause me to examine myself and to grow closer to God. I'm a better person now than when I struggled under the stress of my marriage. Even though I do not believe I sinned in divorcing Jim, I have asked for and received forgiveness for sins committed during our years together.

Second, I have a new understanding of what the Bible says regarding divorce. I recently read the book, *Divorce and Remarriage in the Church*, by David Instone-Brewer, an esteemed scholar on first-century Judaism and its bearing on the New Testament. This book gives a fresh interpretation of biblical passages on the subject. I found the following quote to be enlightening:

> There were no debates about the validity of neglect and abuse as grounds for divorce in *any* ancient Jewish literature, for the same reason that there are none about the oneness of God: these principles were unanimously agreed on. Rather than indicating that Jesus did not accept the validity of divorce for neglect and abuse, his silence about it highlights the fact that he did accept it, like all other Jews at that time.[7]

This acceptance of abuse and neglect as grounds for divorce indicates that those actions fall under the heading of marital unfaithfulness, as mentioned by Jesus in Matthew 5:32. A husband who neglects or abuses his wife is being unfaithful to her every bit as much as through sexual infidelity. The same applies to the wife.

Third, I found intriguing another theme in Instone-Brewer's book: the concept of a marriage covenant. The biblical passages that deal with covenant and contract can be confusing. Today, we understand a contract as having conditions. If the agreed-upon conditions are not met, the contract can be broken. A covenant on the other hand, is understood to be unbreakable. However, according to Instone-Brewer, "... *covenant* and *contract* are both translations of the same Hebrew word, so the idea [of marriage as an unbreakable covenant] does not exist in the Bible."[8] For instance, God made a covenant with Noah not to flood the earth ever again, period. No conditions were attached. On the other hand, God's covenant with the Israelites at Mt. Sinai can be considered a contract, since it had stipulations. The marriage covenant in the Bible has the characteristics of a contract, since it can be broken by unfaithfulness.

I believe my intuition, common sense, and whisperings of the Holy Spirit have been God's guidance concerning divorce. Unfortunately, the disagreement among Christians about divorce remains an issue. Take the recent controversy between the Pope and conservative or traditionalist Catholics. The pope has cracked open the door for the possibility that divorced and civilly remarried Catholics can take communion. But the debate over marriage, divorce, and remarriage among the Catholic Church promises to continue for a long time to come. That's true in Protestant denominations as well. I believe we should not ignore our disagreements concerning divorce and remarriage but rather continue with scholarly study and engage in respectful dialogue. Divorce is difficult enough without condemnation from one's spiritual community.

What I believe about marriage

In this memoir, I've touched on the concept of submission between husbands and wives. Paul speaks of submission in Ephesians.

> Wives, submit yourselves to your own husbands as you do to the Lord. For the husband is the head of the wife as Christ is the head of the church, His body, of which He is the Savior. Now as the church submits to Christ, so also wives should submit to their husbands in everything. (Ephesians 5:22-24)

Christians have struggled with this passage for generations, often ignoring the rest of it, "However, each one of you [husbands] also must love his wife as he loves himself, and the wife must respect her husband." I understand that Paul means a mutual submission. An article by Margaret Mowczko explains it this way:

Both Peter and Paul instructed wives to be submissive to their own husbands (Ephesians 5:21-22; Colossians 3:18-19; Titus 2:5; 1 Peter 3:1). However the concept of submission has been exaggerated by many Christians. Submission is really just the opposite of resistance and rebellion. Peter and Paul wanted wives to be allied with their husbands, in supportive and harmonious marriages, and not alienated from them. Also, neither Peter or Paul wrote that wives must obey their husbands.[9]

The Galatians passage applies to mutual submission as well, and bears repeating:

"You, my brothers and sisters, were called to be free. But do not use your freedom to indulge the sinful nature; rather, serve one another humbly in love. For the entire law is fulfilled in keeping this one command: 'Love your neighbor as yourself.'" (Galatians 5:13-14).

I'll paraphrase: "Wives, treat your husbands as you would have them treat you. Likewise, husbands, treat your wives as you would have them treat you." That's the essence of mutual submission. There is need for respectful dialogue over this issue as well.

What does the fruit indicate?

I imagine some of you think I've got it all wrong. Before you judge, though, consider "A good tree cannot bear bad fruit, and a bad tree cannot bear good fruit. Every tree that does not bear good fruit is cut down and thrown into the fire. Thus, by their fruit you will recognize them." (Matthew 7:18-20). God has poured many blessings on me since the divorce. Bill and I have the kind of marriage we both desired. We submit to each other each day. We serve as beloved members of our church. We have a warm and inviting home. Our joy and gratitude in the Lord is boundless. We believe the fruit we produce displays God's work in us.

What I believe about courtship

Let's face it, Bill and I put ourselves on the fast track of L-O-V-E. Our mutual desire to stay celibate until marriage gave us a strong indication that God had put us together at just the right time. After going through a vetted counseling program at my church, we felt confident we had done what we could to be ready for marriage. Still, I suggest that committed couples take their time getting to know one another. Make sure you are committed to being equally yoked, that is, you share the same or similar Christian beliefs. Read *Finding the Love of Your Life*, and learn from it. Obtain feedback from a respected Christian marriage counseling service and work out any issues that arise before setting a wedding date.

I once met an older couple who'd been married a year and had not yet settled on where they would live—his house or hers. I detected simmering resentment and wondered if they would be able to settle their dispute or decide to return to their single lives. Don't be like that couple. Seek God's direction early on.

Above all

Let us love one another as Christ loved us, putting aside legalism, respecting God's law, and extending His grace in our marriages, in our churches, our communities, and in our world.

Suggested Reading & Resources

Books

Chapman, Gary. *The Five Love Languages: The Secret to Love That Lasts.* Chicago: Northfield Publishing, 1st ed, 2015

Cron, Ian Morgan and Stabile, Suzanne. *The Road Back to You: An Enneagram Journey to Self-Discovery,* Downers Grove: IVP Books, 2016

Foster, Richard J. *Money, Sex and Power: The Challenge of a Disciplined Life Paperback* New York: HarperCollins, 1985

Gottman, John M. Harmony, Silver, Nina. *The Seven Principles for Making Marriage Work.* New York: Random House, revised ed, 2015

Gundry, Patricia. *Heirs Together: Applying the Biblical Principle of Mutual Submission in Your Marriage.* Grand Rapids: Suitcase Books, 1999 (out of print but worth searching for)

Gungor, Mark. *Laugh Your Way to a Better Marriage: Unlocking the Secrets to Life, Love, and Marriage.* New York: Simon & Shuster, 2008

Hoffman, Natalie. *Is It Me? Making Sense of Your Confusing Marriage: A Christian Woman's Guide to Hidden Emotional and Spiritual Abuse,* Flying Fee Media, 2018

Instone-Brewer, David. *Divorce and Remarriage in the Church: Biblical Solutions for Pastoral Realities,* Downers Grove: IVP Books, 2007

Kimmel, Tim. *Grace-Filled Marriage: The Missing Piece. The Place to Start*, Brentwood: Worthy Publishing, 2015

Lamott, Anne. *Traveling Mercies: Some Thoughts on Faith*, New York: Anchor Books, 2000

Smedes, Lewis B. *Forgive and Forget: Healing the Hurts We Don't Deserve,* New York: HarperOne, 2007

Warren, Neil Clark. *Finding the Love of Your Life: Ten Principles for Choosing the Right Marriage Partner.* New York: Pocket Books, 1992 (out of print but worth searching for)

Yetkovich, Kay, Milan. *How We Love: Discover Your Love Style, Enhance Your Marriage*, Colorado Springs: Waterbrook Press, 2008

Other

Boundless (a segment of Focus on the Family). *The Biblical Dating Series*
http://www.boundless.org/relationships/2012/biblical-dating-how-its-different-from-modern-dating

International Forgiveness Institute, https://internationalforgiveness.com

Stauffer, Erich. *Dr. James Dobson's Twelve Steps of Intimacy*
http://www.erichstauffer.com/pop-culture/dr-james-dobsons-twelve-steps-of-intimacy

Endnotes

1. M. Scott Peck, *The Road Less Traveled* (New York: Simon & Schuster, 1978), 85.

2. Richard J. Foster, *Money, Sex and Power: The Challenge of a Disciplined Life Paperback* (San Francisco: Harper & Row, 1985), 144-145.

3. M. Scott Peck, *The Different Drum: Community Making and Peace* (New York: Simon & Schuster, 1998), 220.

4. Anne Lamott, *Traveling Mercies: Some Thoughts on Faith,* (Anchor, 2000), 19.

5. Louis Smedes, *Forgive and Forget: Healing the Hurts We Don't Deserve,* (New York: Pocket Books, 1990), 45.

6. Warren, Neil Clark. *Finding the Love of Your Life: Ten Principles for Choosing the Right Marriage Partner.* (New York: Pocket Books, 1992), 88.

7. David Instone-Brewer, *Divorce and Remarriage in the Church: Biblical Solutions for Pastoral Realities* (Downers Grove: Inter Varsity Press, 2003), 96.

8. Instone-Brewer, *Divorce and Remarriage in the Church: Biblical Solutions for Pastoral Realities,* 39.

9. Margaret Mowczko, "Double Standards in the Practice and Promotion of Submission," (CBI International.org/blogs 8/2/2013).

Thank you for taking the time to read this book. Now that you've finished, please take a moment to head back to Amazon and leave me a review. It helps me to establish myself and for others to find the book. (For *Reviews Made Easy*, go here.) I hope you'll also visit my website, www.LindaMKurth.com and sign up for my mailing list. I so appreciate your support.

Linda

About The Author

Linda M. Kurth is the author of both children's and adult books. She also writes the blog, *Help and Healing for Divorced Christians*, where she advocates for the healing of divorced people within the church. Linda and her husband, Bill, of seventeen years have settled in their "home of the heart" in western Washington State where they participate in their church. She sings in a local music group, enjoys entertaining family  and friends, maintains a large garden, and is inspired by their big trees and wild bird visits. Visit Linda's website at www.LindaMKurth.com

Other Books by the Author

Home of the Heart

A clean, contemporary romance about two high-powered careers, two stubborn egos, and too many miles between. Can Meg and Matt alter their career paths and embrace the chance for love? Spoiler Alert— look for the romantic cabin scene on Oregon's Mt. Hood. Available as an eBook on Amazon.com

Quick Reads

Welcome to the Land of Enchantment: A Short Memoir of a Young Marriage

(Prequel to *God, the Devil, and Divorce*)

Set in Albuquerque, New Mexico, Linda M. Kurth paints a colorful picture of life as a young newlywed far from home in the late 60s. With a dash of humor, the author explores her transformation into adulthood, becoming part of Rex's dysfunctional family, and her growing love of the Southwest. Available as an eBook on Amazon.com

Ballroom Dancing and Other Life Lessons

Four essays in living life. Even if you never get out on the dance floor, you'll likely find the twelve lessons in *Ballroom Dancing* applicable. *Singing in Church Choir* includes spiritual as well as practical lessons. In *Being a Step-Grandparent,* the author shares how she's been able to stay on good terms with her step-grandchildren and their parents while enjoying her role of step-grandmother to six. *Dealing with Chronic Pain* gives encouragement by example for those who suffer from chronic pain. Available as an eBook on Amazon.com

Finding Joy in Being Single after Divorce

Kurth writes, "The feeling of being alone [after my divorce] washed over me and seemed to permeate every cell of my body." The author explores the difference between being alone and being single, and encourages the newly divorced to learn to embrace singlehood. This three-part booklet includes *12 Steps to a More Joyful Life after Divorce, Single or Alone?* and *30 Fun Things to Do When You're Single*. Available as an eBook on Amazon. com

CPSIA information can be obtained
at www.ICGtesting.com
Printed in the USA
JSHW031453100221
11789JS00001B/60